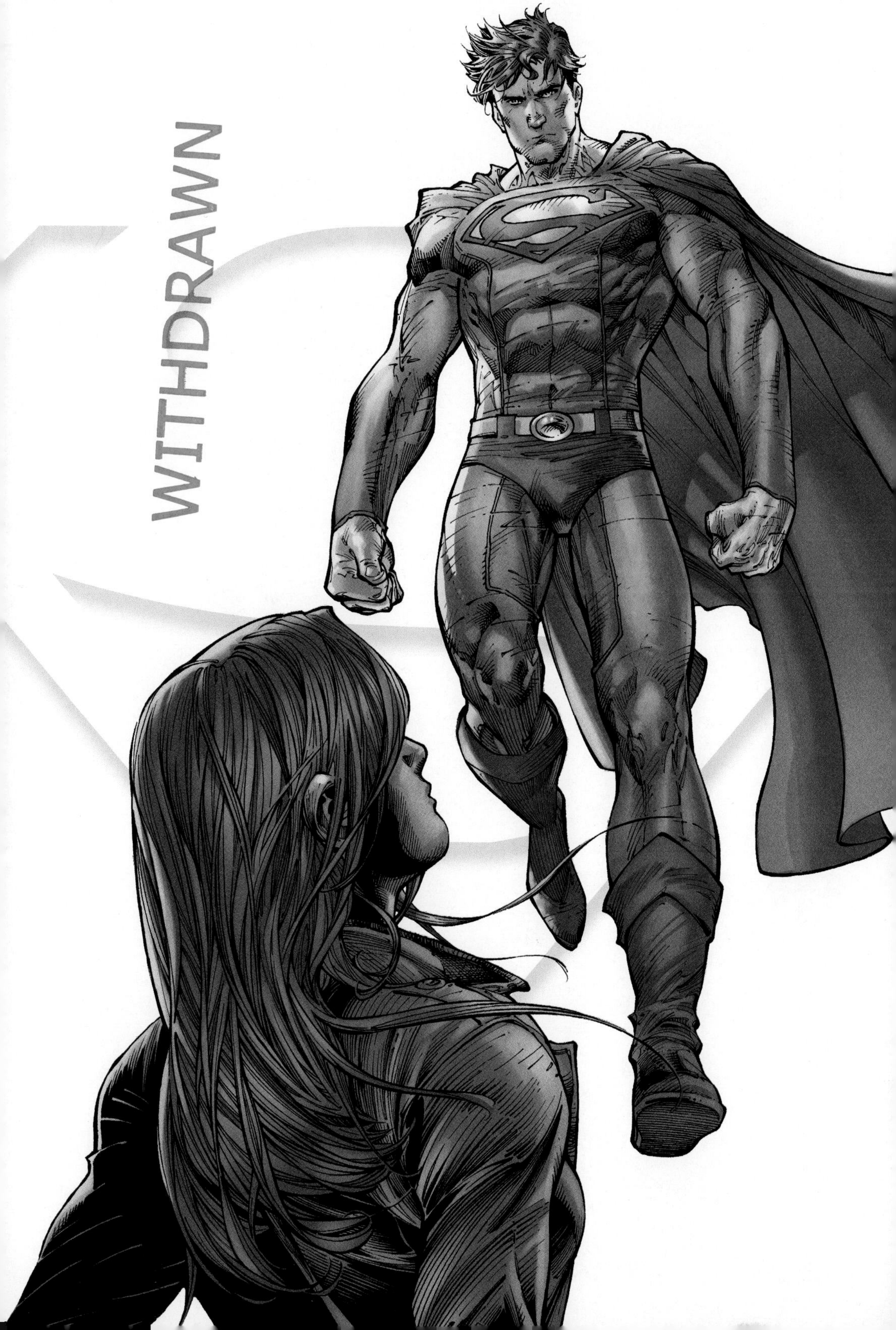

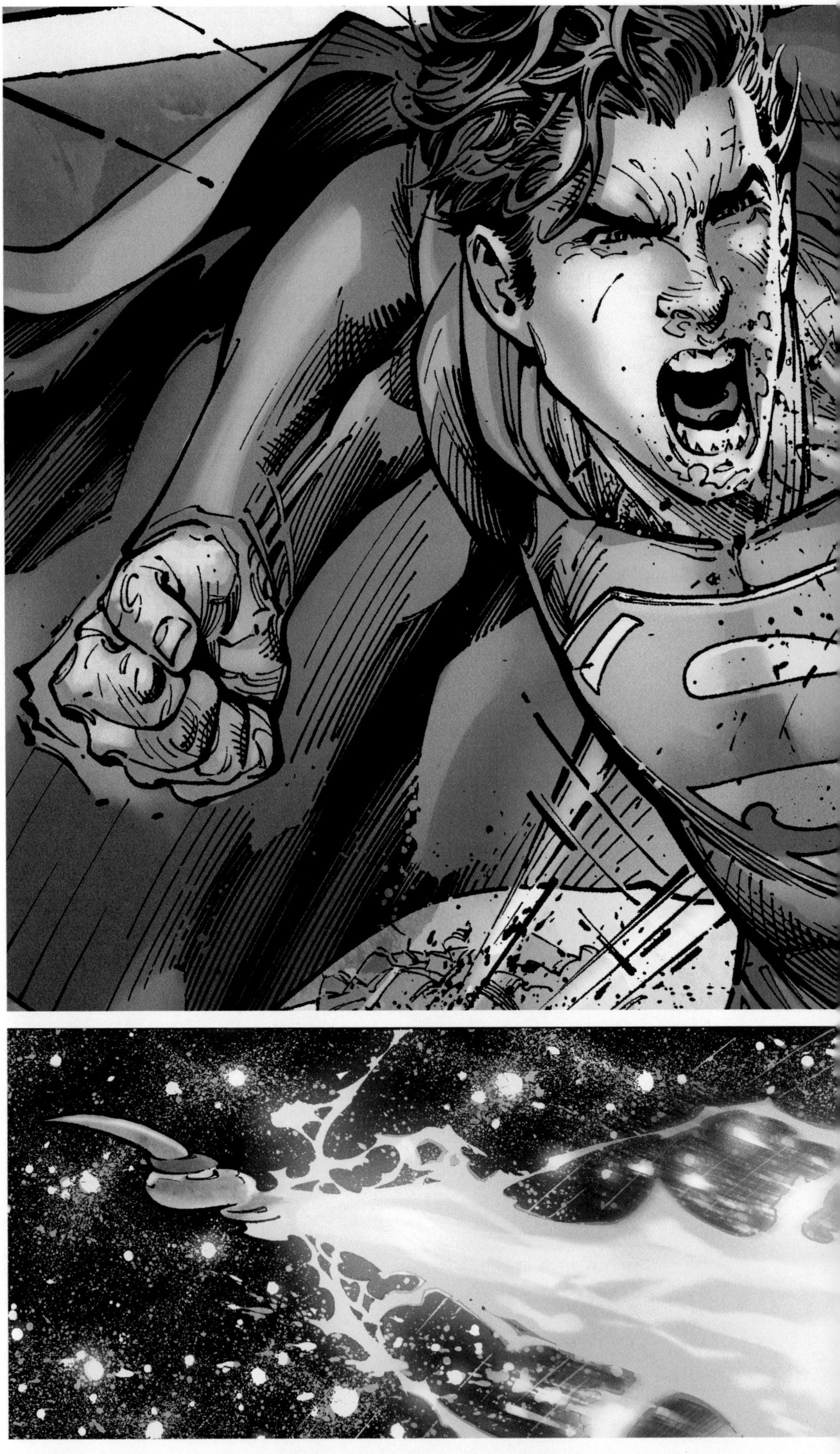

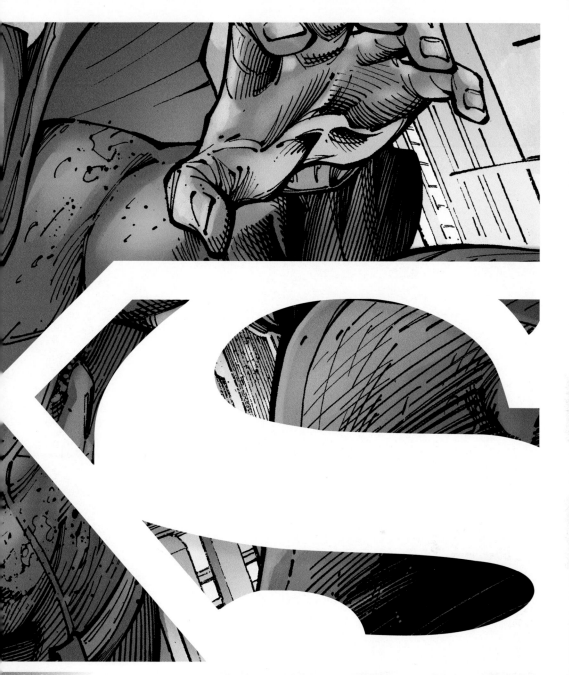

EARTH ONE

Written by **J. Michael Straczynski**   Pencils by **Ardian Syaf**

Inks by **Sandra Hope**   Colors by **Barbara Ciardo**   Lettered by **Rob Leigh**

SUPERMAN created by Jerry Siegel & Joe Shuster

By special arrangement with the Jerry Siegel family.

Eddie Berganza & **Darren Shan** Editors
Robbin Brosterman Design Director – Books
Louis Prandi Art Director

Bob Harras Senior VP – Editor-in-Chief, DC Comics

Diane Nelson President
Dan DiDio and **Jim Lee** Co-Publishers
Geoff Johns Chief Creative Officer
Amit Desai Senior VP – Marketing & Franchise Management
Amy Genkins Senior VP – Business & Legal Affairs
Nairi Gardiner Senior VP – Finance
Jeff Boison VP – Publishing Planning
Mark Chiarello VP – Art Direction & Design
John Cunningham VP – Marketing
Terri Cunningham VP – Editorial Administration
Larry Ganem VP – Talent Relations & Services
Alison Gill Senior VP – Manufacturing & Operations
Hank Kanalz Senior VP – Vertigo & Integrated Publishing
Jay Kogan VP – Business & Legal Affairs, Publishing
Jack Mahan VP – Business Affairs, Talent
Nick Napolitano VP – Manufacturing Administration
Sue Pohja VP – Book Sales
Fred Ruiz VP – Manufacturing Operations
Courtney Simmons Senior VP – Publicity
Bob Wayne Senior VP – Sales

 SUPERMAN:EARTH ONE VOLUME THREE

Published by DC Comics, 1700 Broadway, New York, NY 10019. Copy
© 2014 by DC Comics. All Rights Reserved. All characters featured i
publication, the distinctive likenesses thereof and related element
trademarks of DC Comics. Printed by RR Donnelley, Salem, VA, USA.
First Printing. DC Comics, a Warner Bros. Entertainment Company.
HC ISBN: 978-1-4012-4184-1

Library of Congress Cataloging-in-Publication Data

Straczynski, J. Michael, 1954- author.
  Superman earth one volume 3 / J. Michael Straczynski, Ardian Syaf.
    pages cm
   ISBN 978-1-4012-4184-1 (hardback)
  1. Graphic novels. I. Syaf, Ardian, illustrator. II. Title.

PN6728.S9S774 2015
741.5'973—dc23

                                            2014032787

DEDICATIONS

Every generation grows up with a version of Superman that is "their" Superman. For me, that was the Silver Age Superman, whose face was kind and thoughtful and wise and compassionate and yet impossibly strong. Unyielding. Honorable. So this third volume of Superman: Earth One is dedicated to the memory of CURT SWAN, who was my gateway drug to a deep and abiding love of the Superman mythos.

J. Michael Straczynski

To the memory of my father, Tamsir AS, who bought me my first comics and taught me how to draw, my mother, wife and my little son, Fahri.

Ardian Syaf

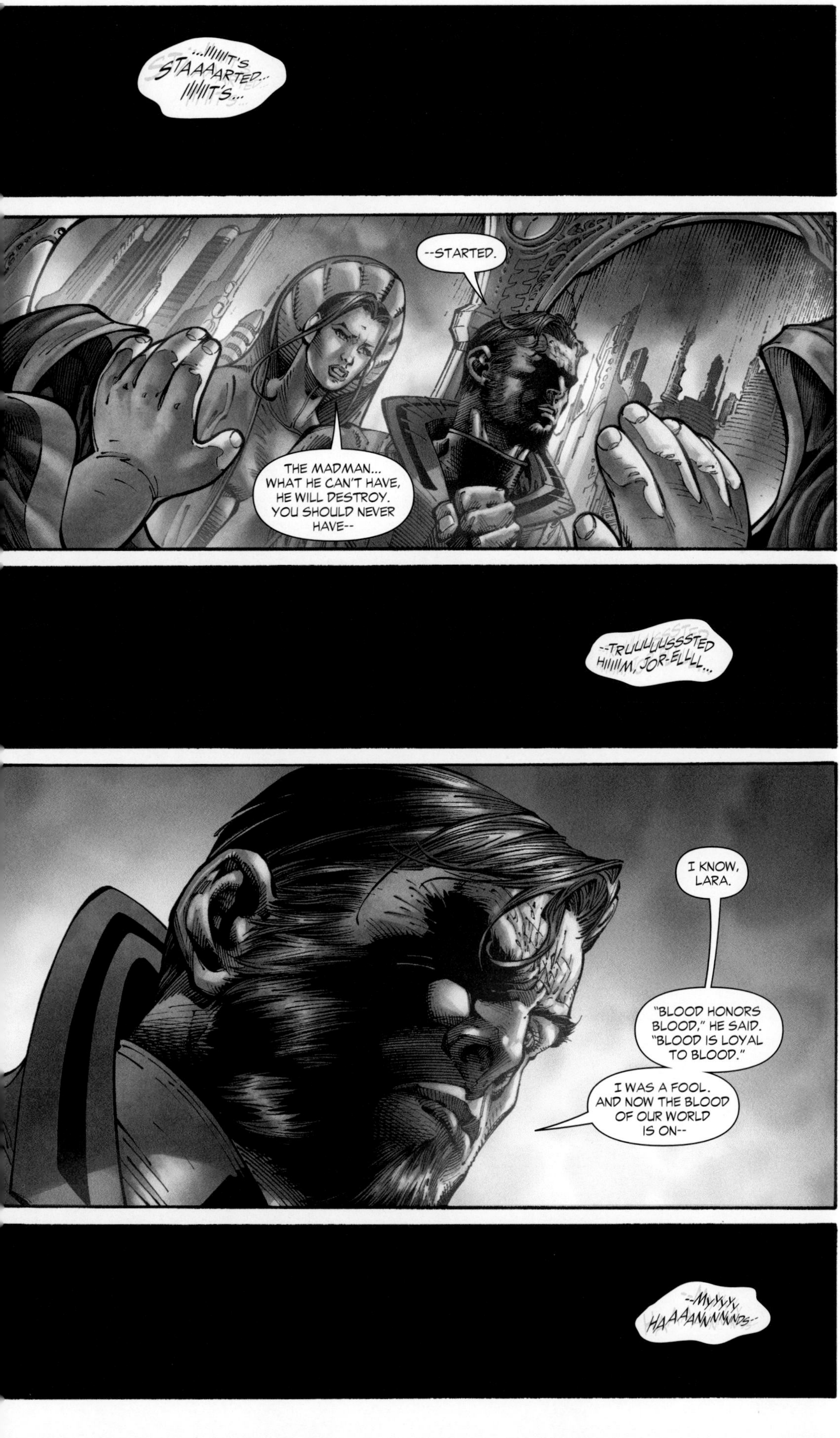
...IIIIIT'S STAAAARTED... IIIIIT'S...
--STARTED.
THE MADMAN... WHAT HE CAN'T HAVE, HE WILL DESTROY. YOU SHOULD NEVER HAVE--
--TRUUUUSSSTED HIIIIM, JOR-ELLLL...
I KNOW, LARA.
"BLOOD HONORS BLOOD," HE SAID. "BLOOD IS LOYAL TO BLOOD."
I WAS A FOOL. AND NOW THE BLOOD OF OUR WORLD IS ON--
--MYYYYY HAAAANNNNNDS--

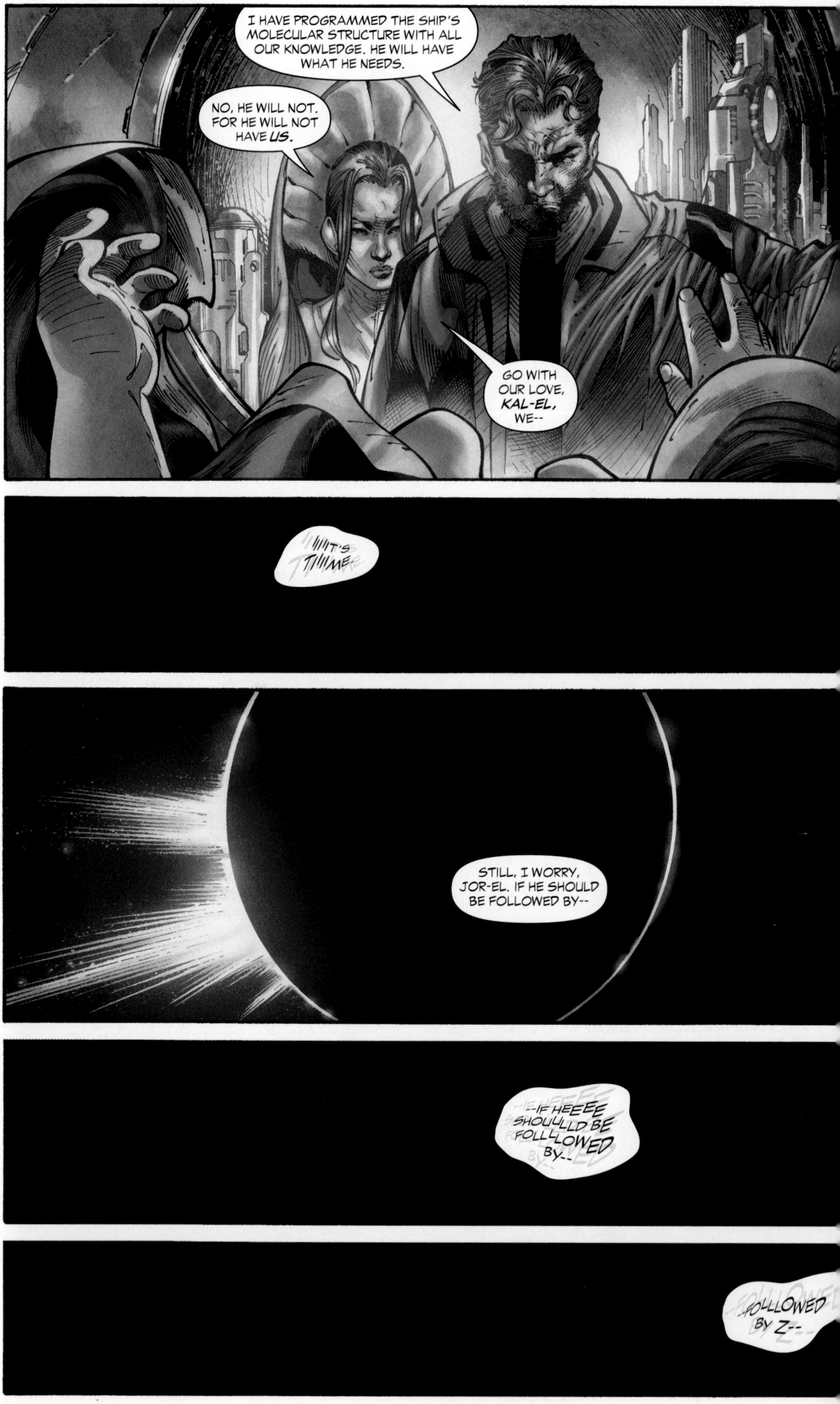
I HAVE PROGRAMMED THE SHIP'S MOLECULAR STRUCTURE WITH ALL OUR KNOWLEDGE. HE WILL HAVE WHAT HE NEEDS.
NO, HE WILL NOT. FOR HE WILL NOT HAVE US.
GO WITH OUR LOVE, KAL-EL, WE--
IIIIT'S TIIIME.
STILL, I WORRY, JOR-EL. IF HE SHOULD BE FOLLOWED BY--
--IF HEEEE SHOULLLLD BE FOLLLLOWED BY--
--FOLLLOWED BY Z--

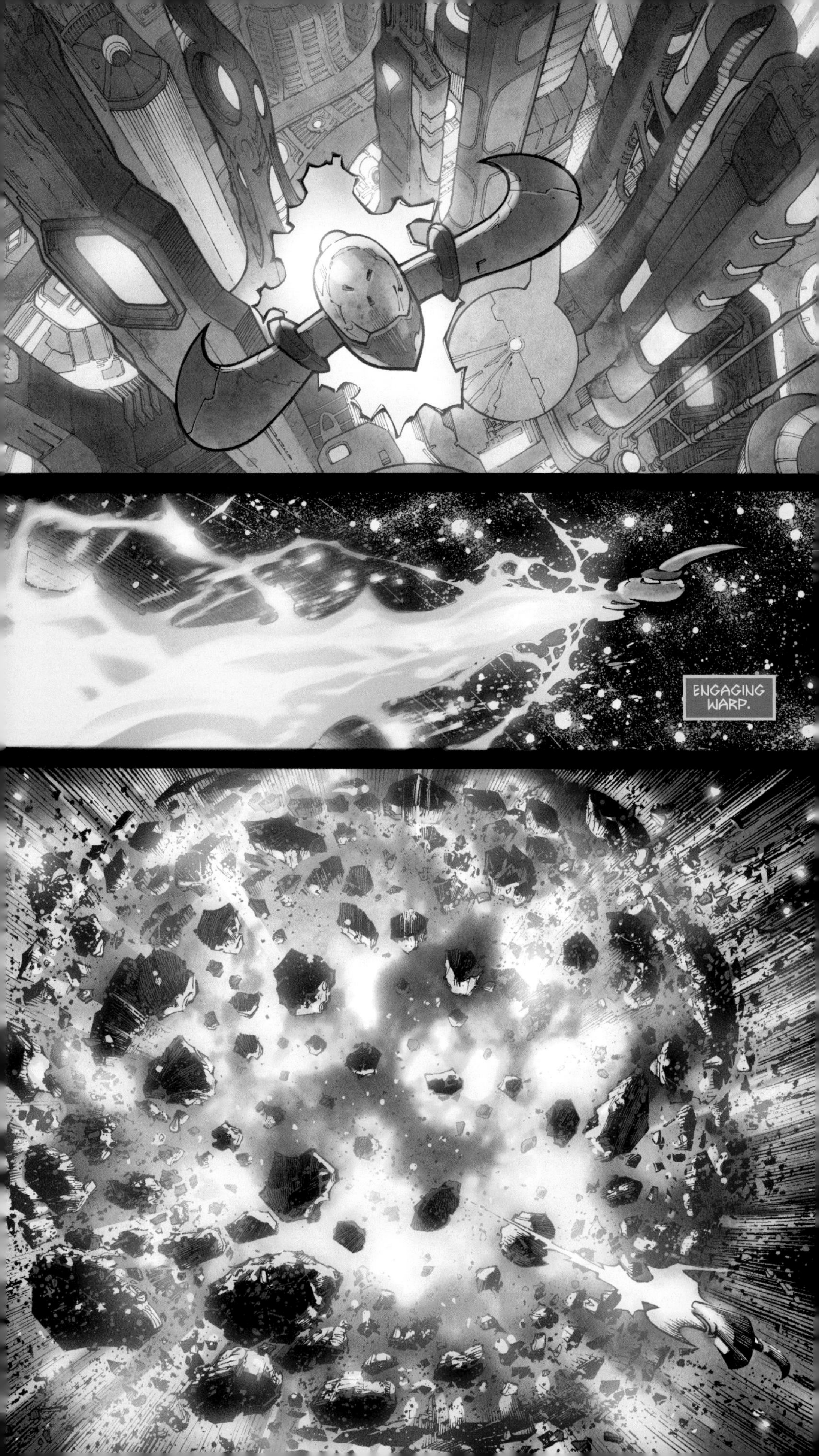
ENGAGING WARP.

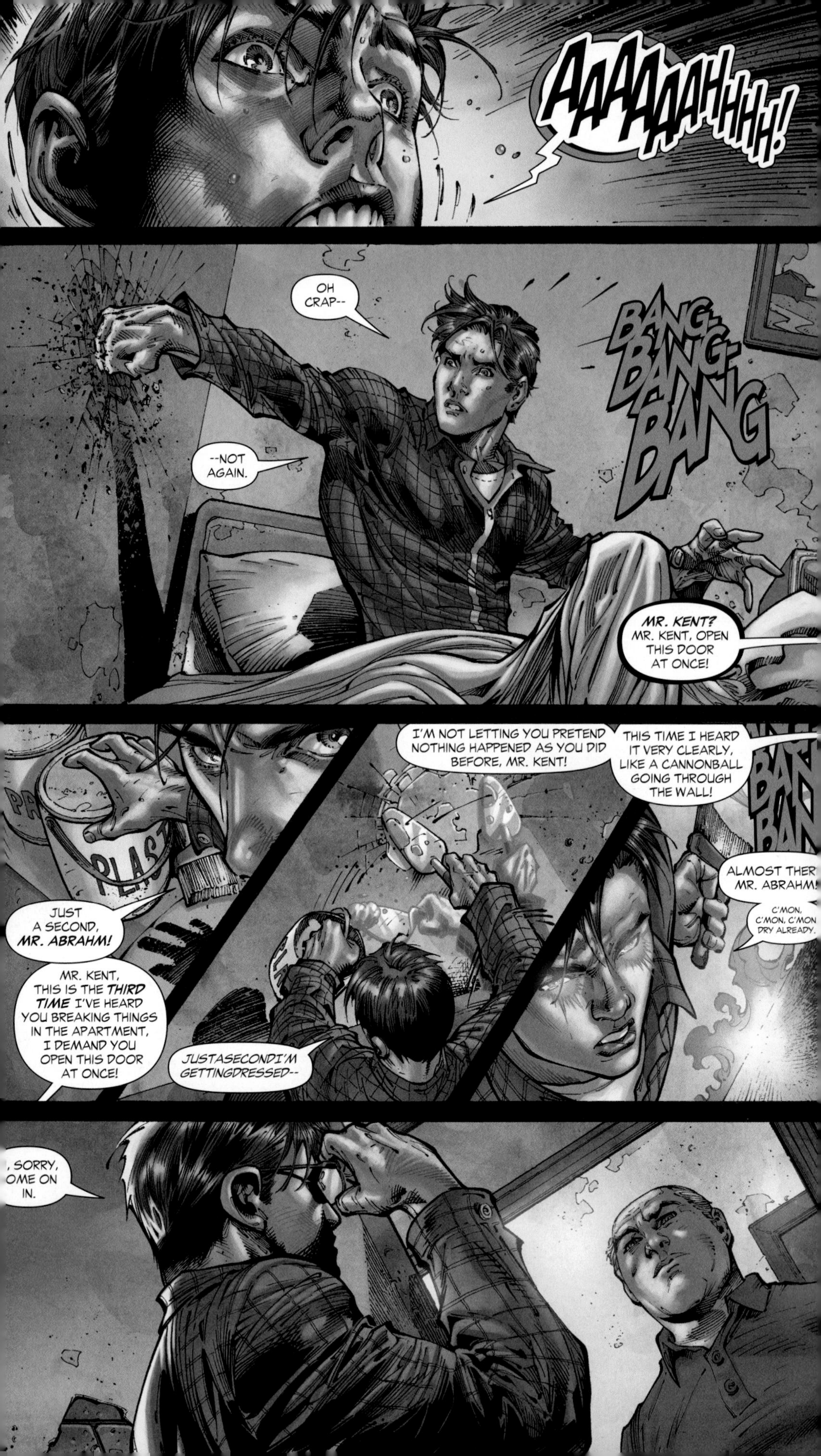

AAAAAAHHHH!
OH CRAP--
--NOT AGAIN.
BANG-BANG-BANG
MR. KENT? MR. KENT, OPEN THIS DOOR AT ONCE!
JUST A SECOND, MR. ABRAHM!
MR. KENT, THIS IS THE THIRD TIME I'VE HEARD YOU BREAKING THINGS IN THE APARTMENT, I DEMAND YOU OPEN THIS DOOR AT ONCE!
I'M NOT LETTING YOU PRETEND NOTHING HAPPENED AS YOU DID BEFORE, MR. KENT!
JUSTASECONDI'M GETTINGDRESSED--
THIS TIME I HEARD IT VERY CLEARLY, LIKE A CANNONBALL GOING THROUGH THE WALL!
ALMOST THER MR. ABRAHM!
C'MON, C'MON, C'MON DRY ALREADY.
, SORY, OME ON IN.

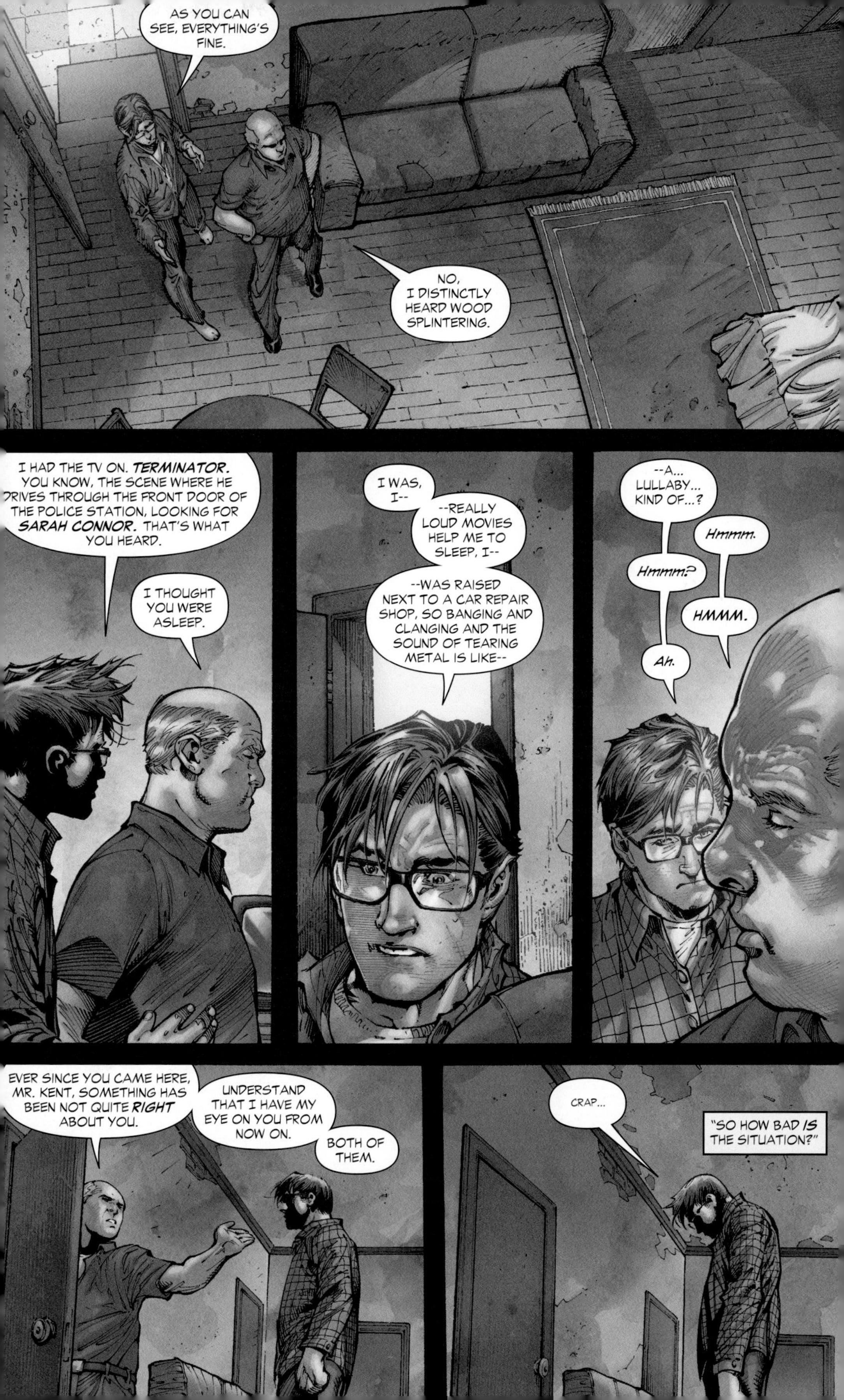
AS YOU CAN SEE, EVERYTHING'S FINE.
NO, I DISTINCTLY HEARD WOOD SPLINTERING.
I HAD THE TV ON. TERMINATOR. YOU KNOW, THE SCENE WHERE HE DRIVES THROUGH THE FRONT DOOR OF THE POLICE STATION, LOOKING FOR SARAH CONNOR. THAT'S WHAT YOU HEARD.
I THOUGHT YOU WERE ASLEEP.
I WAS, I--
--REALLY LOUD MOVIES HELP ME TO SLEEP, I--
--WAS RAISED NEXT TO A CAR REPAIR SHOP, SO BANGING AND CLANGING AND THE SOUND OF TEARING METAL IS LIKE--
--A... LULLABY... KIND OF...?
Hmmm.
Hmmm?
HMMM.
Ah.
EVER SINCE YOU CAME HERE, MR. KENT, SOMETHING HAS BEEN NOT QUITE RIGHT ABOUT YOU.
UNDERSTAND THAT I HAVE MY EYE ON YOU FROM NOW ON.
BOTH OF THEM.
CRAP...
"SO HOW BAD IS THE SITUATION?"

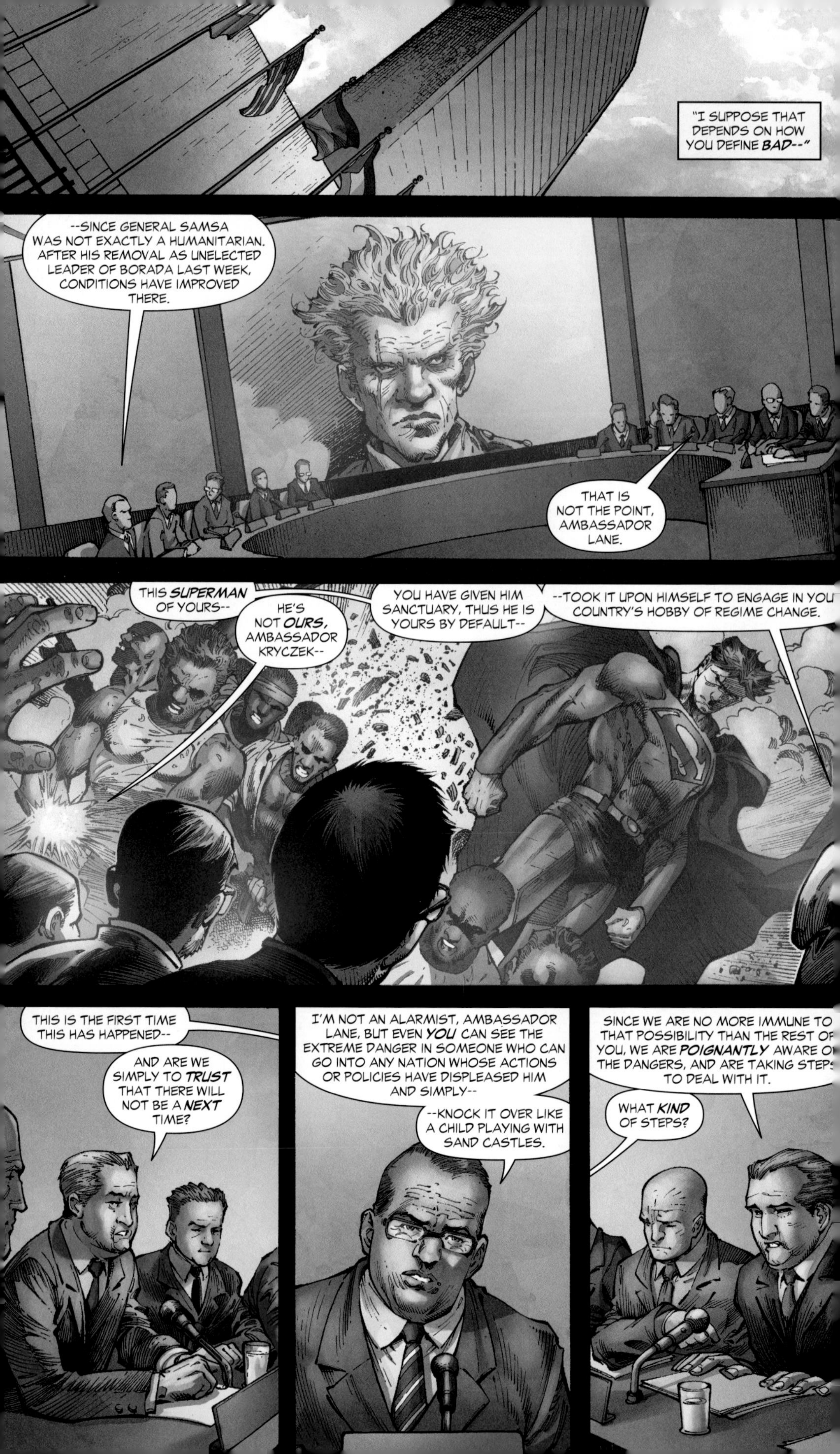
"I SUPPOSE THAT DEPENDS ON HOW YOU DEFINE BAD--"
--SINCE GENERAL SAMSA WAS NOT EXACTLY A HUMANITARIAN. AFTER HIS REMOVAL AS UNELECTED LEADER OF BORADA LAST WEEK, CONDITIONS HAVE IMPROVED THERE.
THAT IS NOT THE POINT, AMBASSADOR LANE.
THIS SUPERMAN OF YOURS--
HE'S NOT OURS, AMBASSADOR KRYCZEK--
YOU HAVE GIVEN HIM SANCTUARY, THUS HE IS YOURS BY DEFAULT--
--TOOK IT UPON HIMSELF TO ENGAGE IN YOU COUNTRY'S HOBBY OF REGIME CHANGE.
THIS IS THE FIRST TIME THIS HAS HAPPENED--
AND ARE WE SIMPLY TO TRUST THAT THERE WILL NOT BE A NEXT TIME?
I'M NOT AN ALARMIST, AMBASSADOR LANE, BUT EVEN YOU CAN SEE THE EXTREME DANGER IN SOMEONE WHO CAN GO INTO ANY NATION WHOSE ACTIONS OR POLICIES HAVE DISPLEASED HIM AND SIMPLY--
--KNOCK IT OVER LIKE A CHILD PLAYING WITH SAND CASTLES.
SINCE WE ARE NO MORE IMMUNE TO THAT POSSIBILITY THAN THE REST OF YOU, WE ARE POIGNANTLY AWARE O THE DANGERS, AND ARE TAKING STEPS TO DEAL WITH IT.
WHAT KIND OF STEPS?

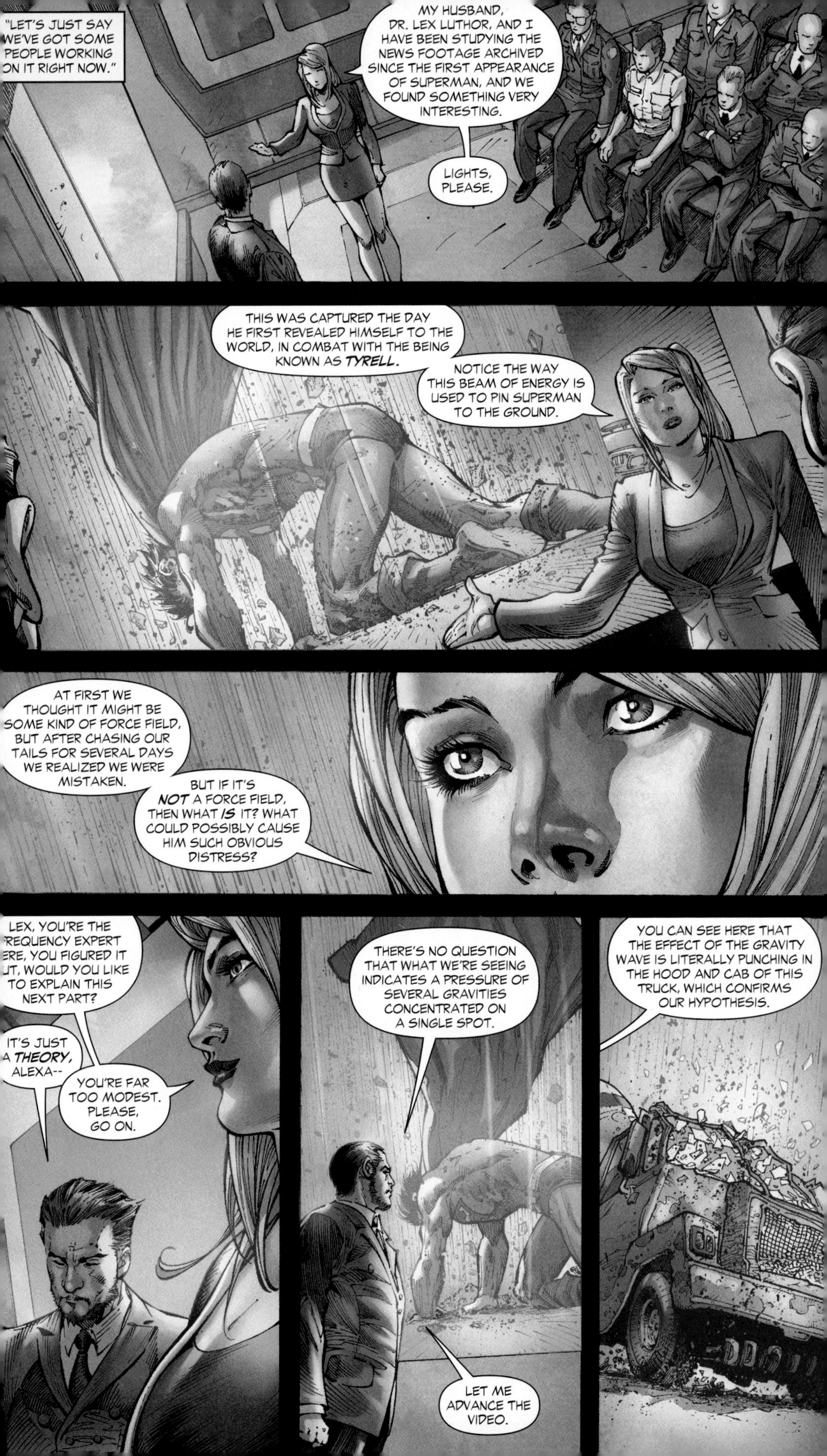
"LET'S JUST SAY WE'VE GOT SOME PEOPLE WORKING ON IT RIGHT NOW."
MY HUSBAND, DR. LEX LUTHOR, AND I HAVE BEEN STUDYING THE NEWS FOOTAGE ARCHIVED SINCE THE FIRST APPEARANCE OF SUPERMAN, AND WE FOUND SOMETHING VERY INTERESTING.
LIGHTS, PLEASE.
THIS WAS CAPTURED THE DAY HE FIRST REVEALED HIMSELF TO THE WORLD, IN COMBAT WITH THE BEING KNOWN AS TYRELL.
NOTICE THE WAY THIS BEAM OF ENERGY IS USED TO PIN SUPERMAN TO THE GROUND.
AT FIRST WE THOUGHT IT MIGHT BE SOME KIND OF FORCE FIELD, BUT AFTER CHASING OUR TAILS FOR SEVERAL DAYS WE REALIZED WE WERE MISTAKEN.
BUT IF IT'S NOT A FORCE FIELD, THEN WHAT IS IT? WHAT COULD POSSIBLY CAUSE HIM SUCH OBVIOUS DISTRESS?
LEX, YOU'RE THE FREQUENCY EXPERT HERE, YOU FIGURED IT OUT, WOULD YOU LIKE TO EXPLAIN THIS NEXT PART?
IT'S JUST A THEORY, ALEXA--
YOU'RE FAR TOO MODEST. PLEASE, GO ON.
THERE'S NO QUESTION THAT WHAT WE'RE SEEING INDICATES A PRESSURE OF SEVERAL GRAVITIES CONCENTRATED ON A SINGLE SPOT.
LET ME ADVANCE THE VIDEO.
YOU CAN SEE HERE THAT THE EFFECT OF THE GRAVITY WAVE IS LITERALLY PUNCHING IN THE HOOD AND CAB OF THIS TRUCK, WHICH CONFIRMS OUR HYPOTHESIS.

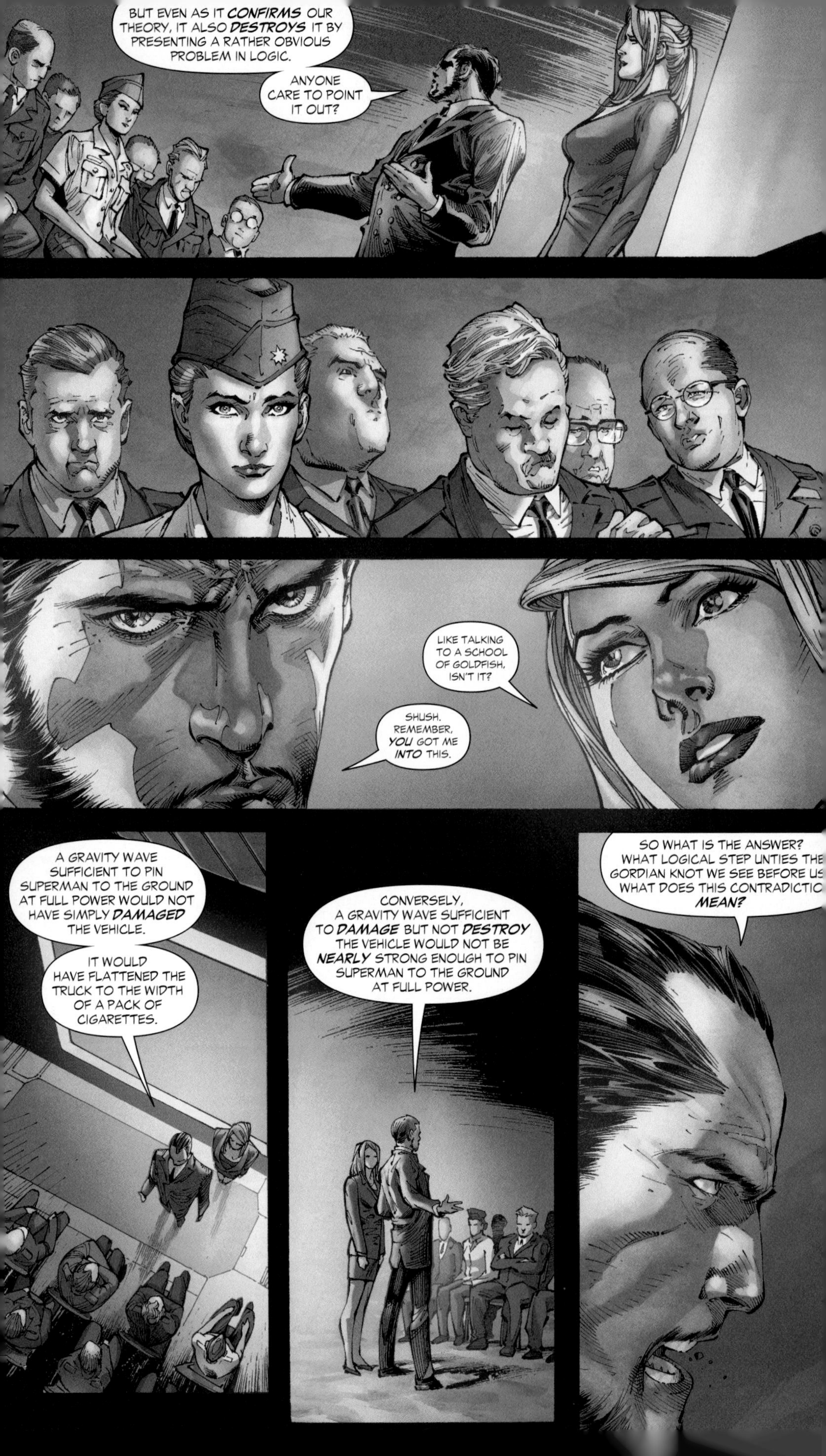
BUT EVEN AS IT CONFIRMS OUR THEORY, IT ALSO DESTROYS IT BY PRESENTING A RATHER OBVIOUS PROBLEM IN LOGIC.
ANYONE CARE TO POINT IT OUT?
LIKE TALKING TO A SCHOOL OF GOLDFISH, ISN'T IT?
SHUSH. REMEMBER, YOU GOT ME INTO THIS.
A GRAVITY WAVE SUFFICIENT TO PIN SUPERMAN TO THE GROUND AT FULL POWER WOULD NOT HAVE SIMPLY DAMAGED THE VEHICLE.
IT WOULD HAVE FLATTENED THE TRUCK TO THE WIDTH OF A PACK OF CIGARETTES.
CONVERSELY, A GRAVITY WAVE SUFFICIENT TO DAMAGE BUT NOT DESTROY THE VEHICLE WOULD NOT BE NEARLY STRONG ENOUGH TO PIN SUPERMAN TO THE GROUND AT FULL POWER.
SO WHAT IS THE ANSWER? WHAT LOGICAL STEP UNTIES THE GORDIAN KNOT WE SEE BEFORE US WHAT DOES THIS CONTRADICTIC MEAN?

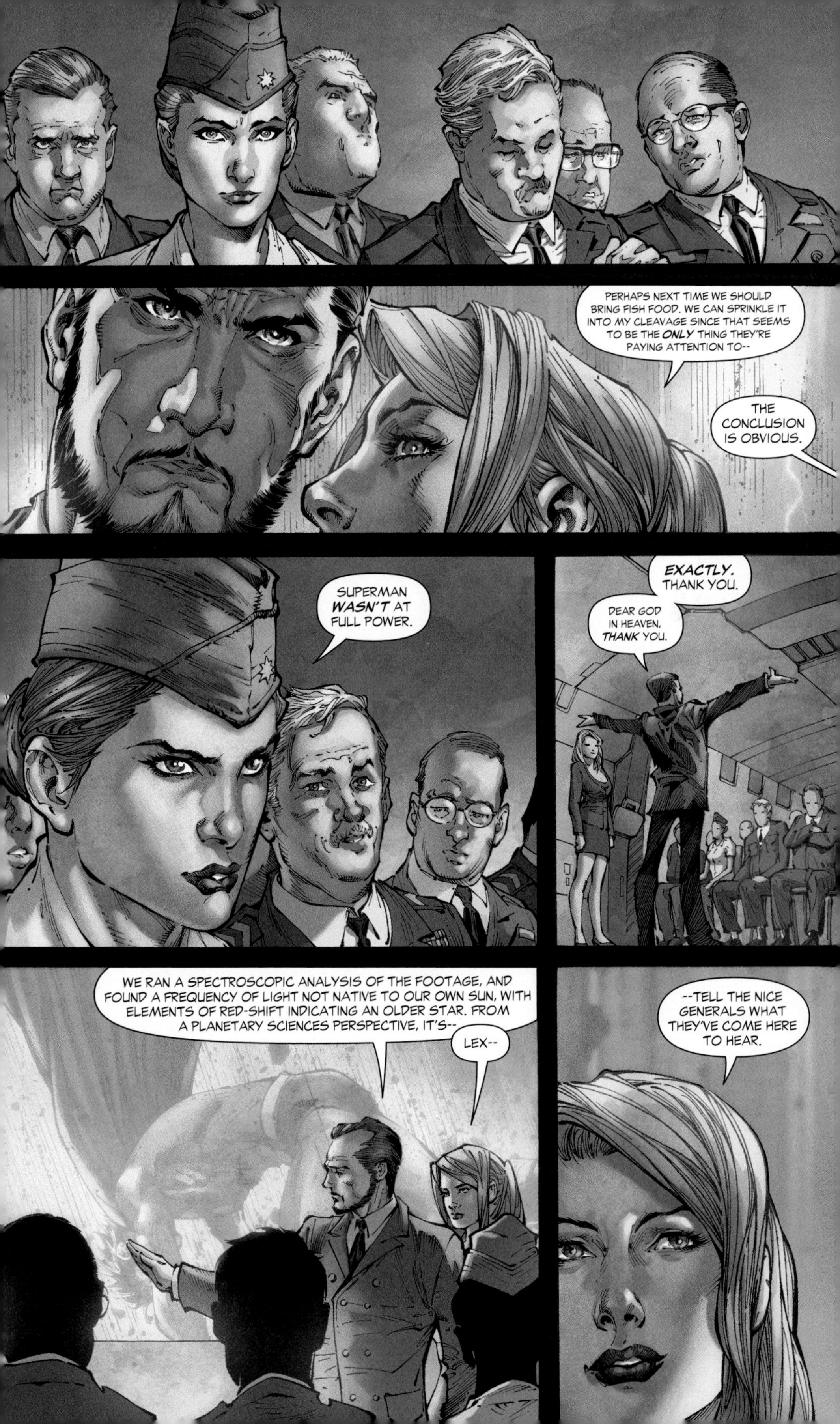
PERHAPS NEXT TIME WE SHOULD BRING FISH FOOD. WE CAN SPRINKLE IT INTO MY CLEAVAGE SINCE THAT SEEMS TO BE THE ONLY THING THEY'RE PAYING ATTENTION TO--
THE CONCLUSION IS OBVIOUS.
SUPERMAN WASN'T AT FULL POWER.
EXACTLY. THANK YOU.
DEAR GOD IN HEAVEN, THANK YOU.
WE RAN A SPECTROSCOPIC ANALYSIS OF THE FOOTAGE, AND FOUND A FREQUENCY OF LIGHT NOT NATIVE TO OUR OWN SUN, WITH ELEMENTS OF RED-SHIFT INDICATING AN OLDER STAR. FROM A PLANETARY SCIENCES PERSPECTIVE, IT'S--
LEX--
--TELL THE NICE GENERALS WHAT THEY'VE COME HERE TO HEAR.

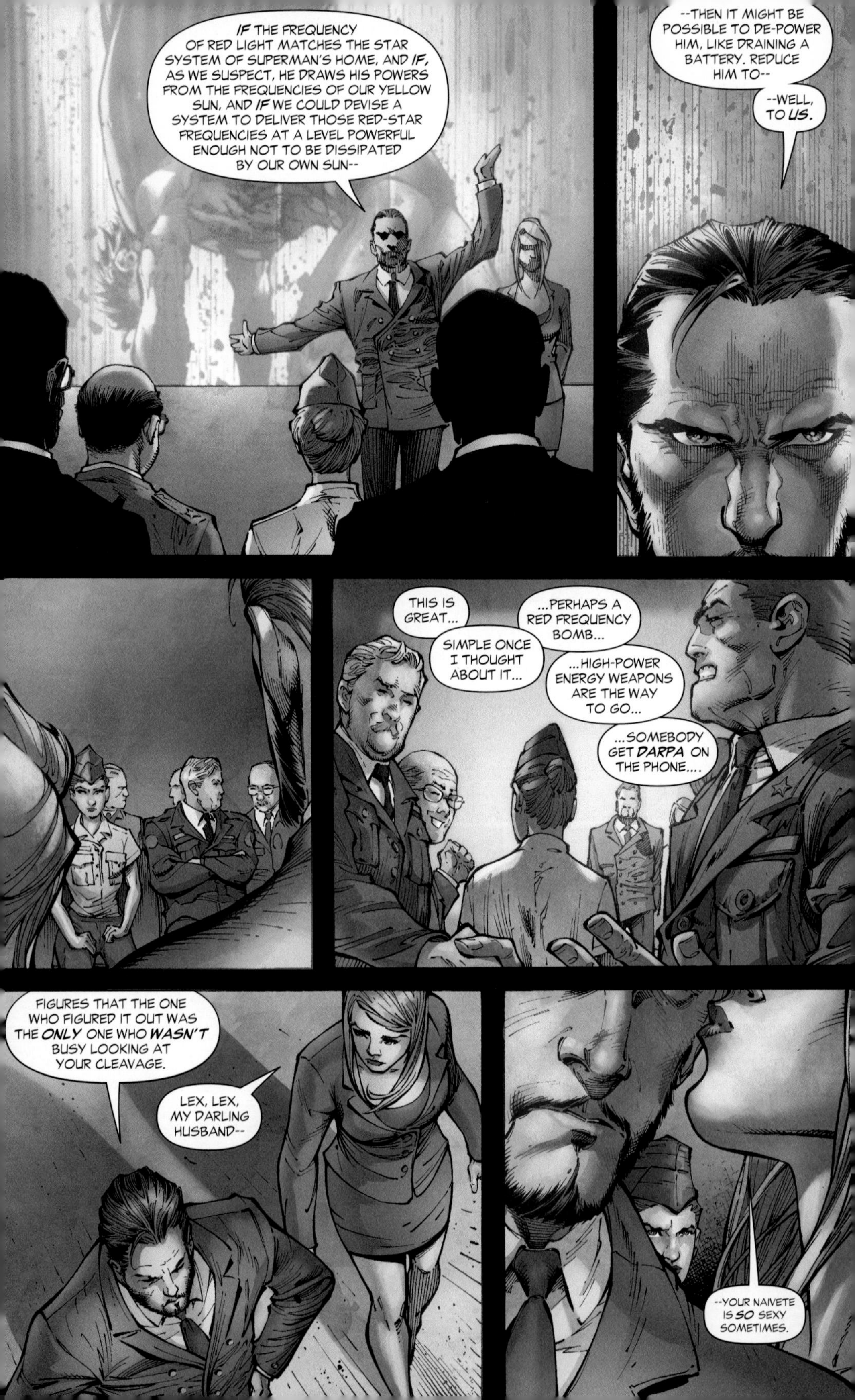
IF THE FREQUENCY OF RED LIGHT MATCHES THE STAR SYSTEM OF SUPERMAN'S HOME, AND IF, AS WE SUSPECT, HE DRAWS HIS POWERS FROM THE FREQUENCIES OF OUR YELLOW SUN, AND IF WE COULD DEVISE A SYSTEM TO DELIVER THOSE RED-STAR FREQUENCIES AT A LEVEL POWERFUL ENOUGH NOT TO BE DISSIPATED BY OUR OWN SUN--
--THEN IT MIGHT BE POSSIBLE TO DE-POWER HIM, LIKE DRAINING A BATTERY. REDUCE HIM TO--
--WELL, TO US.
THIS IS GREAT...
SIMPLE ONCE I THOUGHT ABOUT IT...
...PERHAPS A RED FREQUENCY BOMB...
...HIGH-POWER ENERGY WEAPONS ARE THE WAY TO GO...
...SOMEBODY GET DARPA ON THE PHONE....
FIGURES THAT THE ONE WHO FIGURED IT OUT WAS THE ONLY ONE WHO WASN'T BUSY LOOKING AT YOUR CLEAVAGE.
LEX, LEX, MY DARLING HUSBAND--
--YOUR NAIVETE IS SO SEXY SOMETIMES.

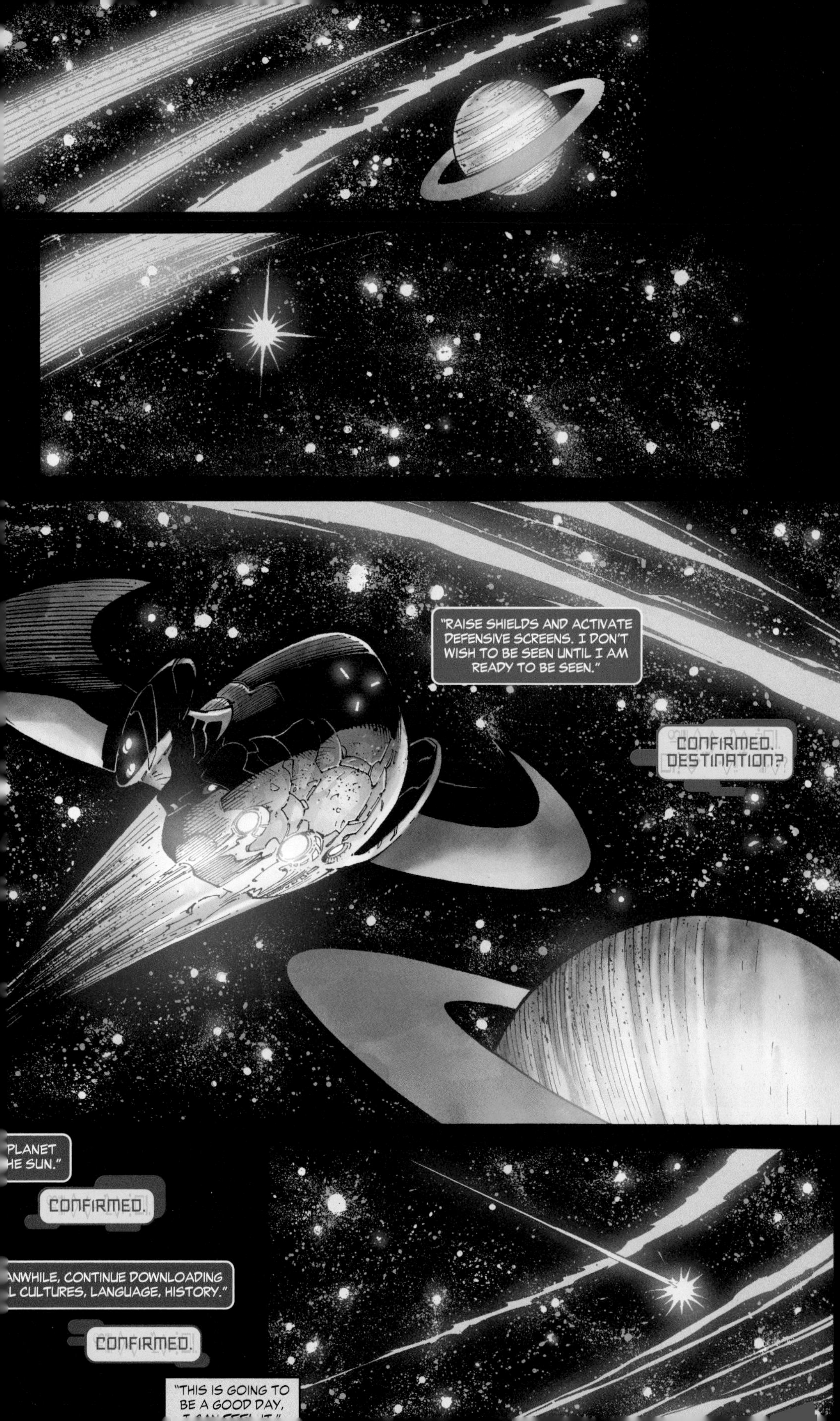
"RAISE SHIELDS AND ACTIVATE DEFENSIVE SCREENS. I DON'T WISH TO BE SEEN UNTIL I AM READY TO BE SEEN."
CONFIRMED. DESTINATION?
PLANET
HE SUN."
CONFIRMED.
ANWHILE, CONTINUE DOWNLOADING
L CULTURES, LANGUAGE, HISTORY."
CONFIRMED.
"THIS IS GOING TO BE A GOOD DAY.

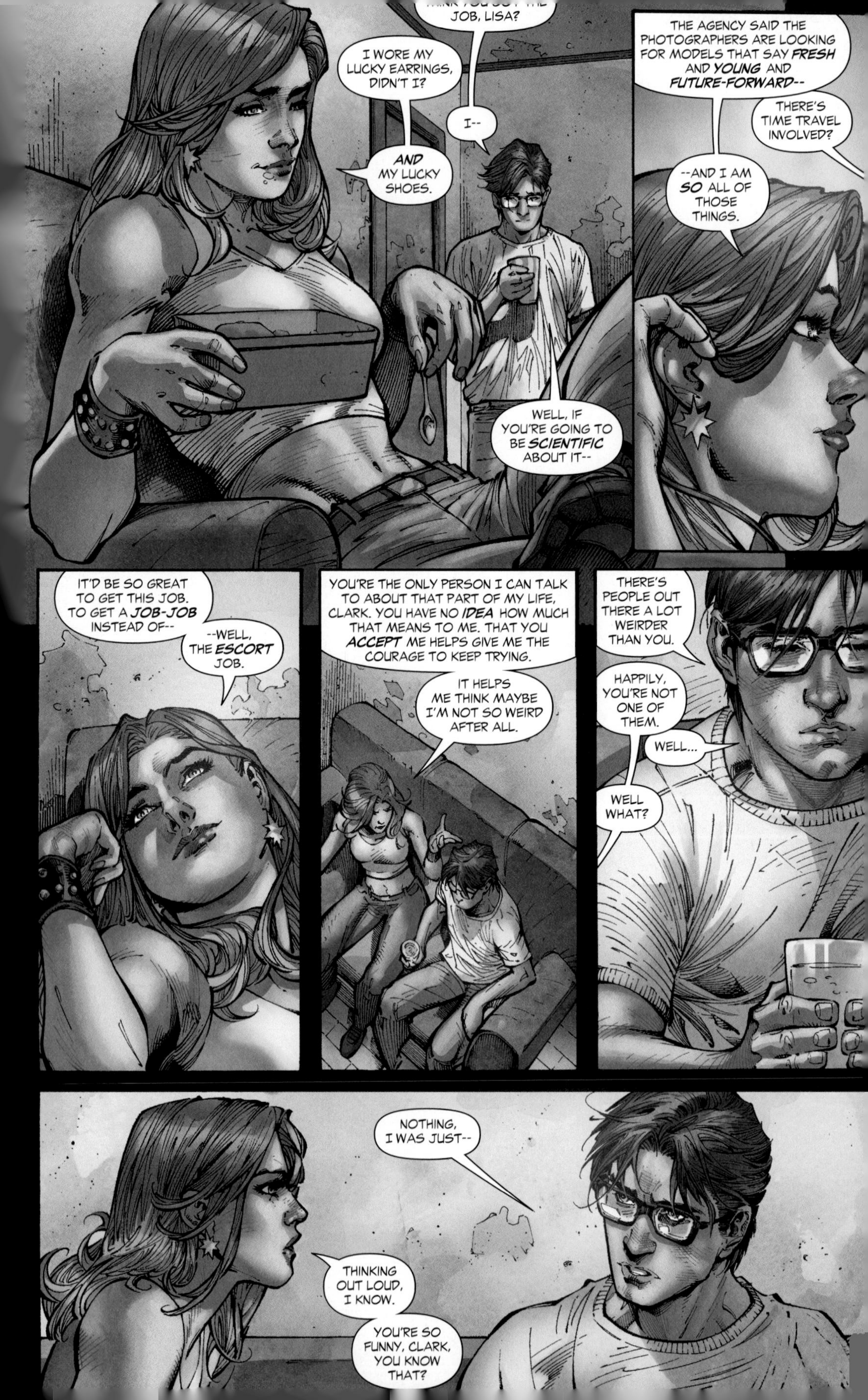

JOB, LISA?
I WORE MY LUCKY EARRINGS, DIDN'T I?
I--
AND MY LUCKY SHOES.
WELL, IF YOU'RE GOING TO BE SCIENTIFIC ABOUT IT--
THE AGENCY SAID THE PHOTOGRAPHERS ARE LOOKING FOR MODELS THAT SAY FRESH AND YOUNG AND FUTURE-FORWARD--
THERE'S TIME TRAVEL INVOLVED?
--AND I AM SO ALL OF THOSE THINGS.
IT'D BE SO GREAT TO GET THIS JOB. TO GET A JOB-JOB INSTEAD OF--
--WELL, THE ESCORT JOB.
YOU'RE THE ONLY PERSON I CAN TALK TO ABOUT THAT PART OF MY LIFE, CLARK. YOU HAVE NO IDEA HOW MUCH THAT MEANS TO ME. THAT YOU ACCEPT ME HELPS GIVE ME THE COURAGE TO KEEP TRYING.
IT HELPS ME THINK MAYBE I'M NOT SO WEIRD AFTER ALL.
THERE'S PEOPLE OUT THERE A LOT WEIRDER THAN YOU.
HAPPILY, YOU'RE NOT ONE OF THEM.
WELL...
WELL WHAT?
NOTHING, I WAS JUST--
THINKING OUT LOUD, I KNOW.
YOU'RE SO FUNNY, CLARK, YOU KNOW THAT?

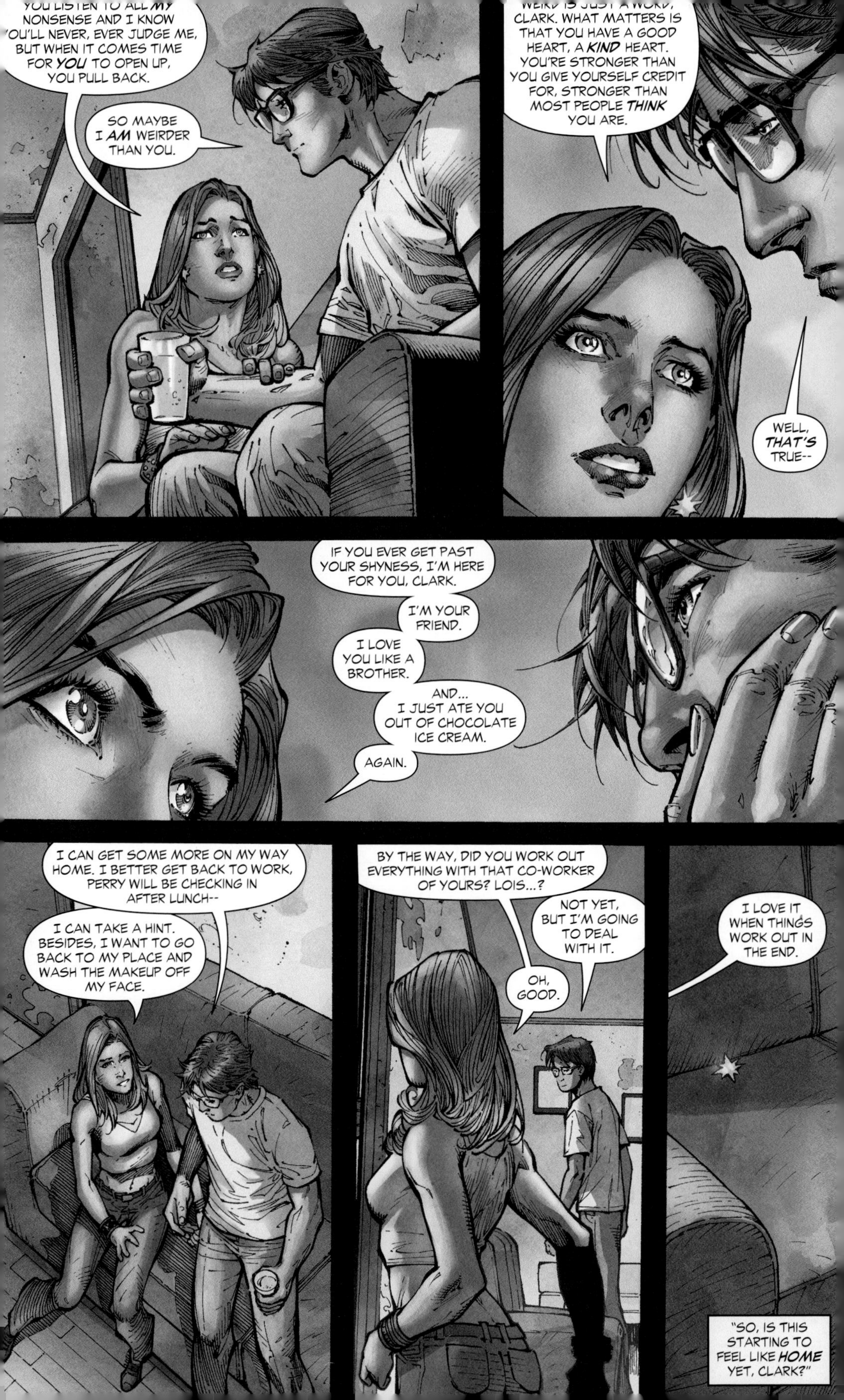
YOU LISTEN TO ALL MY NONSENSE AND I KNOW YOU'LL NEVER, EVER JUDGE ME, BUT WHEN IT COMES TIME FOR YOU TO OPEN UP, YOU PULL BACK.
SO MAYBE I AM WEIRDER THAN YOU.
WEIRD IS JUST A WORD, CLARK. WHAT MATTERS IS THAT YOU HAVE A GOOD HEART, A KIND HEART. YOU'RE STRONGER THAN YOU GIVE YOURSELF CREDIT FOR, STRONGER THAN MOST PEOPLE THINK YOU ARE.
WELL, THAT'S TRUE--
IF YOU EVER GET PAST YOUR SHYNESS, I'M HERE FOR YOU, CLARK.
I'M YOUR FRIEND.
I LOVE YOU LIKE A BROTHER.
AND... I JUST ATE YOU OUT OF CHOCOLATE ICE CREAM.
AGAIN.
I CAN GET SOME MORE ON MY WAY HOME. I BETTER GET BACK TO WORK, PERRY WILL BE CHECKING IN AFTER LUNCH--
I CAN TAKE A HINT. BESIDES, I WANT TO GO BACK TO MY PLACE AND WASH THE MAKEUP OFF MY FACE.
BY THE WAY, DID YOU WORK OUT EVERYTHING WITH THAT CO-WORKER OF YOURS? LOIS...?
NOT YET, BUT I'M GOING TO DEAL WITH IT.
OH, GOOD.
I LOVE IT WHEN THINGS WORK OUT IN THE END.
"SO, IS THIS STARTING TO FEEL LIKE HOME YET, CLARK?"

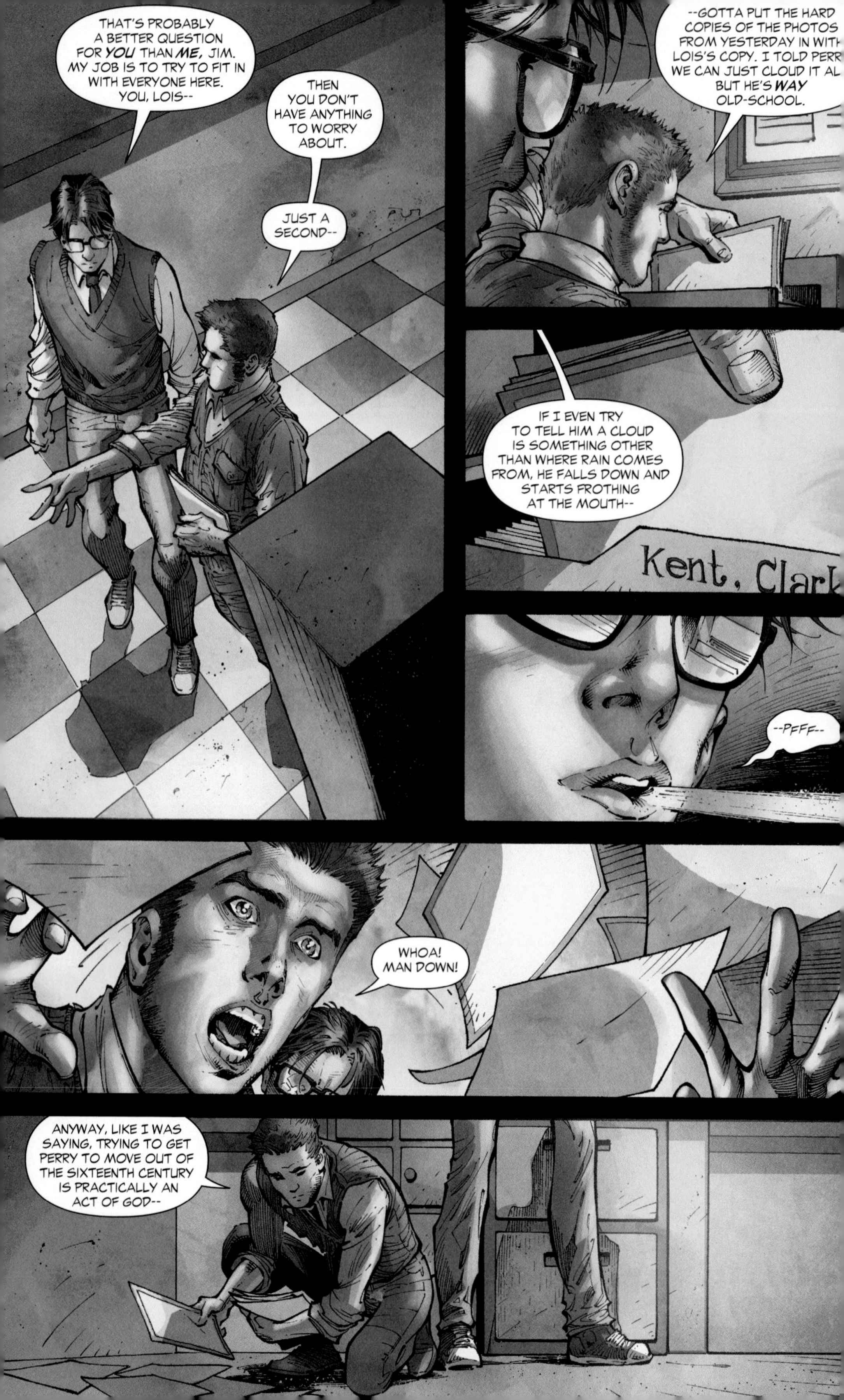
THAT'S PROBABLY A BETTER QUESTION FOR *YOU* THAN *ME,* JIM. MY JOB IS TO TRY TO FIT IN WITH EVERYONE HERE. YOU, LOIS--
THEN YOU DON'T HAVE ANYTHING TO WORRY ABOUT.
JUST A SECOND--
--GOTTA PUT THE HARD COPIES OF THE PHOTOS FROM YESTERDAY IN WITH LOIS'S COPY. I TOLD PERR WE CAN JUST CLOUD IT AL BUT HE'S *WAY* OLD-SCHOOL.
IF I EVEN TRY TO TELL HIM A CLOUD IS SOMETHING OTHER THAN WHERE RAIN COMES FROM, HE FALLS DOWN AND STARTS FROTHING AT THE MOUTH--
Kent, Clark
--PFFF--
WHOA! MAN DOWN!
ANYWAY, LIKE I WAS SAYING, TRYING TO GET PERRY TO MOVE OUT OF THE SIXTEENTH CENTURY IS PRACTICALLY AN ACT OF GOD--

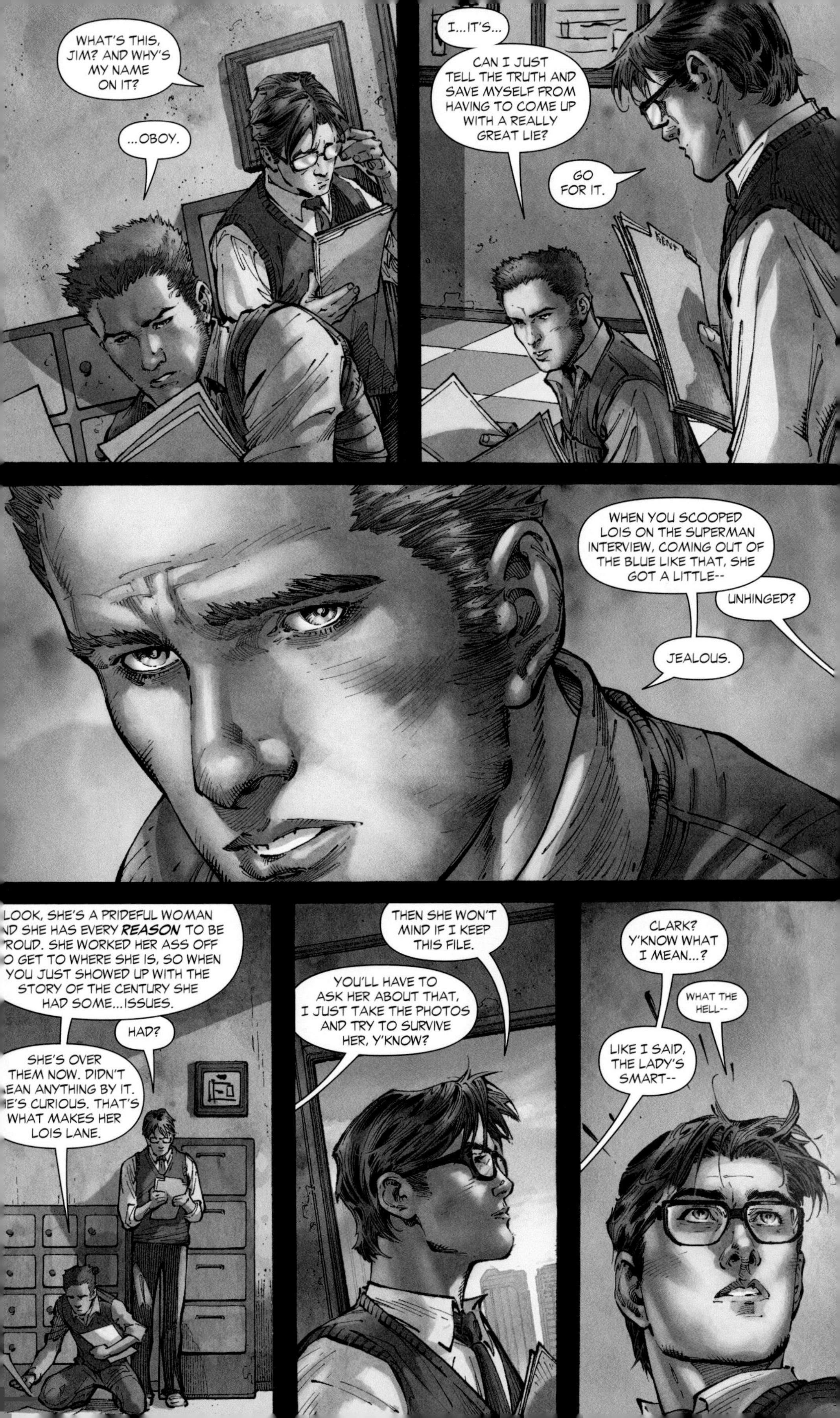
WHAT'S THIS, JIM? AND WHY'S MY NAME ON IT?
...OBOY.
I...IT'S...
CAN I JUST TELL THE TRUTH AND SAVE MYSELF FROM HAVING TO COME UP WITH A REALLY GREAT LIE?
GO FOR IT.
WHEN YOU SCOOPED LOIS ON THE SUPERMAN INTERVIEW, COMING OUT OF THE BLUE LIKE THAT, SHE GOT A LITTLE--
UNHINGED?
JEALOUS.
LOOK, SHE'S A PRIDEFUL WOMAN ND SHE HAS EVERY REASON TO BE ROUD. SHE WORKED HER ASS OFF O GET TO WHERE SHE IS, SO WHEN YOU JUST SHOWED UP WITH THE STORY OF THE CENTURY SHE HAD SOME...ISSUES.
HAD?
SHE'S OVER THEM NOW. DIDN'T EAN ANYTHING BY IT. E'S CURIOUS. THAT'S WHAT MAKES HER LOIS LANE.
THEN SHE WON'T MIND IF I KEEP THIS FILE.
YOU'LL HAVE TO ASK HER ABOUT THAT, I JUST TAKE THE PHOTOS AND TRY TO SURVIVE HER, Y'KNOW?
CLARK? Y'KNOW WHAT I MEAN...?
WHAT THE HELL--
LIKE I SAID, THE LADY'S SMART--

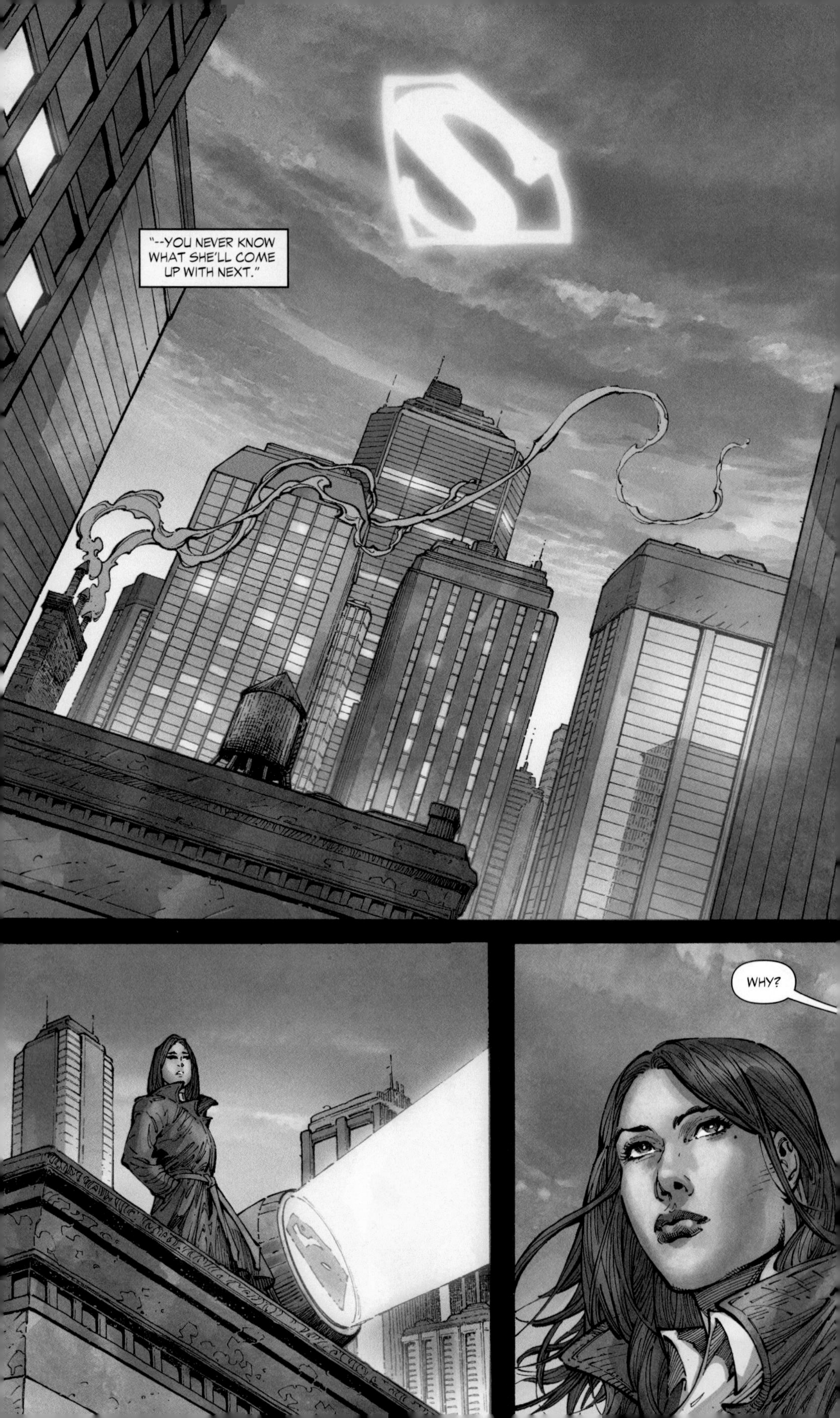
"--YOU NEVER KNOW WHAT SHE'LL COME UP WITH NEXT."
WHY?

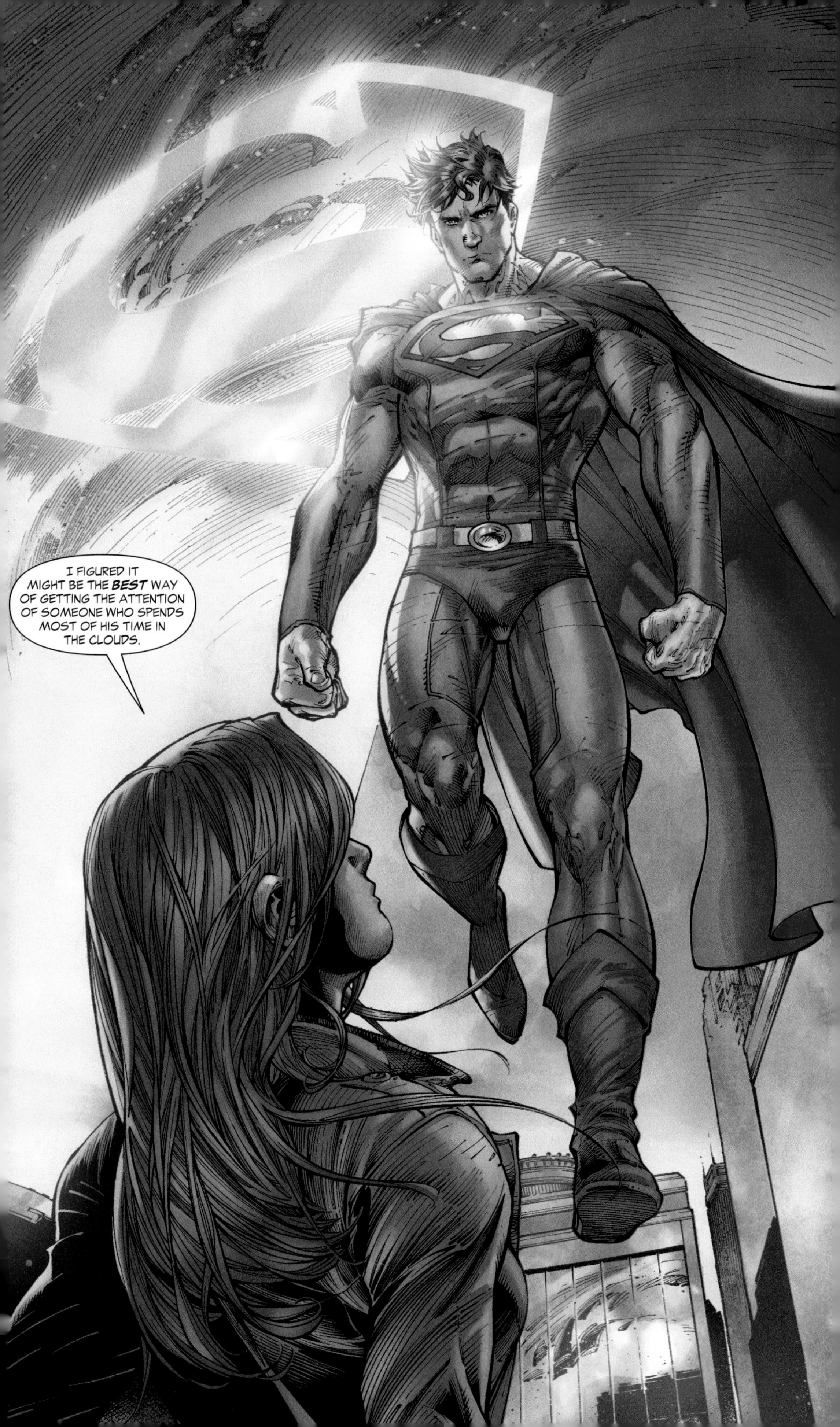
I FIGURED IT MIGHT BE THE BEST WAY OF GETTING THE ATTENTION OF SOMEONE WHO SPENDS MOST OF HIS TIME IN THE CLOUDS.

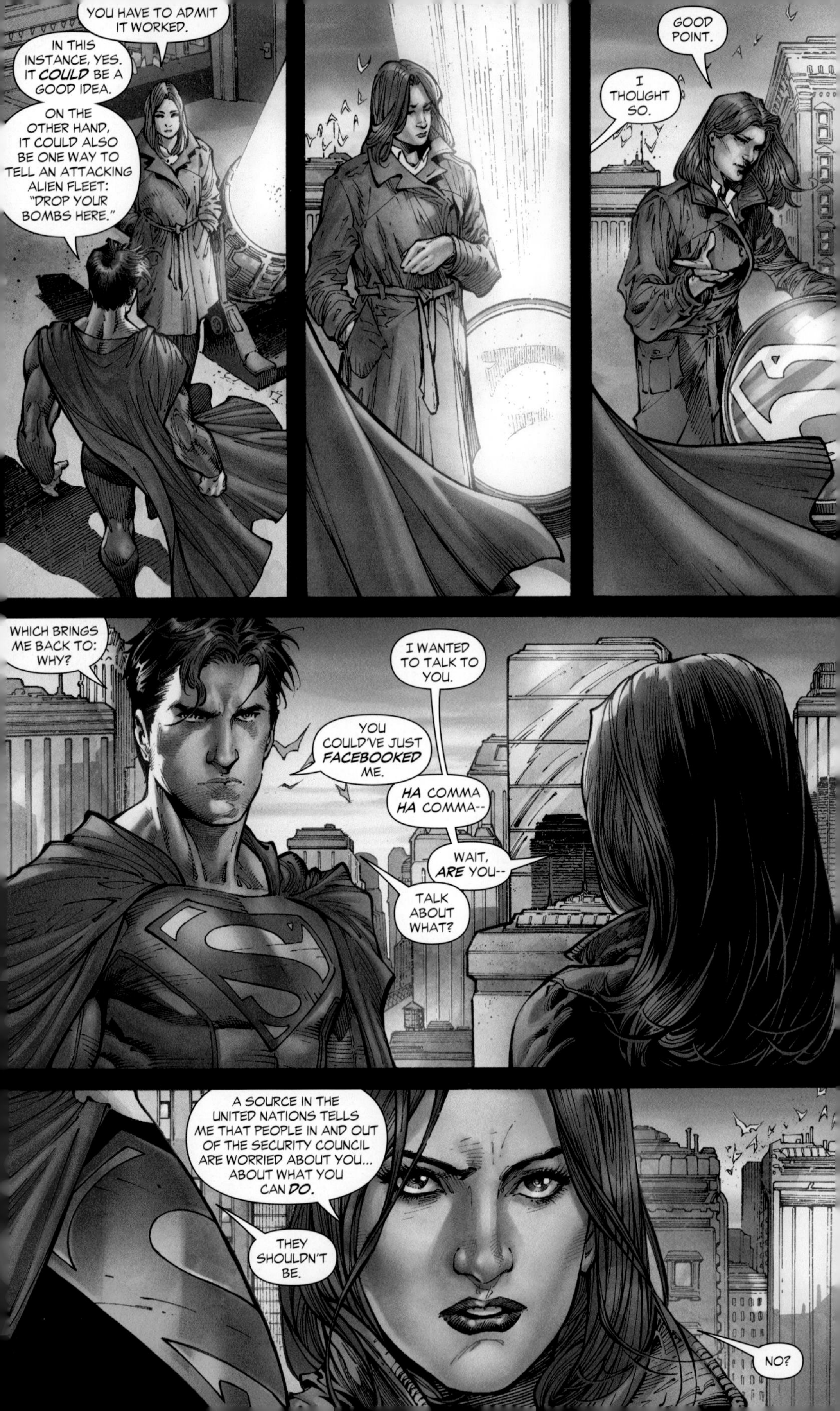
YOU HAVE TO ADMIT IT WORKED.
IN THIS INSTANCE, YES. IT COULD BE A GOOD IDEA.
ON THE OTHER HAND, IT COULD ALSO BE ONE WAY TO TELL AN ATTACKING ALIEN FLEET: "DROP YOUR BOMBS HERE."
GOOD POINT.
I THOUGHT SO.
WHICH BRINGS ME BACK TO: WHY?
I WANTED TO TALK TO YOU.
YOU COULD'VE JUST FACEBOOKED ME.
HA COMMA HA COMMA--
WAIT, ARE YOU--
TALK ABOUT WHAT?
A SOURCE IN THE UNITED NATIONS TELLS ME THAT PEOPLE IN AND OUT OF THE SECURITY COUNCIL ARE WORRIED ABOUT YOU... ABOUT WHAT YOU CAN DO.
THEY SHOULDN'T BE.
NO?

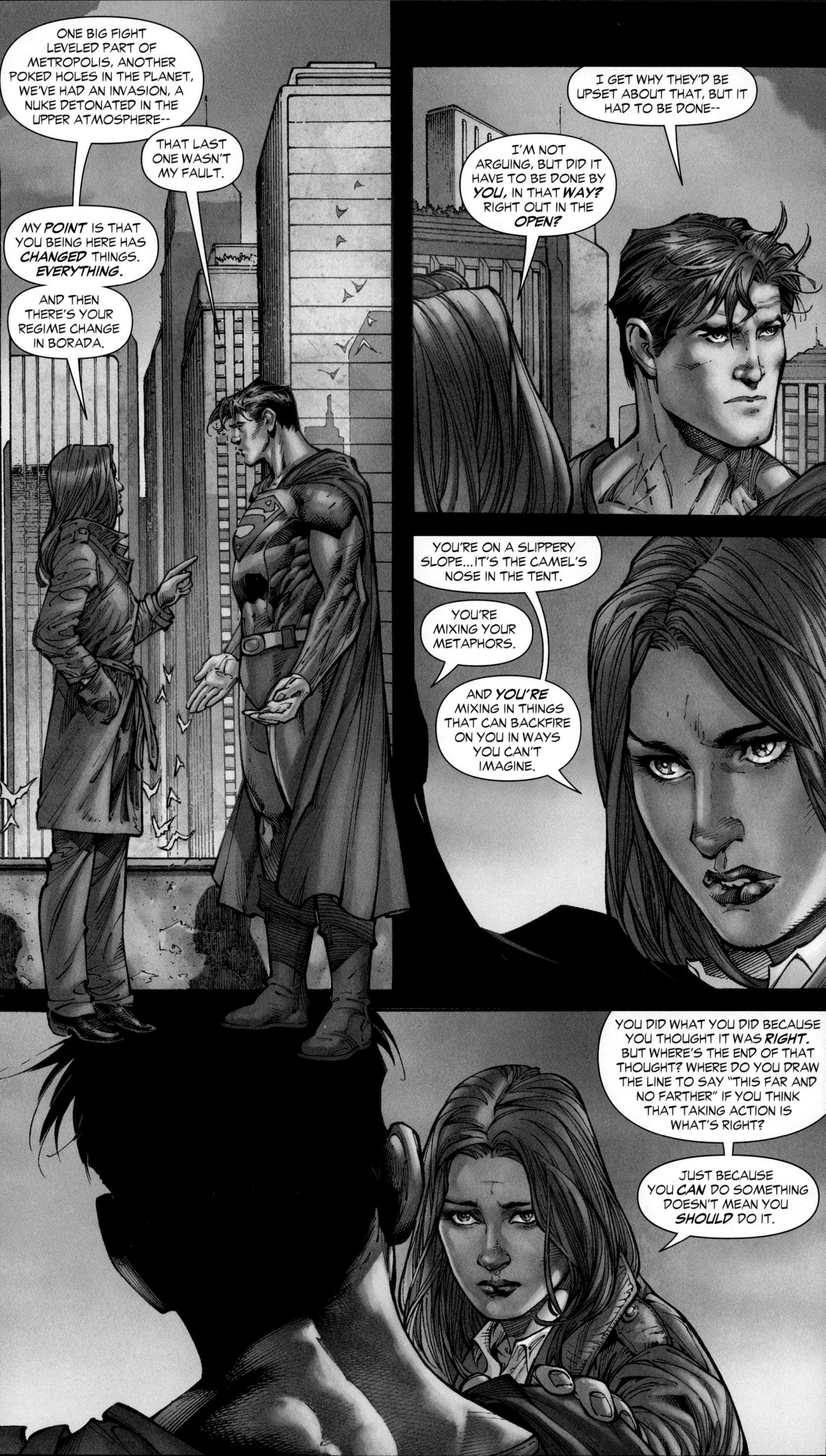
ONE BIG FIGHT LEVELED PART OF METROPOLIS, ANOTHER POKED HOLES IN THE PLANET, WE'VE HAD AN INVASION, A NUKE DETONATED IN THE UPPER ATMOSPHERE--
THAT LAST ONE WASN'T MY FAULT.
MY **POINT** IS THAT YOU BEING HERE HAS **CHANGED** THINGS. **EVERYTHING.**
AND THEN THERE'S YOUR REGIME CHANGE IN BORADA.
I GET WHY THEY'D BE UPSET ABOUT THAT, BUT IT HAD TO BE DONE--
I'M NOT ARGUING, BUT DID IT HAVE TO BE DONE BY **YOU,** IN THAT **WAY?** RIGHT OUT IN THE **OPEN?**
YOU'RE ON A SLIPPERY SLOPE...IT'S THE CAMEL'S NOSE IN THE TENT.
YOU'RE MIXING YOUR METAPHORS.
AND **YOU'RE** MIXING IN THINGS THAT CAN BACKFIRE ON YOU IN WAYS YOU CAN'T IMAGINE.
YOU DID WHAT YOU DID BECAUSE YOU THOUGHT IT WAS **RIGHT.** BUT WHERE'S THE END OF THAT THOUGHT? WHERE DO YOU DRAW THE LINE TO SAY "THIS FAR AND NO FARTHER" IF YOU THINK THAT TAKING ACTION IS WHAT'S RIGHT?
JUST BECAUSE YOU **CAN** DO SOMETHING DOESN'T MEAN YOU **SHOULD** DO IT.

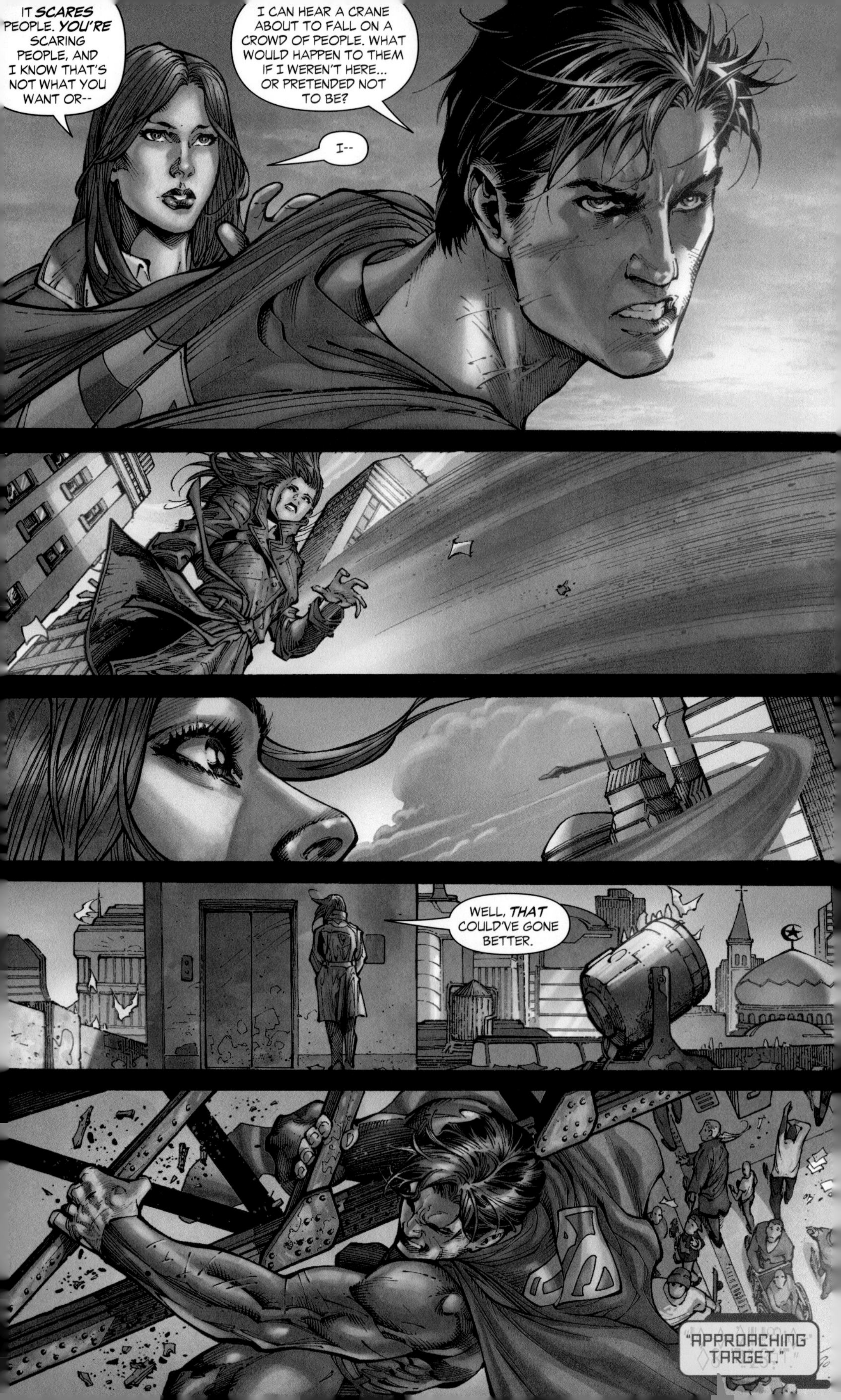

IT SCARES PEOPLE. YOU'RE SCARING PEOPLE, AND I KNOW THAT'S NOT WHAT YOU WANT OR--
I CAN HEAR A CRANE ABOUT TO FALL ON A CROWD OF PEOPLE. WHAT WOULD HAPPEN TO THEM IF I WEREN'T HERE... OR PRETENDED NOT TO BE?
I--
WELL, THAT COULD'VE GONE BETTER.
"APPROACHING TARGET."

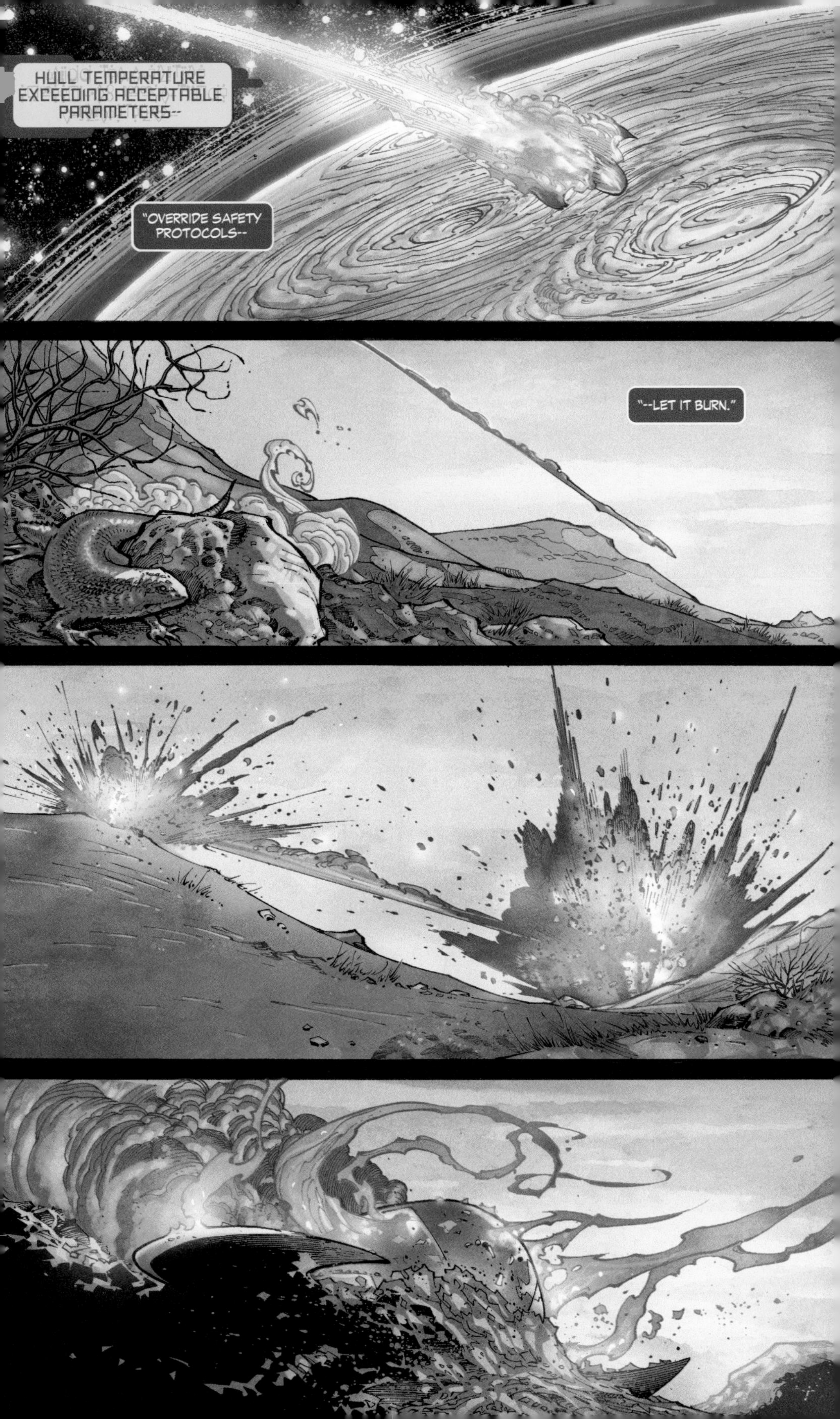
HULL TEMPERATURE EXCEEDING ACCEPTABLE PARAMETERS--
"OVERRIDE SAFETY PROTOCOLS--
"--LET IT BURN."

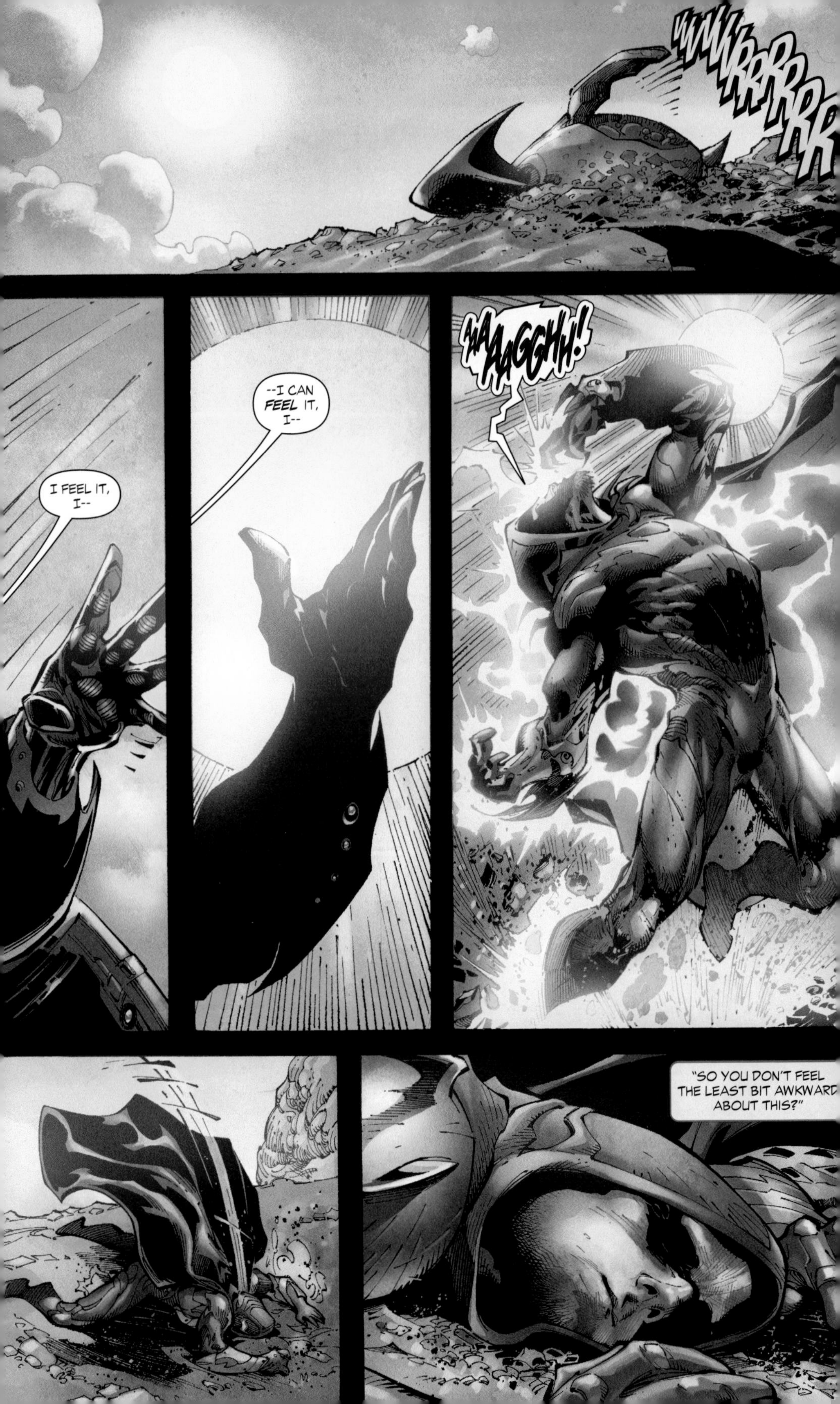

WWWRRRRRRR
I FEEL IT, I--
--I CAN FEEL IT, I--
AAAAGGHH!
"SO YOU DON'T FEEL THE LEAST BIT AWKWARD ABOUT THIS?"

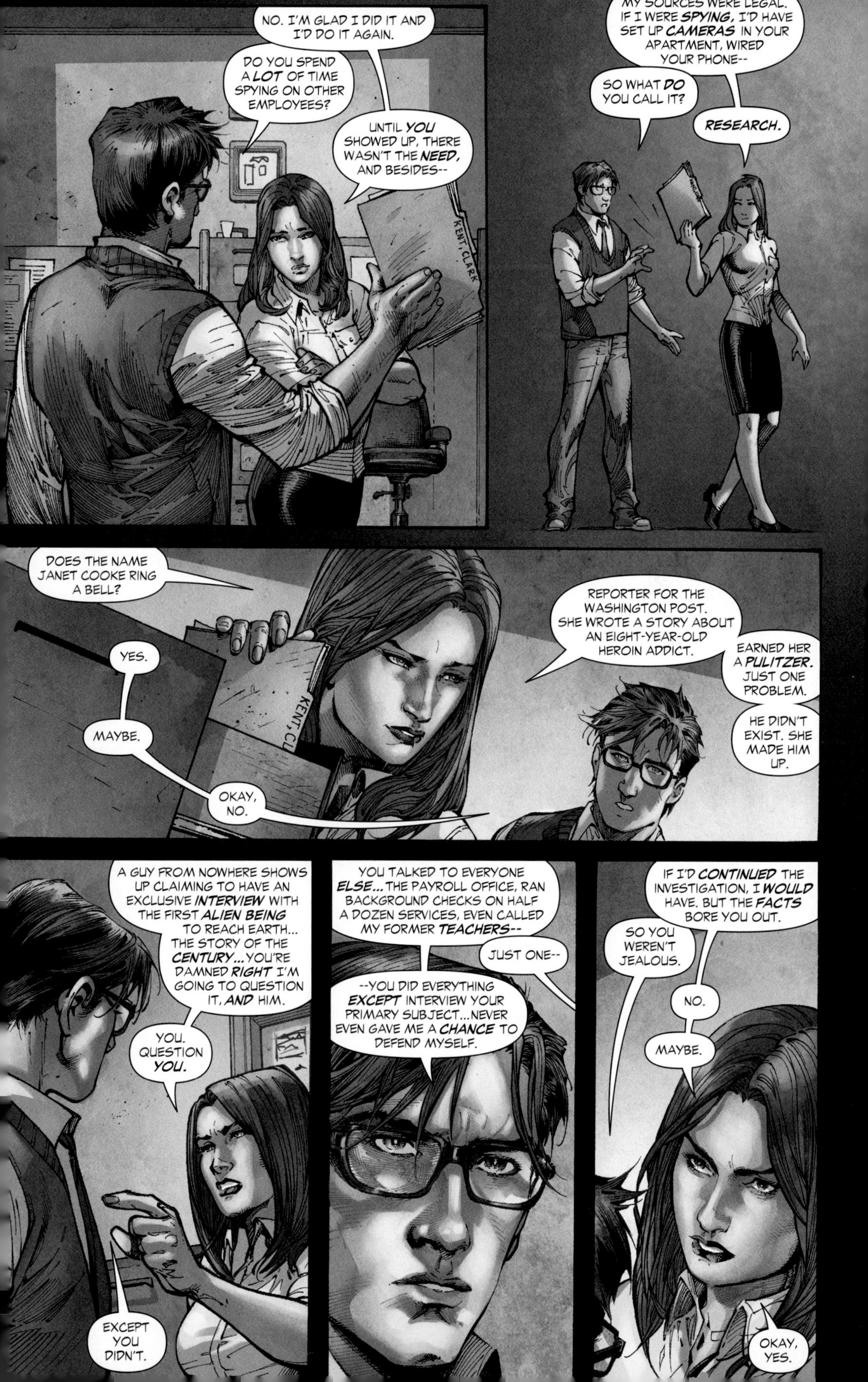
NO. I'M GLAD I DID IT AND I'D DO IT AGAIN.
DO YOU SPEND A LOT OF TIME SPYING ON OTHER EMPLOYEES?
UNTIL YOU SHOWED UP, THERE WASN'T THE NEED, AND BESIDES--
KENT, CLARK
--I WASN'T SPYING. MY SOURCES WERE LEGAL. IF I WERE SPYING, I'D HAVE SET UP CAMERAS IN YOUR APARTMENT, WIRED YOUR PHONE--
SO WHAT DO YOU CALL IT?
RESEARCH.
DOES THE NAME JANET COOKE RING A BELL?
YES.
MAYBE.
OKAY, NO.
REPORTER FOR THE WASHINGTON POST. SHE WROTE A STORY ABOUT AN EIGHT-YEAR-OLD HEROIN ADDICT.
EARNED HER A PULITZER. JUST ONE PROBLEM.
HE DIDN'T EXIST. SHE MADE HIM UP.
A GUY FROM NOWHERE SHOWS UP CLAIMING TO HAVE AN EXCLUSIVE INTERVIEW WITH THE FIRST ALIEN BEING TO REACH EARTH... THE STORY OF THE CENTURY... YOU'RE DAMNED RIGHT I'M GOING TO QUESTION IT, AND HIM.
YOU. QUESTION YOU.
EXCEPT YOU DIDN'T.
YOU TALKED TO EVERYONE ELSE... THE PAYROLL OFFICE, RAN BACKGROUND CHECKS ON HALF A DOZEN SERVICES, EVEN CALLED MY FORMER TEACHERS--
JUST ONE--
--YOU DID EVERYTHING EXCEPT INTERVIEW YOUR PRIMARY SUBJECT... NEVER EVEN GAVE ME A CHANCE TO DEFEND MYSELF.
IF I'D CONTINUED THE INVESTIGATION, I WOULD HAVE. BUT THE FACTS BORE YOU OUT.
SO YOU WEREN'T JEALOUS.
NO.
MAYBE.
OKAY, YES.

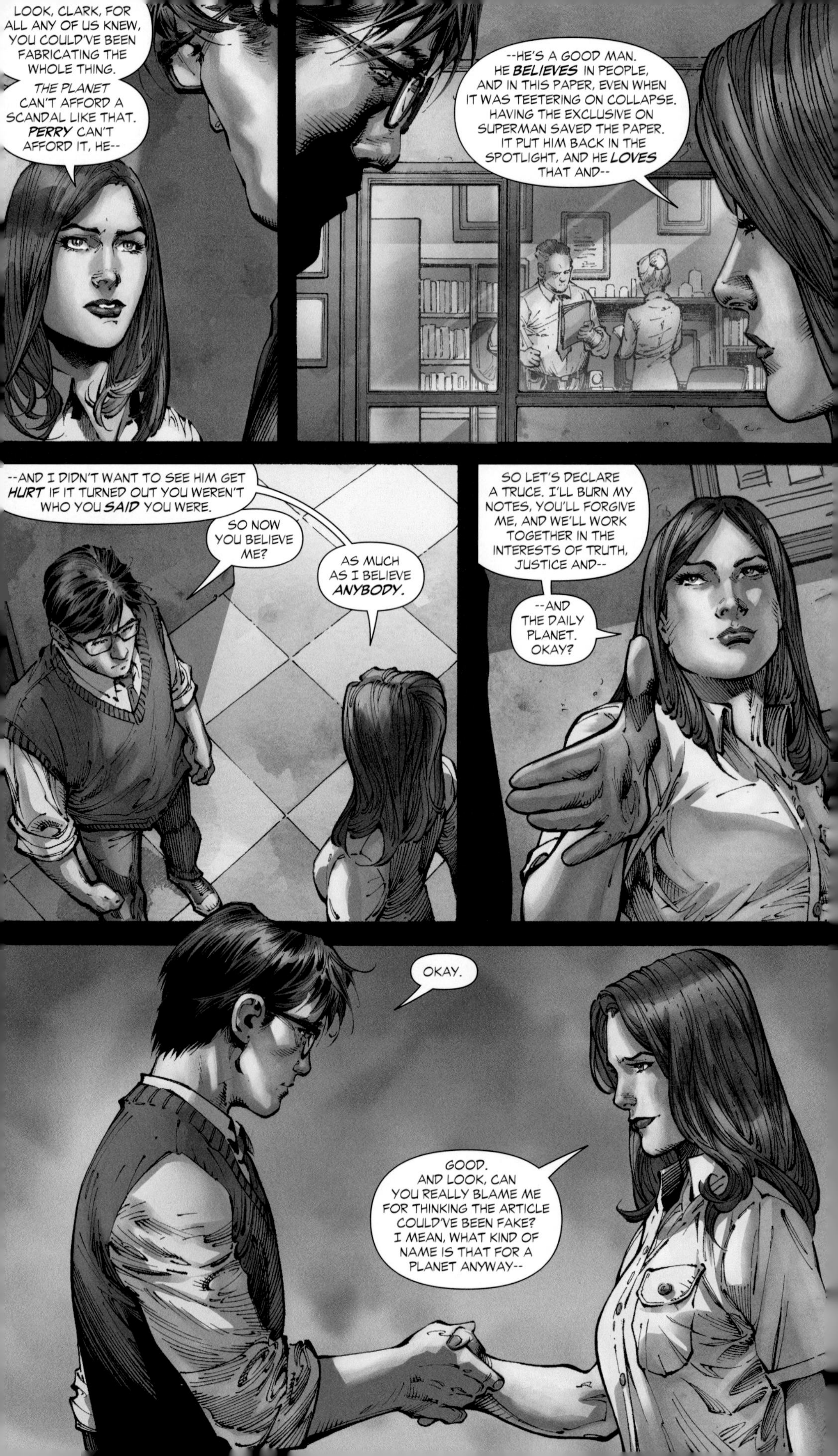
LOOK, CLARK, FOR ALL ANY OF US KNEW, YOU COULD'VE BEEN FABRICATING THE WHOLE THING.
THE PLANET CAN'T AFFORD A SCANDAL LIKE THAT. PERRY CAN'T AFFORD IT, HE--
--HE'S A GOOD MAN. HE BELIEVES IN PEOPLE, AND IN THIS PAPER, EVEN WHEN IT WAS TEETERING ON COLLAPSE. HAVING THE EXCLUSIVE ON SUPERMAN SAVED THE PAPER. IT PUT HIM BACK IN THE SPOTLIGHT, AND HE LOVES THAT AND--
--AND I DIDN'T WANT TO SEE HIM GET HURT IF IT TURNED OUT YOU WEREN'T WHO YOU SAID YOU WERE.
SO NOW YOU BELIEVE ME?
AS MUCH AS I BELIEVE ANYBODY.
SO LET'S DECLARE A TRUCE. I'LL BURN MY NOTES, YOU'LL FORGIVE ME, AND WE'LL WORK TOGETHER IN THE INTERESTS OF TRUTH, JUSTICE AND--
--AND THE DAILY PLANET. OKAY?
OKAY.
GOOD. AND LOOK, CAN YOU REALLY BLAME ME FOR THINKING THE ARTICLE COULD'VE BEEN FAKE? I MEAN, WHAT KIND OF NAME IS THAT FOR A PLANET ANYWAY--

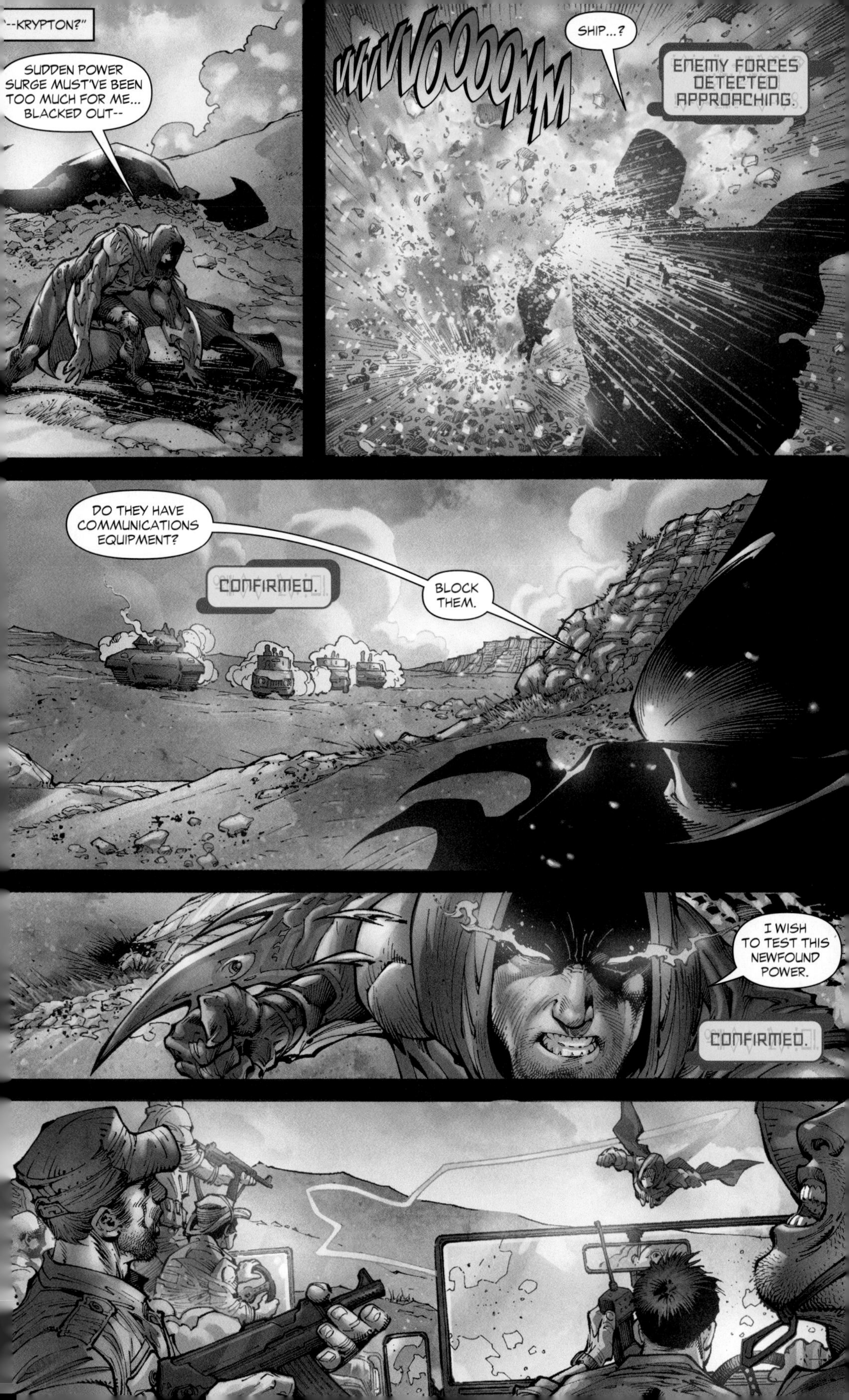
"--KRYPTON?"
SUDDEN POWER SURGE MUST'VE BEEN TOO MUCH FOR ME... BLACKED OUT--
WWVOOOOMM
SHIP...?
ENEMY FORCES DETECTED APPROACHING.
DO THEY HAVE COMMUNICATIONS EQUIPMENT?
CONFIRMED.
BLOCK THEM.
I WISH TO TEST THIS NEWFOUND POWER.
CONFIRMED.

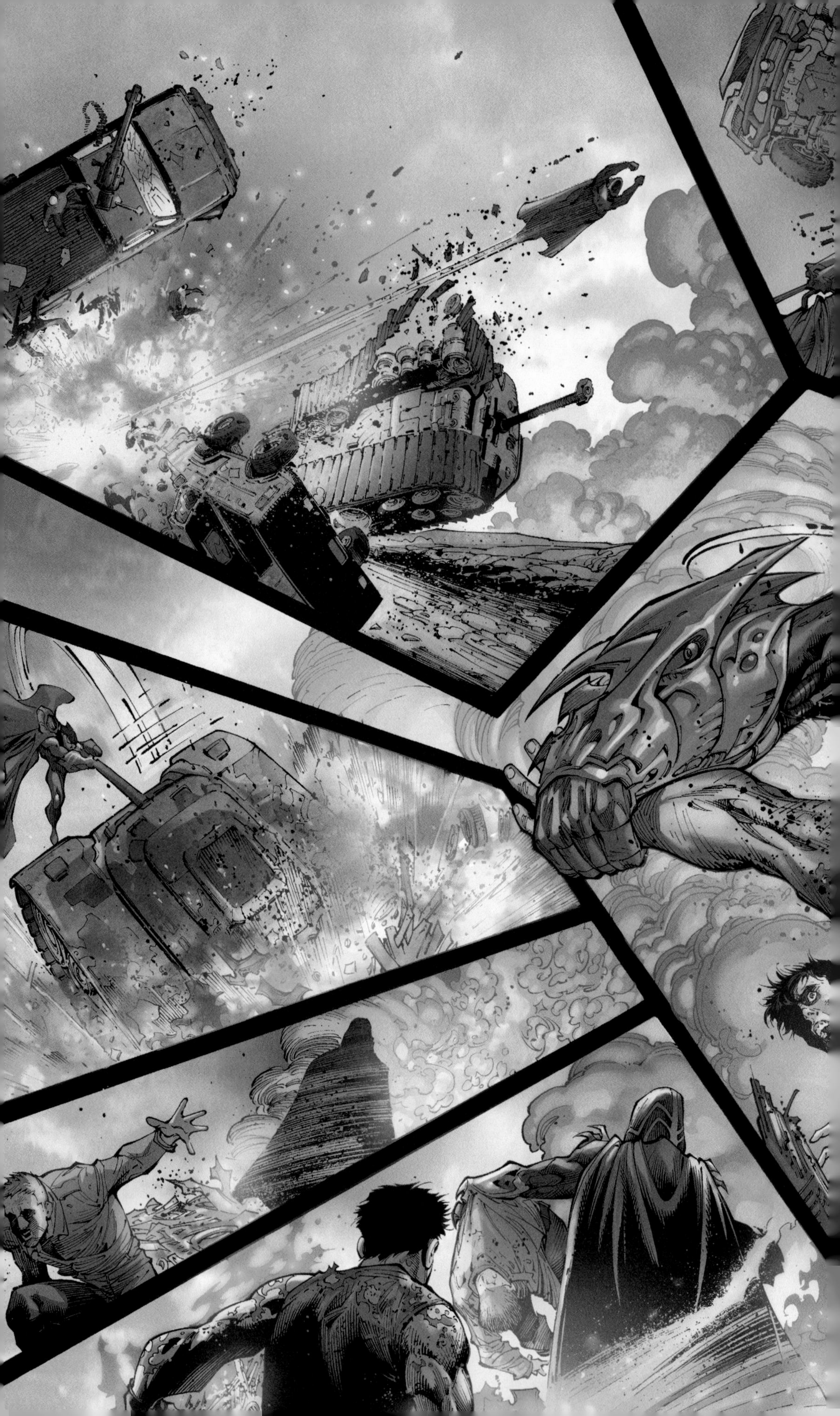

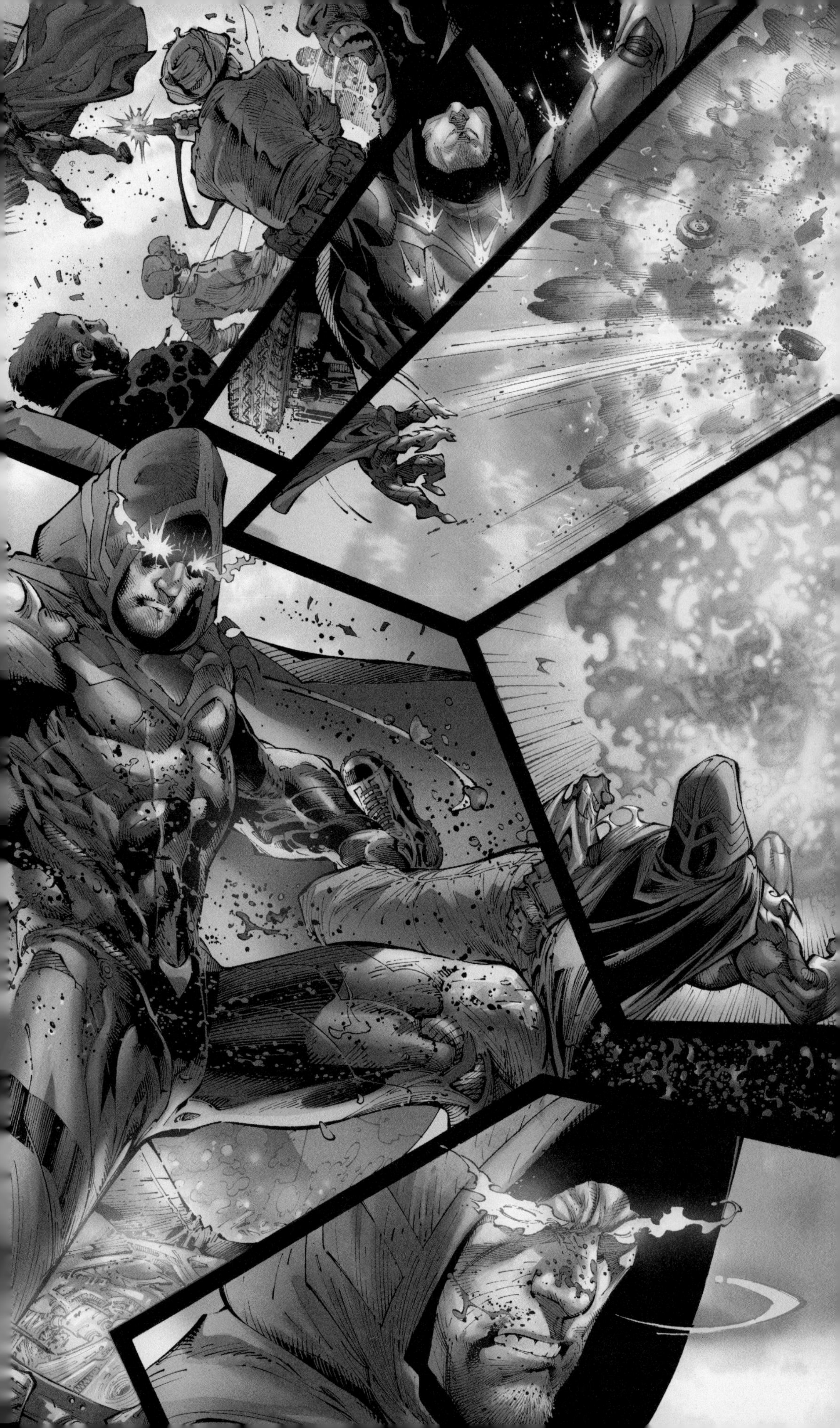

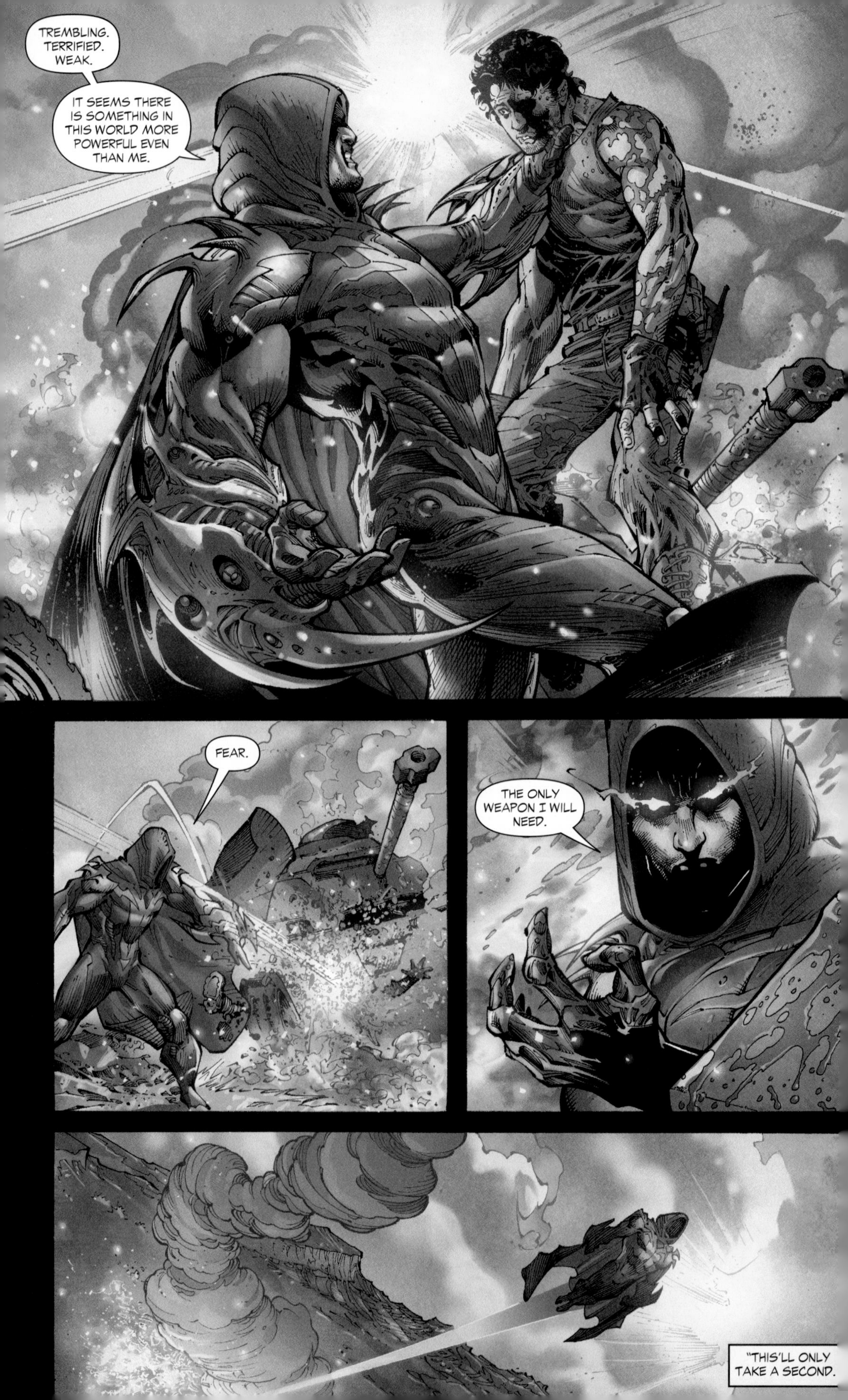
TREMBLING.
TERRIFIED.
WEAK.
IT SEEMS THERE IS SOMETHING IN THIS WORLD MORE POWERFUL EVEN THAN ME.
FEAR.
THE ONLY WEAPON I WILL NEED.
"THIS'LL ONLY TAKE A SECOND.

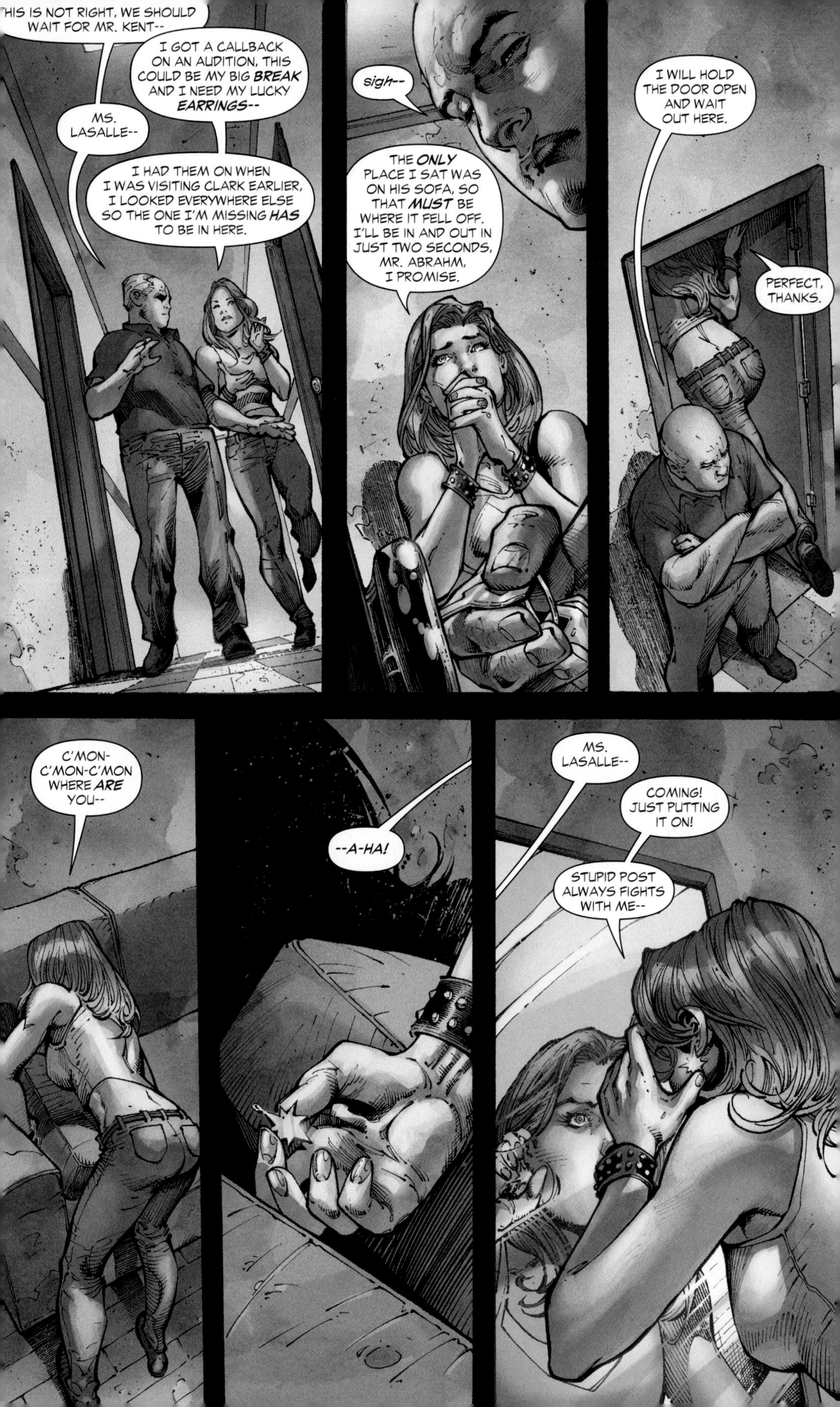
THIS IS NOT RIGHT, WE SHOULD WAIT FOR MR. KENT--
I GOT A CALLBACK ON AN AUDITION, THIS COULD BE MY BIG BREAK AND I NEED MY LUCKY EARRINGS--
MS. LASALLE--
I HAD THEM ON WHEN I WAS VISITING CLARK EARLIER, I LOOKED EVERYWHERE ELSE SO THE ONE I'M MISSING HAS TO BE IN HERE.
sigh--
THE ONLY PLACE I SAT WAS ON HIS SOFA, SO THAT MUST BE WHERE IT FELL OFF. I'LL BE IN AND OUT IN JUST TWO SECONDS, MR. ABRAHM, I PROMISE.
I WILL HOLD THE DOOR OPEN AND WAIT OUT HERE.
PERFECT, THANKS.
C'MON-C'MON-C'MON WHERE ARE YOU--
--A-HA!
MS. LASALLE--
COMING! JUST PUTTING IT ON!
STUPID POST ALWAYS FIGHTS WITH ME--

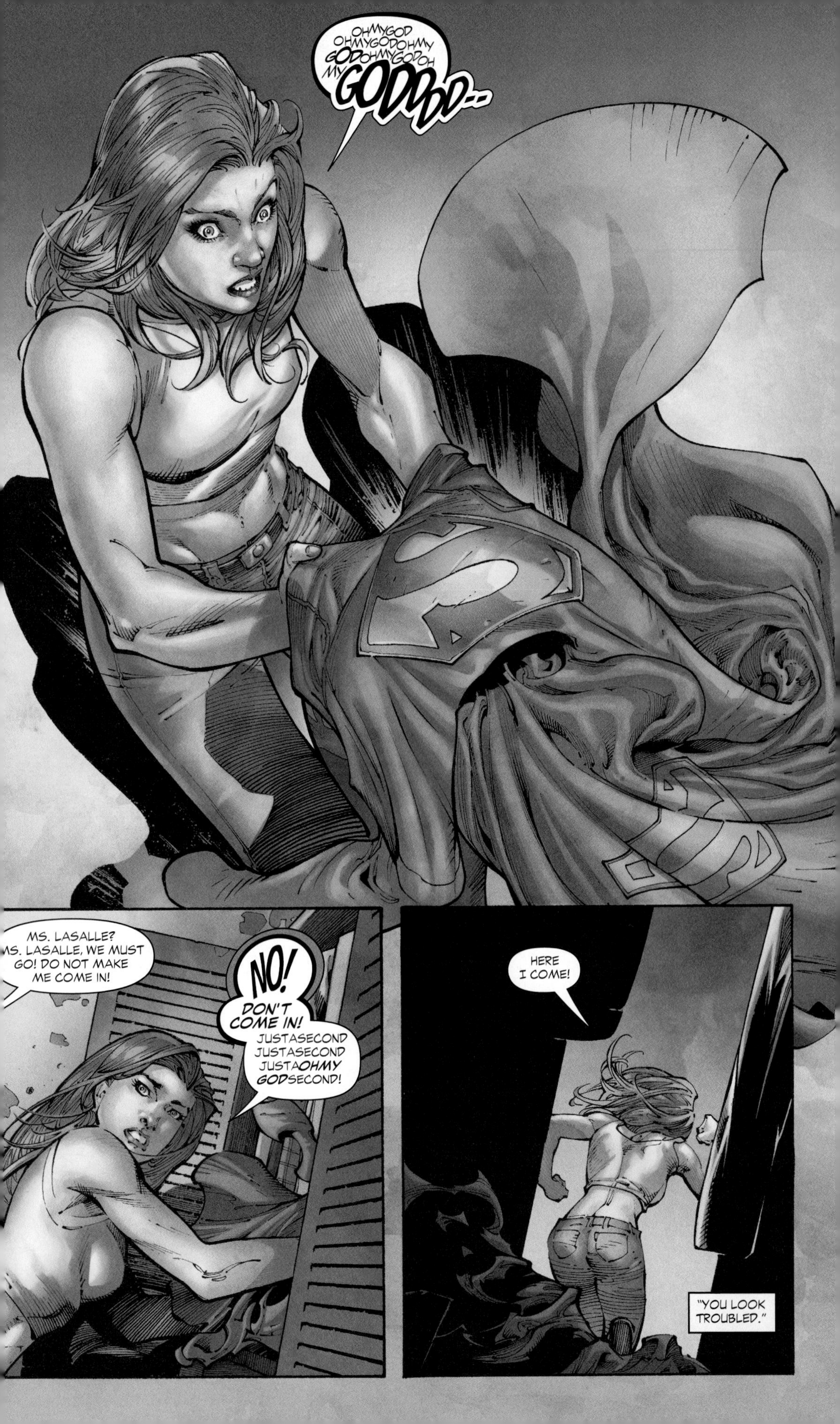
OHMYGOD OHMYGODOHMY GODOHMYGODOH MY GODDDD--
MS. LASALLE? MS. LASALLE, WE MUST GO! DO NOT MAKE ME COME IN!
NO!
DON'T COME IN!
JUSTASECOND JUSTASECOND JUSTAOHMY GODSECOND!
HERE I COME!
"YOU LOOK TROUBLED."

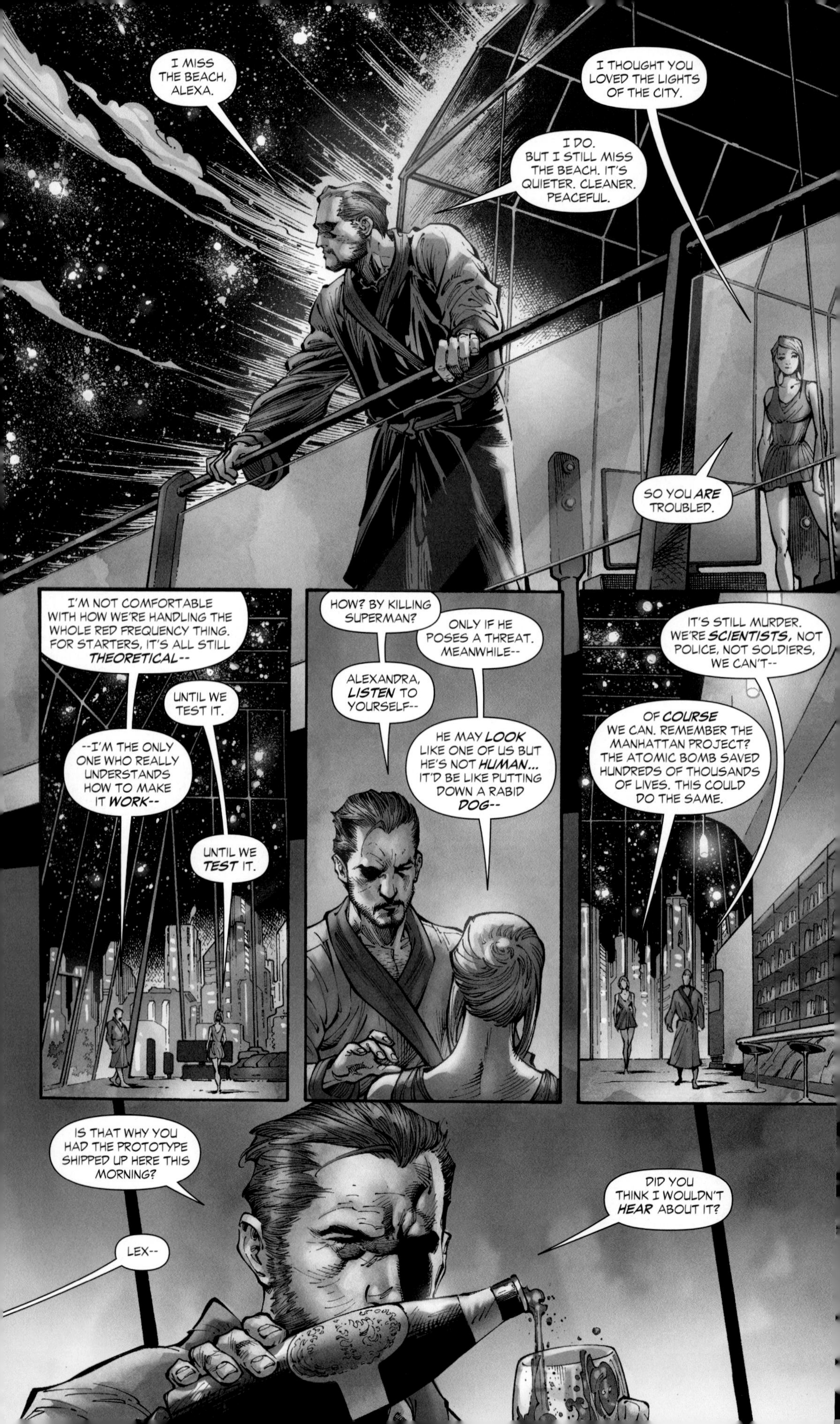
I MISS THE BEACH, ALEXA.
I THOUGHT YOU LOVED THE LIGHTS OF THE CITY.
I DO. BUT I STILL MISS THE BEACH. IT'S QUIETER. CLEANER. PEACEFUL.
SO YOU ARE TROUBLED.
I'M NOT COMFORTABLE WITH HOW WE'RE HANDLING THE WHOLE RED FREQUENCY THING. FOR STARTERS, IT'S ALL STILL THEORETICAL--
UNTIL WE TEST IT.
--I'M THE ONLY ONE WHO REALLY UNDERSTANDS HOW TO MAKE IT WORK--
UNTIL WE TEST IT.
HOW? BY KILLING SUPERMAN?
ONLY IF HE POSES A THREAT. MEANWHILE--
ALEXANDRA, LISTEN TO YOURSELF--
HE MAY LOOK LIKE ONE OF US BUT HE'S NOT HUMAN... IT'D BE LIKE PUTTING DOWN A RABID DOG--
IT'S STILL MURDER. WE'RE SCIENTISTS, NOT POLICE, NOT SOLDIERS, WE CAN'T--
OF COURSE WE CAN. REMEMBER THE MANHATTAN PROJECT? THE ATOMIC BOMB SAVED HUNDREDS OF THOUSANDS OF LIVES. THIS COULD DO THE SAME.
IS THAT WHY YOU HAD THE PROTOTYPE SHIPPED UP HERE THIS MORNING?
LEX--
DID YOU THINK I WOULDN'T HEAR ABOUT IT?

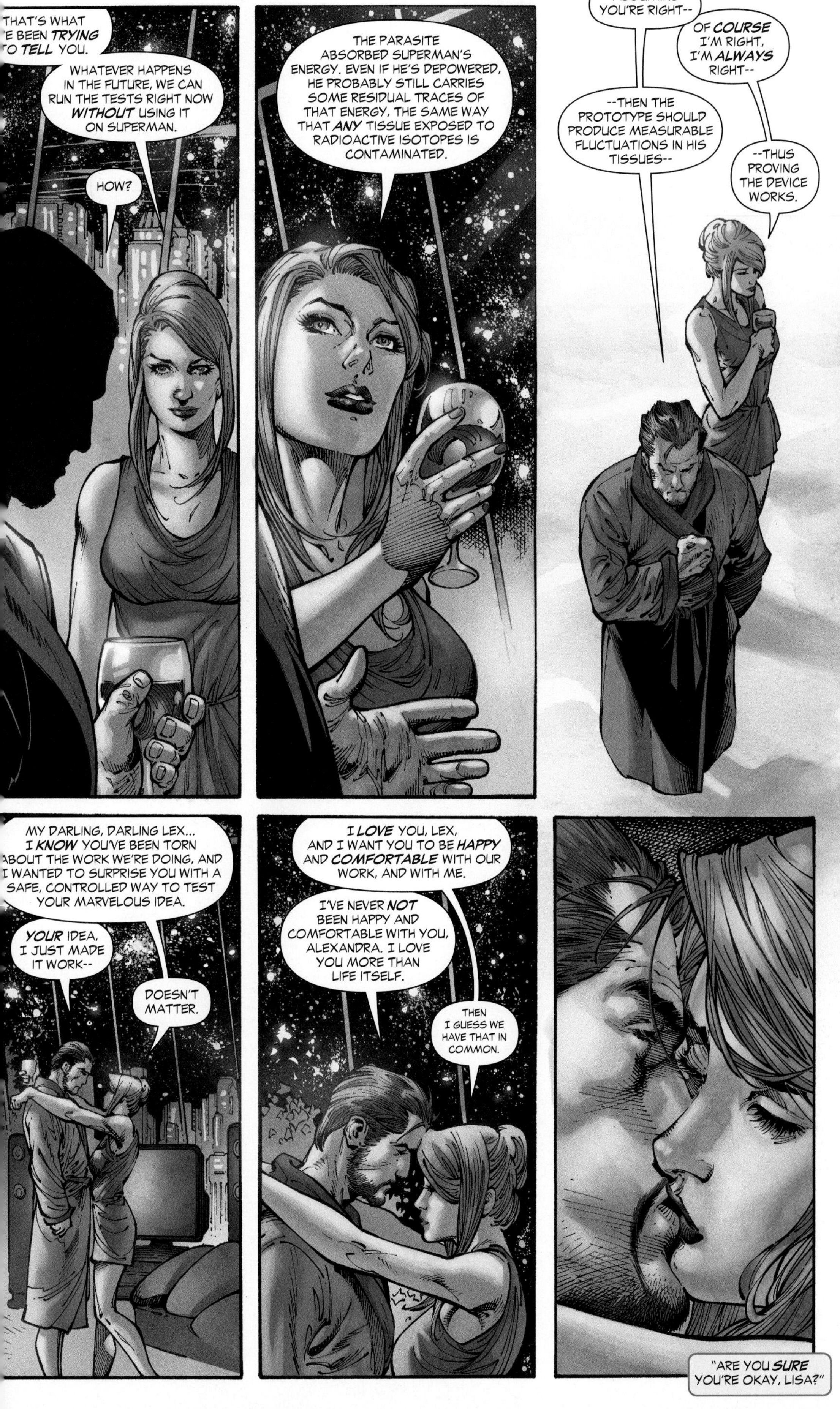
THAT'S WHAT 'E BEEN TRYING TO TELL YOU.
WHATEVER HAPPENS IN THE FUTURE, WE CAN RUN THE TESTS RIGHT NOW WITHOUT USING IT ON SUPERMAN.
HOW?
THE PARASITE ABSORBED SUPERMAN'S ENERGY. EVEN IF HE'S DEPOWERED, HE PROBABLY STILL CARRIES SOME RESIDUAL TRACES OF THAT ENERGY, THE SAME WAY THAT ANY TISSUE EXPOSED TO RADIOACTIVE ISOTOPES IS CONTAMINATED.
ASSUMING YOU'RE RIGHT--
OF COURSE I'M RIGHT, I'M ALWAYS RIGHT--
--THEN THE PROTOTYPE SHOULD PRODUCE MEASURABLE FLUCTUATIONS IN HIS TISSUES--
--THUS PROVING THE DEVICE WORKS.
MY DARLING, DARLING LEX... I KNOW YOU'VE BEEN TORN ABOUT THE WORK WE'RE DOING, AND I WANTED TO SURPRISE YOU WITH A SAFE, CONTROLLED WAY TO TEST YOUR MARVELOUS IDEA.
YOUR IDEA, I JUST MADE IT WORK--
DOESN'T MATTER.
I LOVE YOU, LEX, AND I WANT YOU TO BE HAPPY AND COMFORTABLE WITH OUR WORK, AND WITH ME.
I'VE NEVER NOT BEEN HAPPY AND COMFORTABLE WITH YOU, ALEXANDRA. I LOVE YOU MORE THAN LIFE ITSELF.
THEN I GUESS WE HAVE THAT IN COMMON.
"ARE YOU SURE YOU'RE OKAY, LISA?"

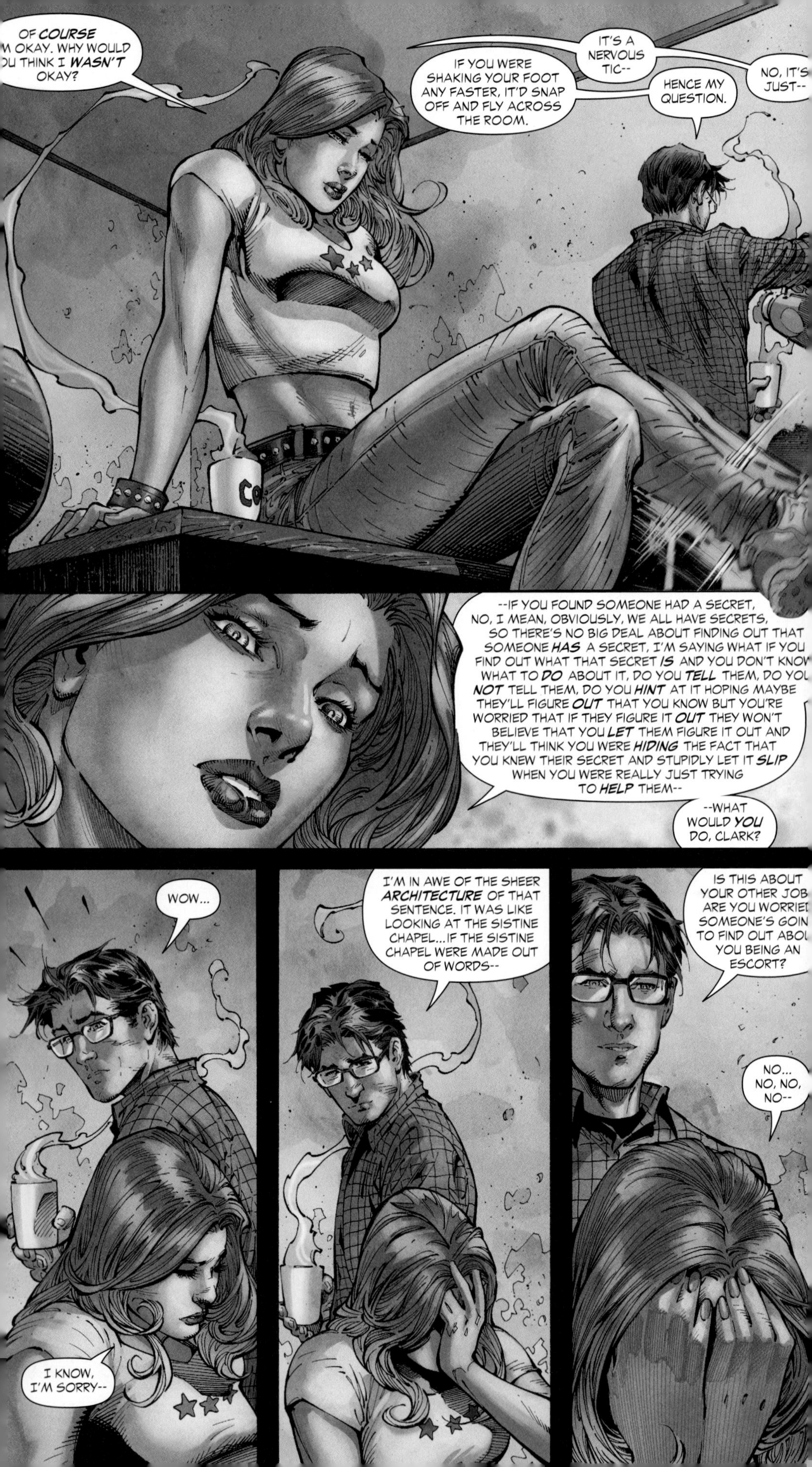
OF COURSE
M OKAY. WHY WOULD
OU THINK I WASN'T
OKAY?
IF YOU WERE SHAKING YOUR FOOT ANY FASTER, IT'D SNAP OFF AND FLY ACROSS THE ROOM.
IT'S A NERVOUS TIC--
HENCE MY QUESTION.
NO, IT'S JUST--
--IF YOU FOUND SOMEONE HAD A SECRET, NO, I MEAN, OBVIOUSLY, WE ALL HAVE SECRETS, SO THERE'S NO BIG DEAL ABOUT FINDING OUT THAT SOMEONE HAS A SECRET, I'M SAYING WHAT IF YOU FIND OUT WHAT THAT SECRET IS AND YOU DON'T KNOW WHAT TO DO ABOUT IT, DO YOU TELL THEM, DO YOU NOT TELL THEM, DO YOU HINT AT IT HOPING MAYBE THEY'LL FIGURE OUT THAT YOU KNOW BUT YOU'RE WORRIED THAT IF THEY FIGURE IT OUT THEY WON'T BELIEVE THAT YOU LET THEM FIGURE IT OUT AND THEY'LL THINK YOU WERE HIDING THE FACT THAT YOU KNEW THEIR SECRET AND STUPIDLY LET IT SLIP WHEN YOU WERE REALLY JUST TRYING TO HELP THEM--
--WHAT WOULD YOU DO, CLARK?
WOW...
I KNOW, I'M SORRY--
I'M IN AWE OF THE SHEER ARCHITECTURE OF THAT SENTENCE. IT WAS LIKE LOOKING AT THE SISTINE CHAPEL...IF THE SISTINE CHAPEL WERE MADE OUT OF WORDS--
IS THIS ABOUT YOUR OTHER JOB ARE YOU WORRIED SOMEONE'S GOIN TO FIND OUT ABOU YOU BEING AN ESCORT?
NO... NO, NO, NO--

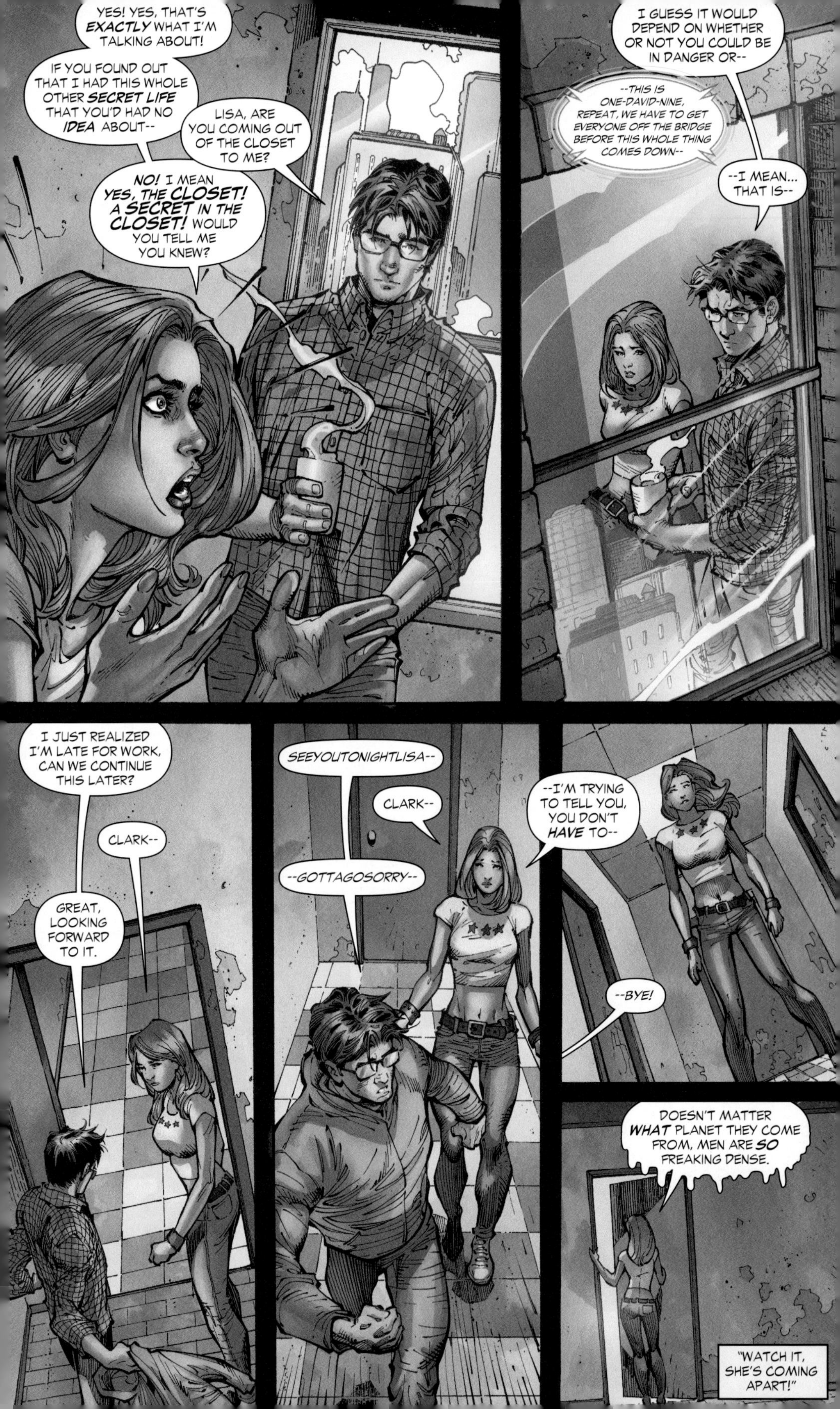

YES! YES, THAT'S *EXACTLY* WHAT I'M TALKING ABOUT!
IF YOU FOUND OUT THAT I HAD THIS WHOLE OTHER *SECRET LIFE* THAT YOU'D HAD NO *IDEA* ABOUT--
LISA, ARE YOU COMING OUT OF THE CLOSET TO ME?
NO! I MEAN *YES, THE CLOSET! A SECRET IN THE CLOSET!* WOULD YOU TELL ME YOU KNEW?
I GUESS IT WOULD DEPEND ON WHETHER OR NOT YOU COULD BE IN DANGER OR--
--THIS IS ONE-DAVID-NINE, REPEAT, WE HAVE TO GET EVERYONE OFF THE BRIDGE BEFORE THIS WHOLE THING COMES DOWN--
--I MEAN... THAT IS--
I JUST REALIZED I'M LATE FOR WORK, CAN WE CONTINUE THIS LATER?
CLARK--
GREAT, LOOKING FORWARD TO IT.
SEEYOUTONIGHTLISA--
CLARK--
--GOTTAGOSORRY--
--I'M TRYING TO TELL YOU, YOU DON'T *HAVE* TO--
--BYE!
DOESN'T MATTER *WHAT* PLANET THEY COME FROM, MEN ARE *SO* FREAKING DENSE.
"WATCH IT, SHE'S COMING APART!"

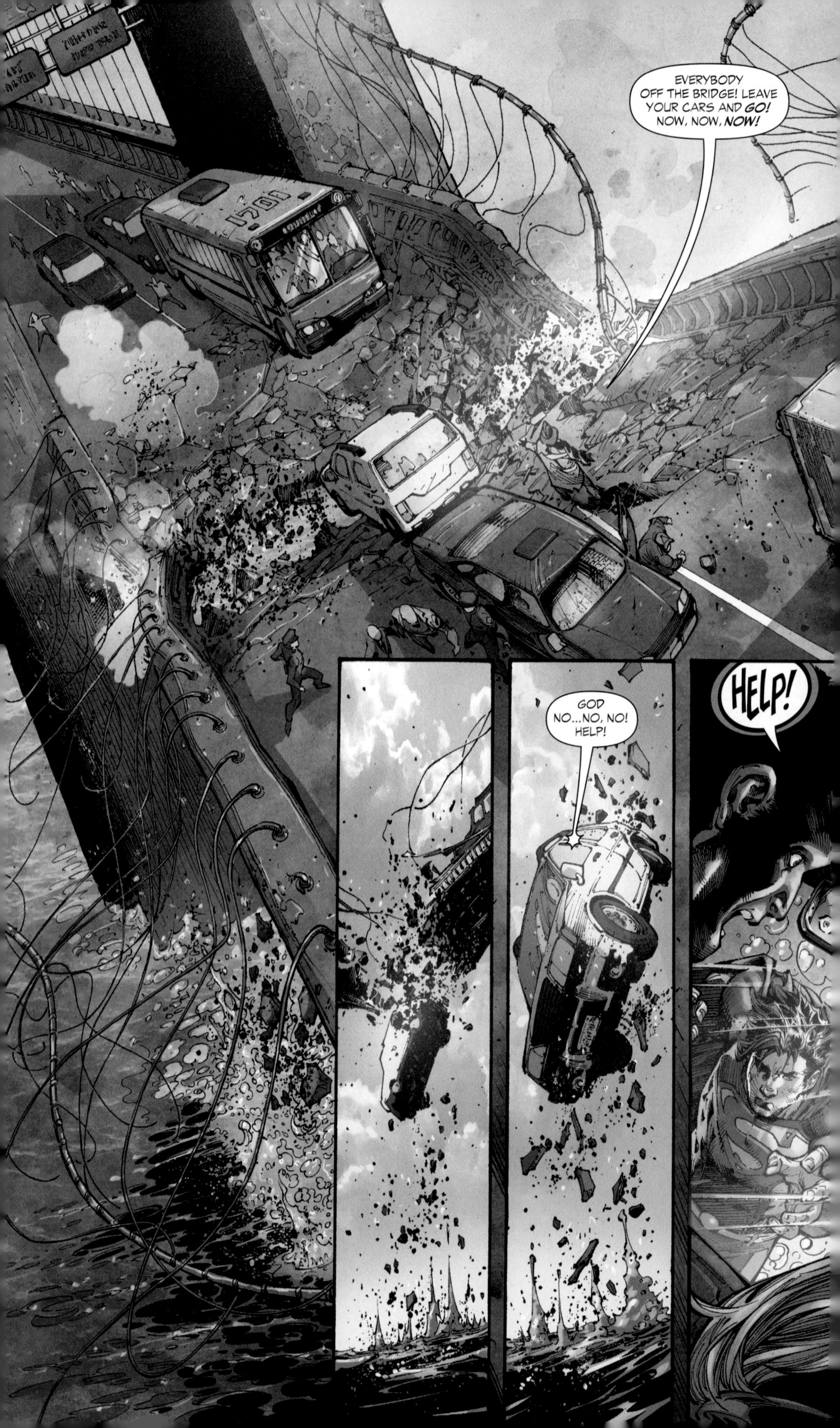
EVERYBODY OFF THE BRIDGE! LEAVE YOUR CARS AND *GO!* NOW, NOW, ***NOW!***
GOD NO...NO, NO! HELP!
HELP!

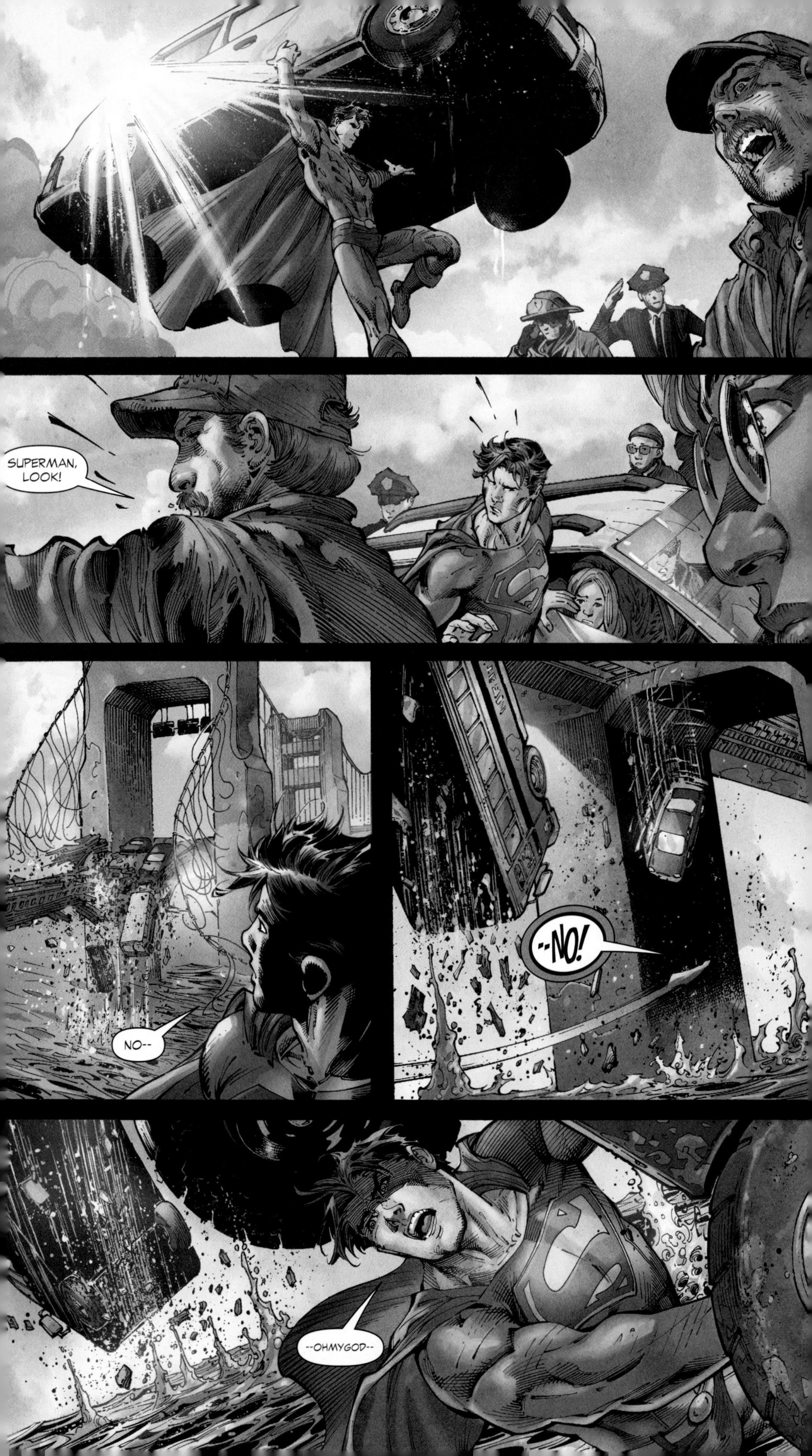
SUPERMAN, LOOK!
NO--
--NO!
--OHMYGOD--

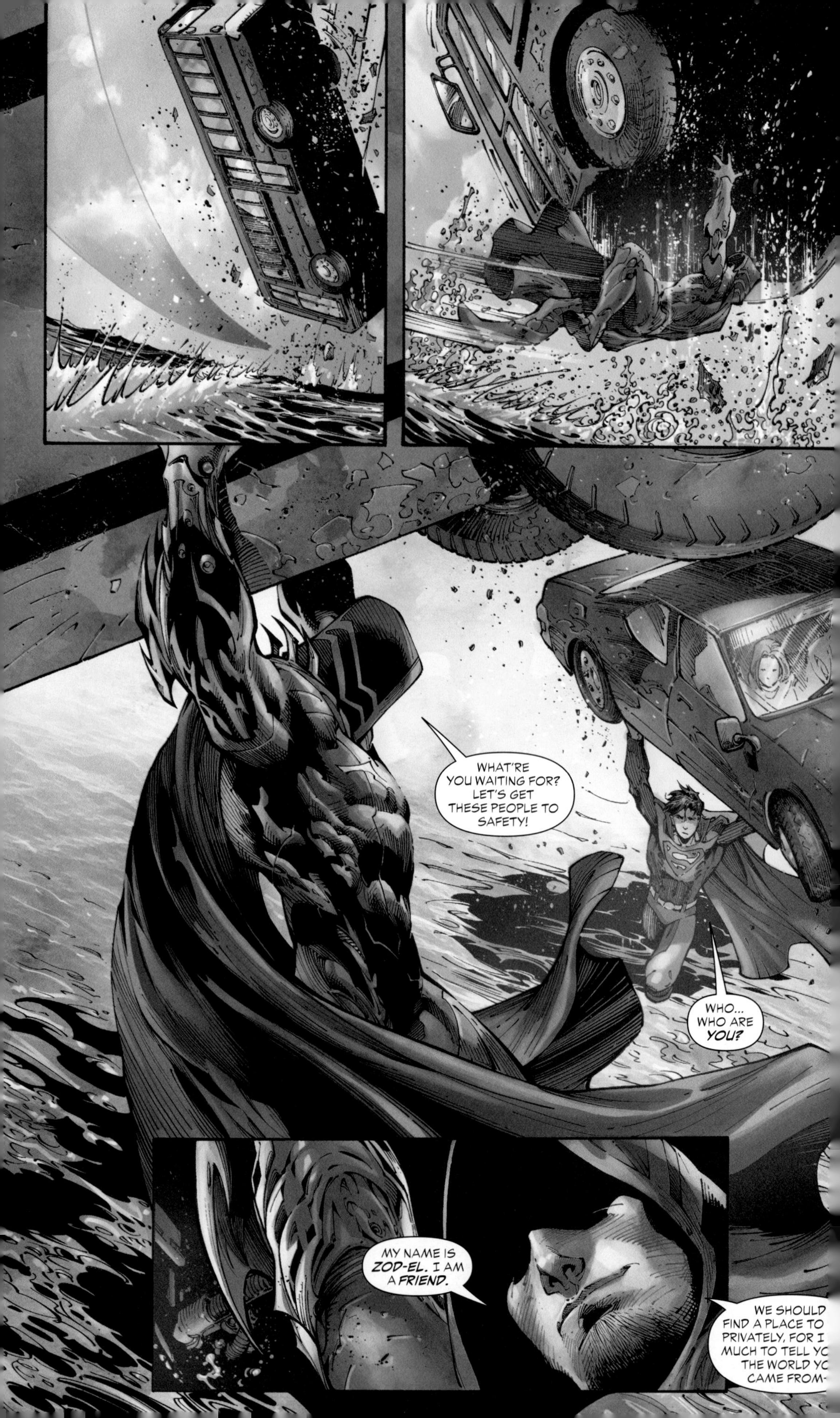
WHAT'RE YOU WAITING FOR? LET'S GET THESE PEOPLE TO SAFETY!
WHO... WHO ARE *YOU?*
MY NAME IS *ZOD-EL.* I AM A *FRIEND.*
WE SHOULD FIND A PLACE TO PRIVATELY, FOR I MUCH TO TELL YO THE WORLD YO CAME FROM-

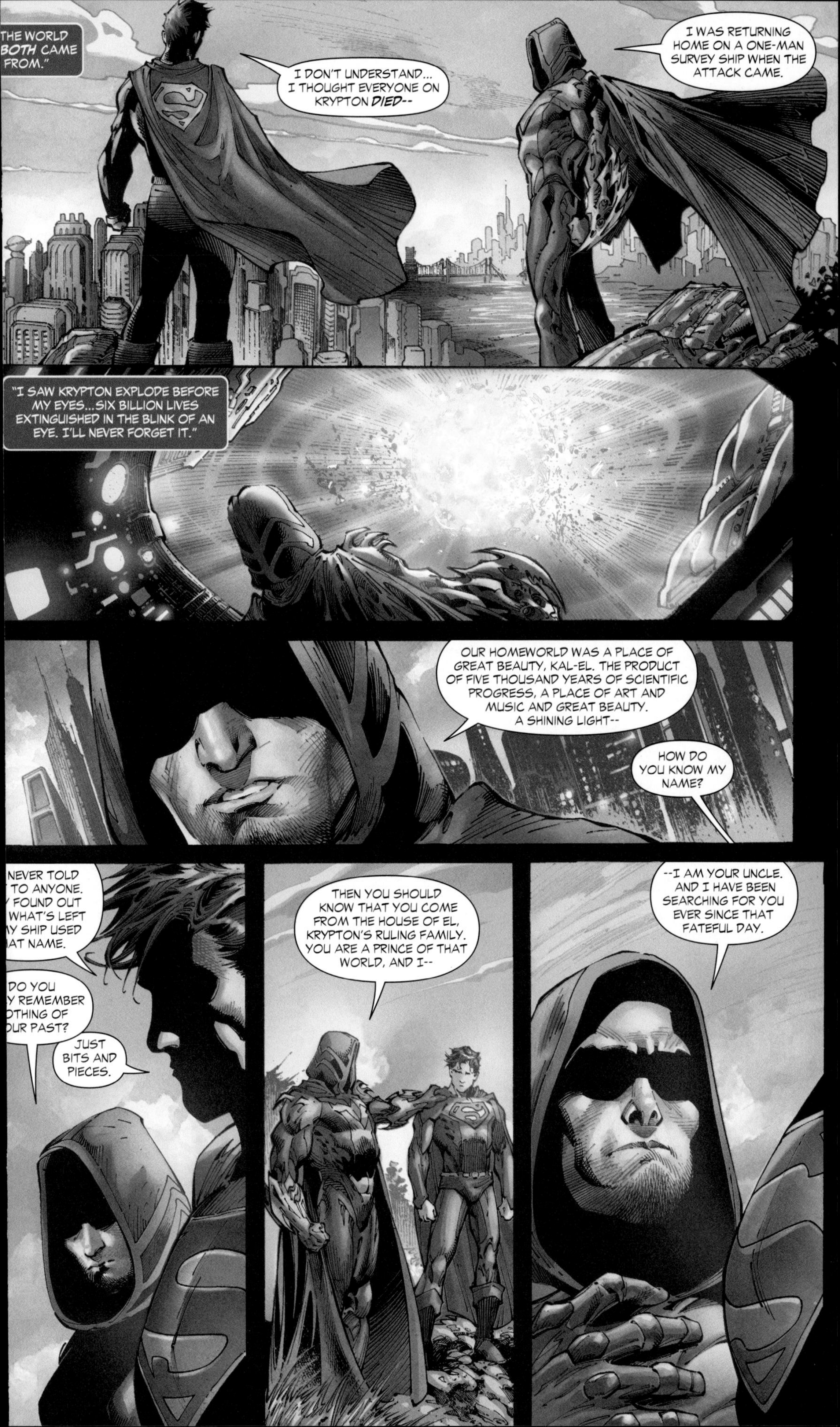
THE WORLD BOTH CAME FROM."
I DON'T UNDERSTAND... I THOUGHT EVERYONE ON KRYPTON DIED--
I WAS RETURNING HOME ON A ONE-MAN SURVEY SHIP WHEN THE ATTACK CAME.
"I SAW KRYPTON EXPLODE BEFORE MY EYES...SIX BILLION LIVES EXTINGUISHED IN THE BLINK OF AN EYE. I'LL NEVER FORGET IT."
OUR HOMEWORLD WAS A PLACE OF GREAT BEAUTY, KAL-EL. THE PRODUCT OF FIVE THOUSAND YEARS OF SCIENTIFIC PROGRESS, A PLACE OF ART AND MUSIC AND GREAT BEAUTY. A SHINING LIGHT--
HOW DO YOU KNOW MY NAME?
NEVER TOLD TO ANYONE. FOUND OUT WHAT'S LEFT SHIP USED NAME.
DO YOU REMEMBER OTHING OF OUR PAST?
JUST BITS AND PIECES.
THEN YOU SHOULD KNOW THAT YOU COME FROM THE HOUSE OF EL, KRYPTON'S RULING FAMILY. YOU ARE A PRINCE OF THAT WORLD, AND I--
--I AM YOUR UNCLE. AND I HAVE BEEN SEARCHING FOR YOU EVER SINCE THAT FATEFUL DAY.

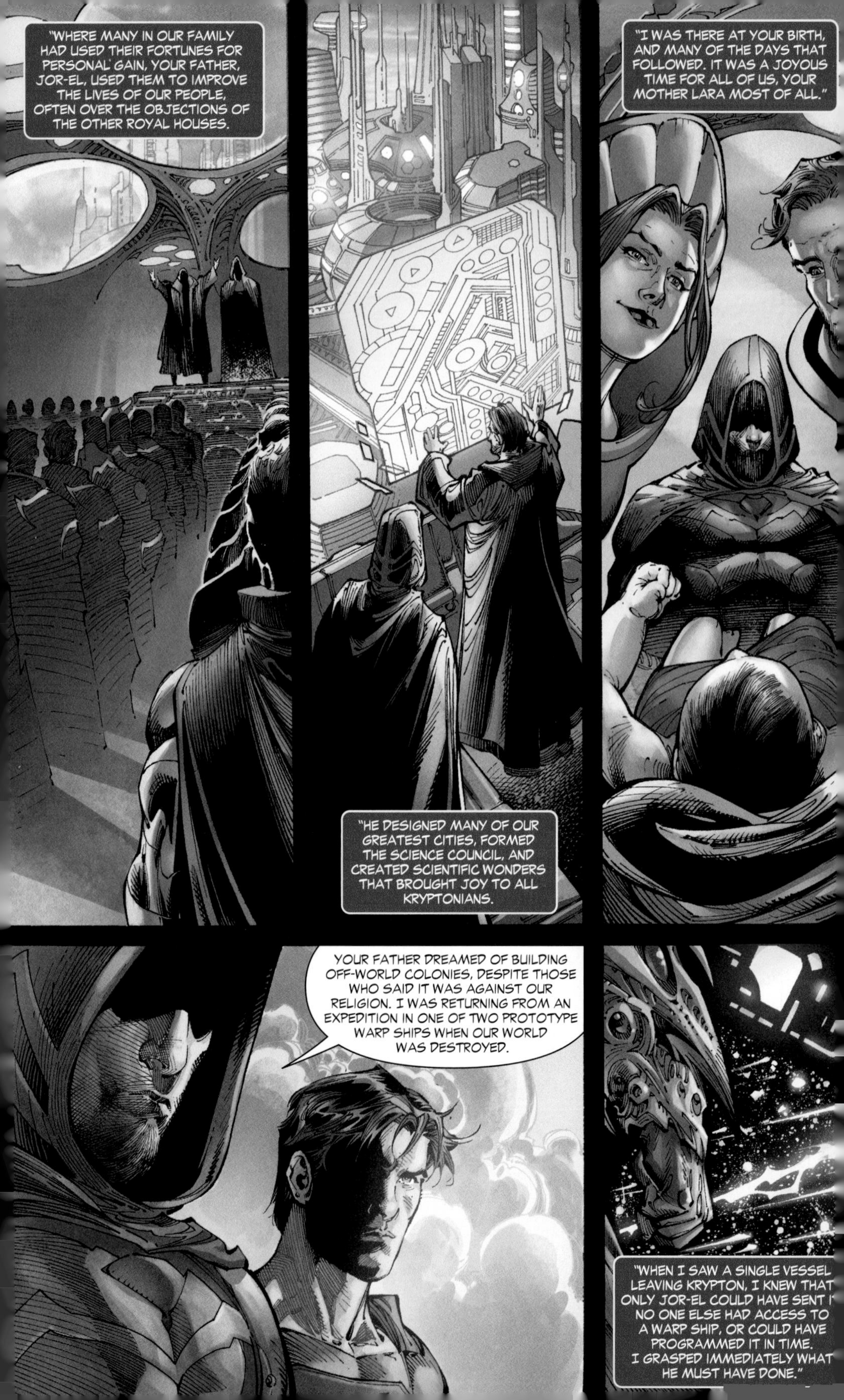
"WHERE MANY IN OUR FAMILY HAD USED THEIR FORTUNES FOR PERSONAL GAIN, YOUR FATHER, JOR-EL, USED THEM TO IMPROVE THE LIVES OF OUR PEOPLE, OFTEN OVER THE OBJECTIONS OF THE OTHER ROYAL HOUSES.
"HE DESIGNED MANY OF OUR GREATEST CITIES, FORMED THE SCIENCE COUNCIL, AND CREATED SCIENTIFIC WONDERS THAT BROUGHT JOY TO ALL KRYPTONIANS.
"I WAS THERE AT YOUR BIRTH, AND MANY OF THE DAYS THAT FOLLOWED. IT WAS A JOYOUS TIME FOR ALL OF US, YOUR MOTHER LARA MOST OF ALL."
YOUR FATHER DREAMED OF BUILDING OFF-WORLD COLONIES, DESPITE THOSE WHO SAID IT WAS AGAINST OUR RELIGION. I WAS RETURNING FROM AN EXPEDITION IN ONE OF TWO PROTOTYPE WARP SHIPS WHEN OUR WORLD WAS DESTROYED.
"WHEN I SAW A SINGLE VESSEL LEAVING KRYPTON, I KNEW THAT ONLY JOR-EL COULD HAVE SENT I NO ONE ELSE HAD ACCESS TO A WARP SHIP, OR COULD HAVE PROGRAMMED IT IN TIME. I GRASPED IMMEDIATELY WHAT HE MUST HAVE DONE."

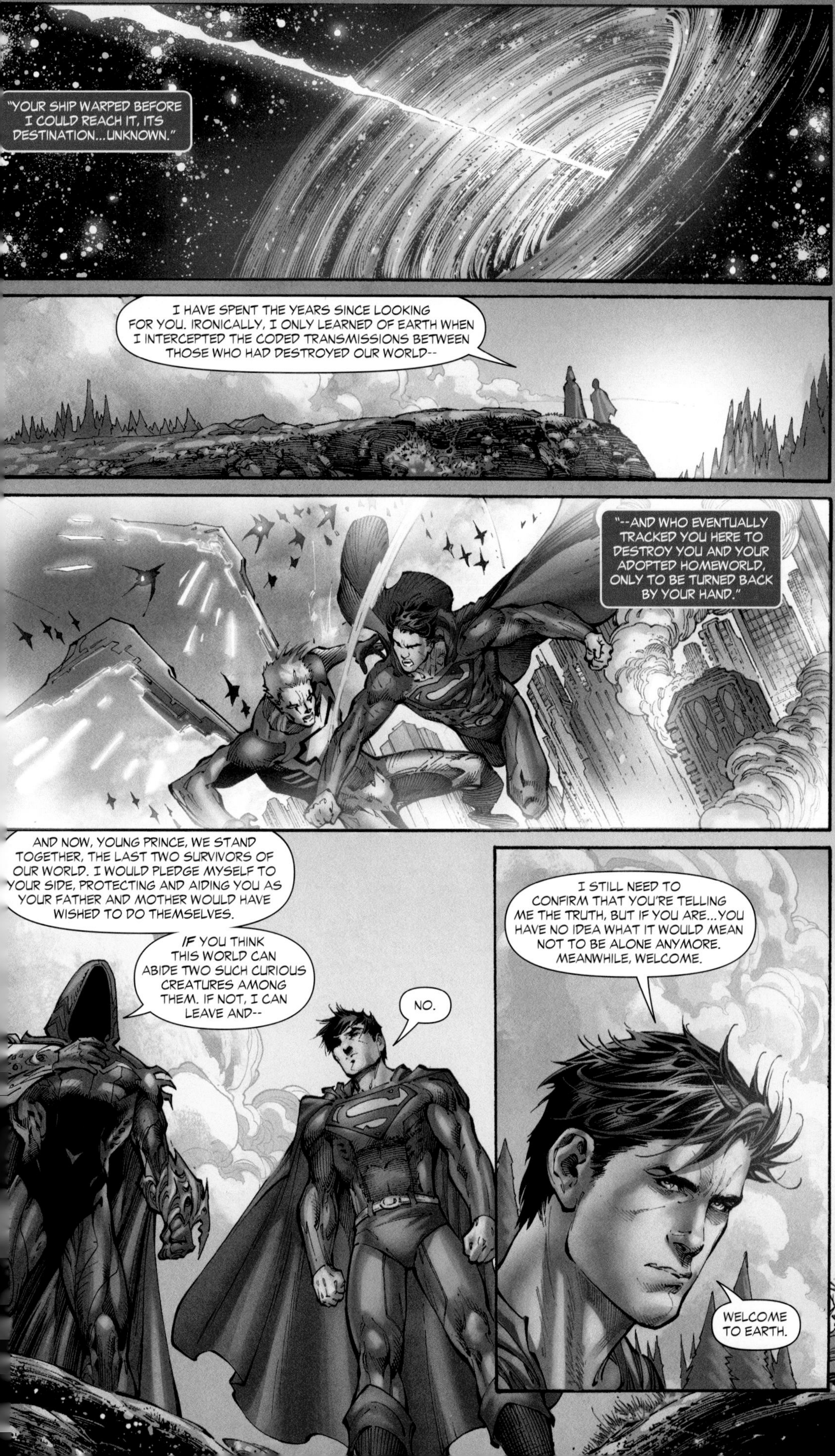
"YOUR SHIP WARPED BEFORE I COULD REACH IT, ITS DESTINATION...UNKNOWN."
I HAVE SPENT THE YEARS SINCE LOOKING FOR YOU. IRONICALLY, I ONLY LEARNED OF EARTH WHEN I INTERCEPTED THE CODED TRANSMISSIONS BETWEEN THOSE WHO HAD DESTROYED OUR WORLD--
"--AND WHO EVENTUALLY TRACKED YOU HERE TO DESTROY YOU AND YOUR ADOPTED HOMEWORLD, ONLY TO BE TURNED BACK BY YOUR HAND."
AND NOW, YOUNG PRINCE, WE STAND TOGETHER, THE LAST TWO SURVIVORS OF OUR WORLD. I WOULD PLEDGE MYSELF TO YOUR SIDE, PROTECTING AND AIDING YOU AS YOUR FATHER AND MOTHER WOULD HAVE WISHED TO DO THEMSELVES.
IF YOU THINK THIS WORLD CAN ABIDE TWO SUCH CURIOUS CREATURES AMONG THEM. IF NOT, I CAN LEAVE AND--
NO.
I STILL NEED TO CONFIRM THAT YOU'RE TELLING ME THE TRUTH, BUT IF YOU ARE...YOU HAVE NO IDEA WHAT IT WOULD MEAN NOT TO BE ALONE ANYMORE. MEANWHILE, WELCOME.
WELCOME TO EARTH.

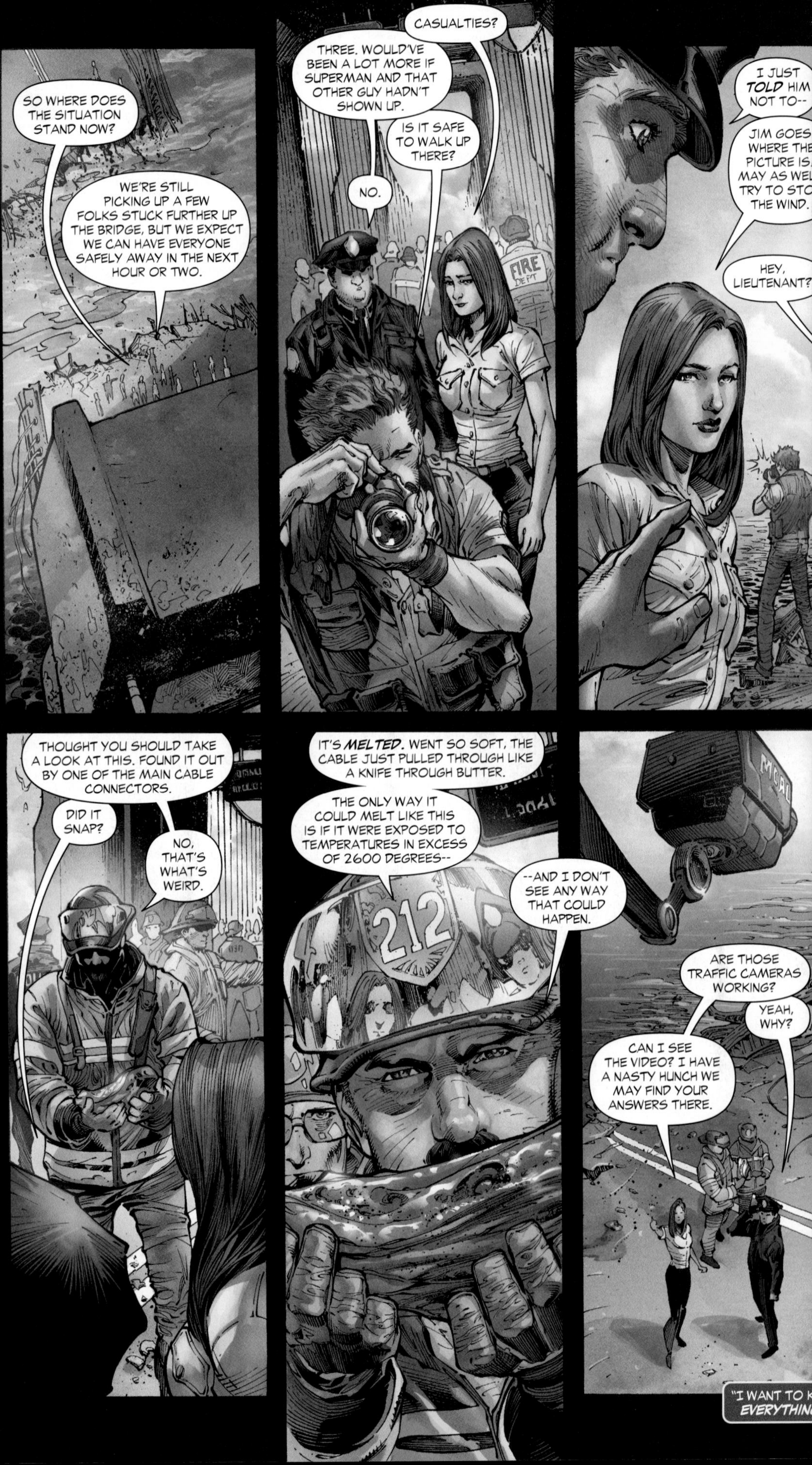
SO WHERE DOES THE SITUATION STAND NOW?
WE'RE STILL PICKING UP A FEW FOLKS STUCK FURTHER UP THE BRIDGE, BUT WE EXPECT WE CAN HAVE EVERYONE SAFELY AWAY IN THE NEXT HOUR OR TWO.
CASUALTIES?
THREE. WOULD'VE BEEN A LOT MORE IF SUPERMAN AND THAT OTHER GUY HADN'T SHOWN UP.
IS IT SAFE TO WALK UP THERE?
NO.
FIRE DEPT
I JUST TOLD HIM NOT TO--
JIM GOES WHERE THE PICTURE IS. MAY AS WEL TRY TO STO THE WIND.
HEY, LIEUTENANT?
THOUGHT YOU SHOULD TAKE A LOOK AT THIS. FOUND IT OUT BY ONE OF THE MAIN CABLE CONNECTORS.
DID IT SNAP?
NO, THAT'S WHAT'S WEIRD.
IT'S MELTED. WENT SO SOFT, THE CABLE JUST PULLED THROUGH LIKE A KNIFE THROUGH BUTTER.
THE ONLY WAY IT COULD MELT LIKE THIS IS IF IT WERE EXPOSED TO TEMPERATURES IN EXCESS OF 2600 DEGREES--
--AND I DON'T SEE ANY WAY THAT COULD HAPPEN.
212
ARE THOSE TRAFFIC CAMERAS WORKING?
YEAH, WHY?
CAN I SEE THE VIDEO? I HAVE A NASTY HUNCH WE MAY FIND YOUR ANSWERS THERE.
"I WANT TO K EVERYTHING

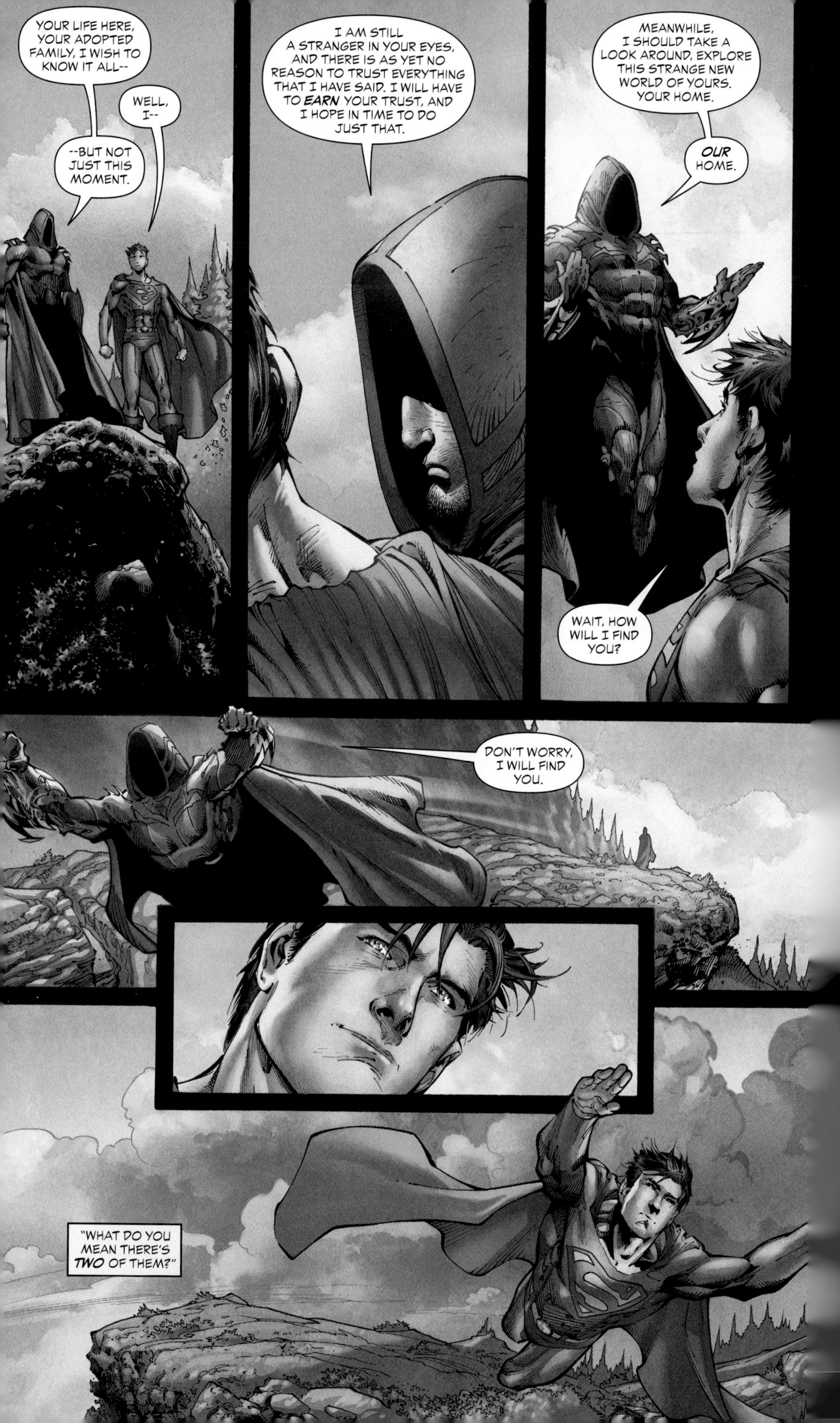
YOUR LIFE HERE, YOUR ADOPTED FAMILY, I WISH TO KNOW IT ALL--
WELL, I--
--BUT NOT JUST THIS MOMENT.
I AM STILL A STRANGER IN YOUR EYES, AND THERE IS AS YET NO REASON TO TRUST EVERYTHING THAT I HAVE SAID. I WILL HAVE TO **EARN** YOUR TRUST, AND I HOPE IN TIME TO DO JUST THAT.
MEANWHILE, I SHOULD TAKE A LOOK AROUND, EXPLORE THIS STRANGE NEW WORLD OF YOURS. YOUR HOME.
OUR HOME.
WAIT, HOW WILL I FIND YOU?
DON'T WORRY, I WILL FIND YOU.
"WHAT DO YOU MEAN THERE'S **TWO** OF THEM?"

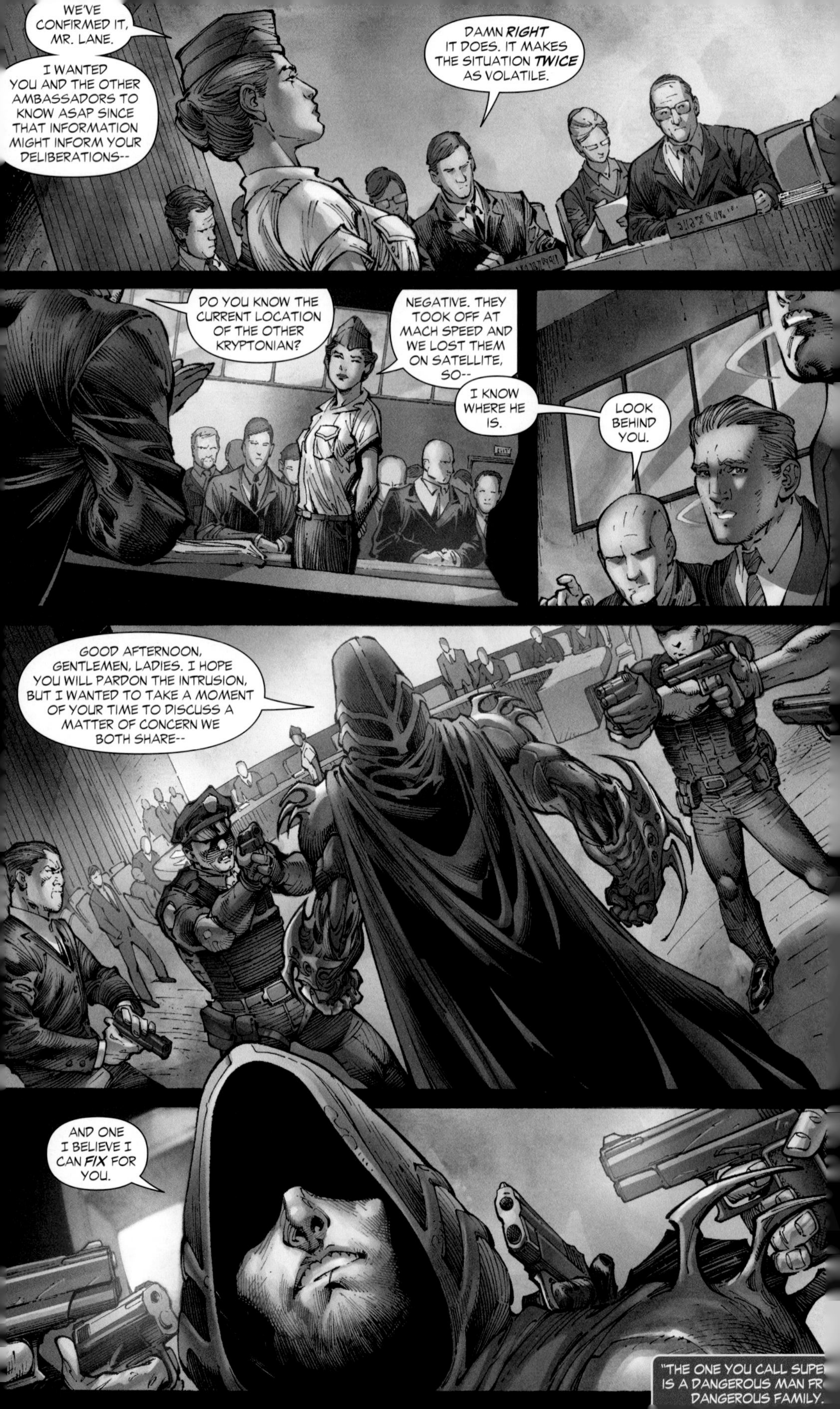
WE'VE CONFIRMED IT, MR. LANE.
I WANTED YOU AND THE OTHER AMBASSADORS TO KNOW ASAP SINCE THAT INFORMATION MIGHT INFORM YOUR DELIBERATIONS--
DAMN RIGHT IT DOES. IT MAKES THE SITUATION TWICE AS VOLATILE.
DO YOU KNOW THE CURRENT LOCATION OF THE OTHER KRYPTONIAN?
NEGATIVE. THEY TOOK OFF AT MACH SPEED AND WE LOST THEM ON SATELLITE, SO--
I KNOW WHERE HE IS.
LOOK BEHIND YOU.
GOOD AFTERNOON, GENTLEMEN, LADIES. I HOPE YOU WILL PARDON THE INTRUSION, BUT I WANTED TO TAKE A MOMENT OF YOUR TIME TO DISCUSS A MATTER OF CONCERN WE BOTH SHARE--
AND ONE I BELIEVE I CAN FIX FOR YOU.
"THE ONE YOU CALL SUPE
IS A DANGEROUS MAN FR
DANGEROUS FAMILY.

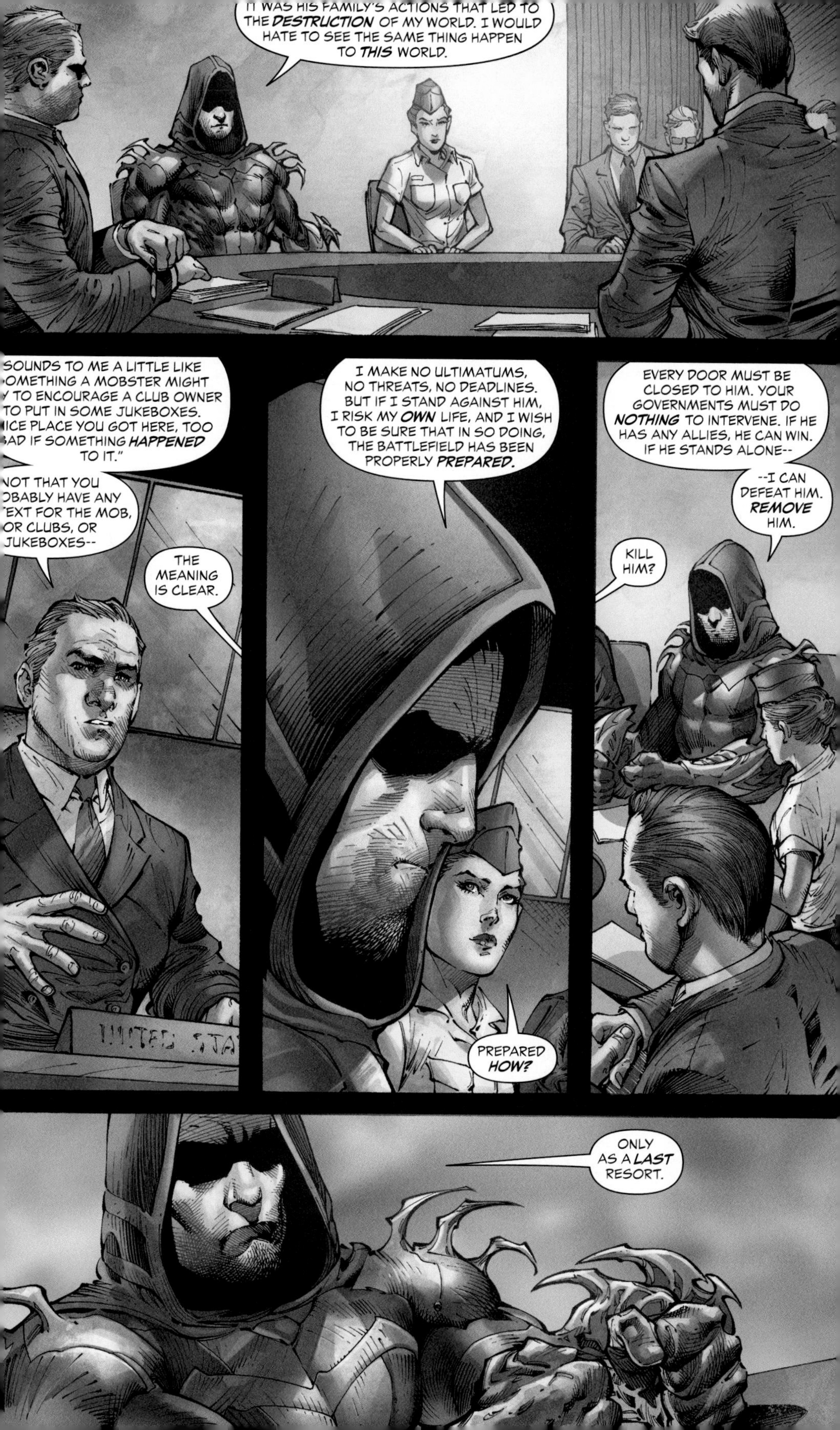
IT WAS HIS FAMILY'S ACTIONS THAT LED TO THE DESTRUCTION OF MY WORLD. I WOULD HATE TO SEE THE SAME THING HAPPEN TO THIS WORLD.
SOUNDS TO ME A LITTLE LIKE OMETHING A MOBSTER MIGHT Y TO ENCOURAGE A CLUB OWNER TO PUT IN SOME JUKEBOXES. ICE PLACE YOU GOT HERE, TOO AD IF SOMETHING HAPPENED TO IT."
NOT THAT YOU OBABLY HAVE ANY TEXT FOR THE MOB, OR CLUBS, OR JUKEBOXES--
THE MEANING IS CLEAR.
I MAKE NO ULTIMATUMS, NO THREATS, NO DEADLINES. BUT IF I STAND AGAINST HIM, I RISK MY OWN LIFE, AND I WISH TO BE SURE THAT IN SO DOING, THE BATTLEFIELD HAS BEEN PROPERLY PREPARED.
PREPARED HOW?
EVERY DOOR MUST BE CLOSED TO HIM. YOUR GOVERNMENTS MUST DO NOTHING TO INTERVENE. IF HE HAS ANY ALLIES, HE CAN WIN. IF HE STANDS ALONE--
--I CAN DEFEAT HIM. REMOVE HIM.
KILL HIM?
ONLY AS A LAST RESORT.

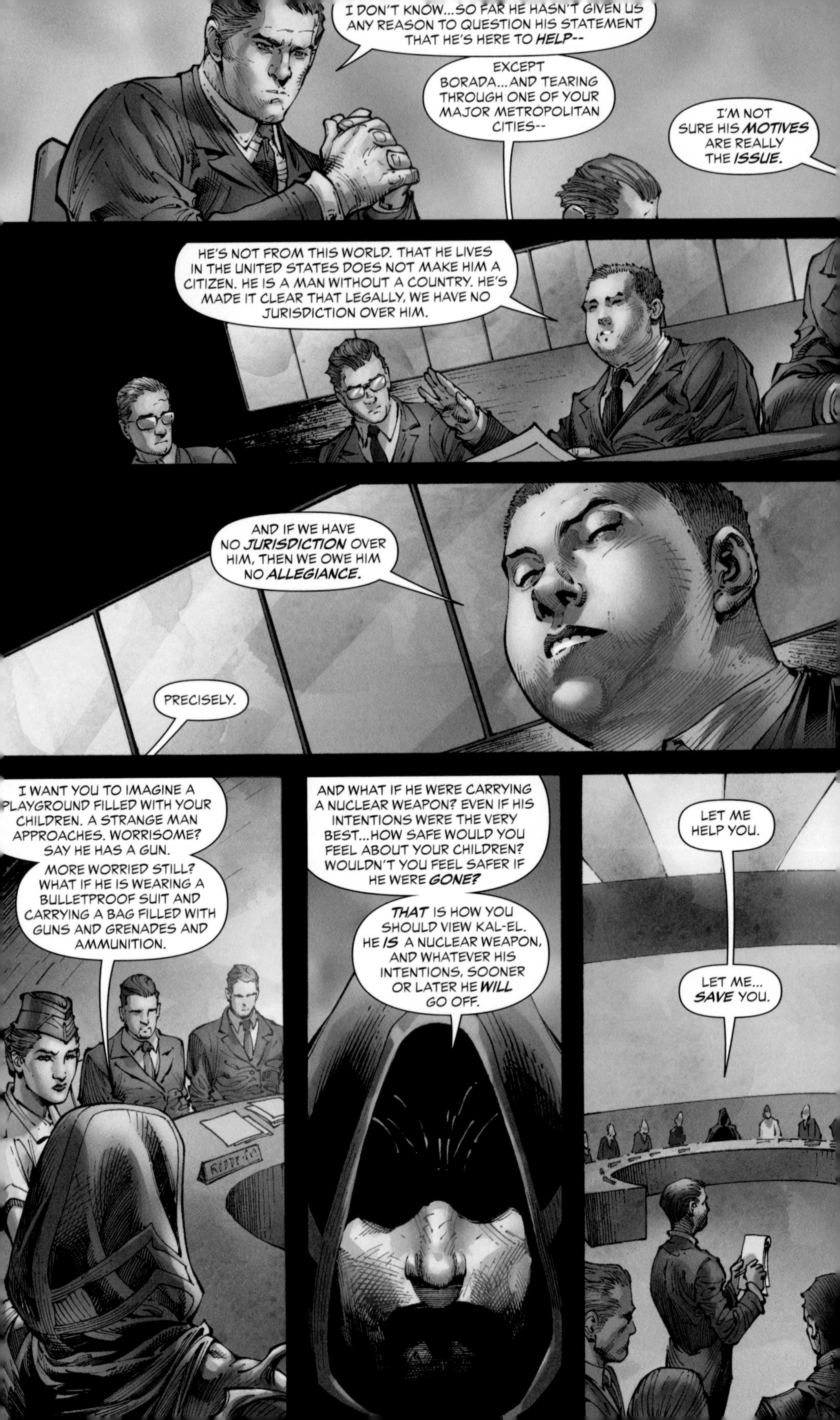
I DON'T KNOW...SO FAR HE HASN'T GIVEN US ANY REASON TO QUESTION HIS STATEMENT THAT HE'S HERE TO HELP--
EXCEPT BORADA...AND TEARING THROUGH ONE OF YOUR MAJOR METROPOLITAN CITIES--
I'M NOT SURE HIS MOTIVES ARE REALLY THE ISSUE.
HE'S NOT FROM THIS WORLD. THAT HE LIVES IN THE UNITED STATES DOES NOT MAKE HIM A CITIZEN. HE IS A MAN WITHOUT A COUNTRY. HE'S MADE IT CLEAR THAT LEGALLY, WE HAVE NO JURISDICTION OVER HIM.
AND IF WE HAVE NO JURISDICTION OVER HIM, THEN WE OWE HIM NO ALLEGIANCE.
PRECISELY.
I WANT YOU TO IMAGINE A PLAYGROUND FILLED WITH YOUR CHILDREN. A STRANGE MAN APPROACHES. WORRISOME? SAY HE HAS A GUN.
MORE WORRIED STILL? WHAT IF HE IS WEARING A BULLETPROOF SUIT AND CARRYING A BAG FILLED WITH GUNS AND GRENADES AND AMMUNITION.
AND WHAT IF HE WERE CARRYING A NUCLEAR WEAPON? EVEN IF HIS INTENTIONS WERE THE VERY BEST...HOW SAFE WOULD YOU FEEL ABOUT YOUR CHILDREN? WOULDN'T YOU FEEL SAFER IF HE WERE GONE?
THAT IS HOW YOU SHOULD VIEW KAL-EL. HE IS A NUCLEAR WEAPON, AND WHATEVER HIS INTENTIONS, SOONER OR LATER HE WILL GO OFF.
LET ME HELP YOU.
LET ME... SAVE YOU.

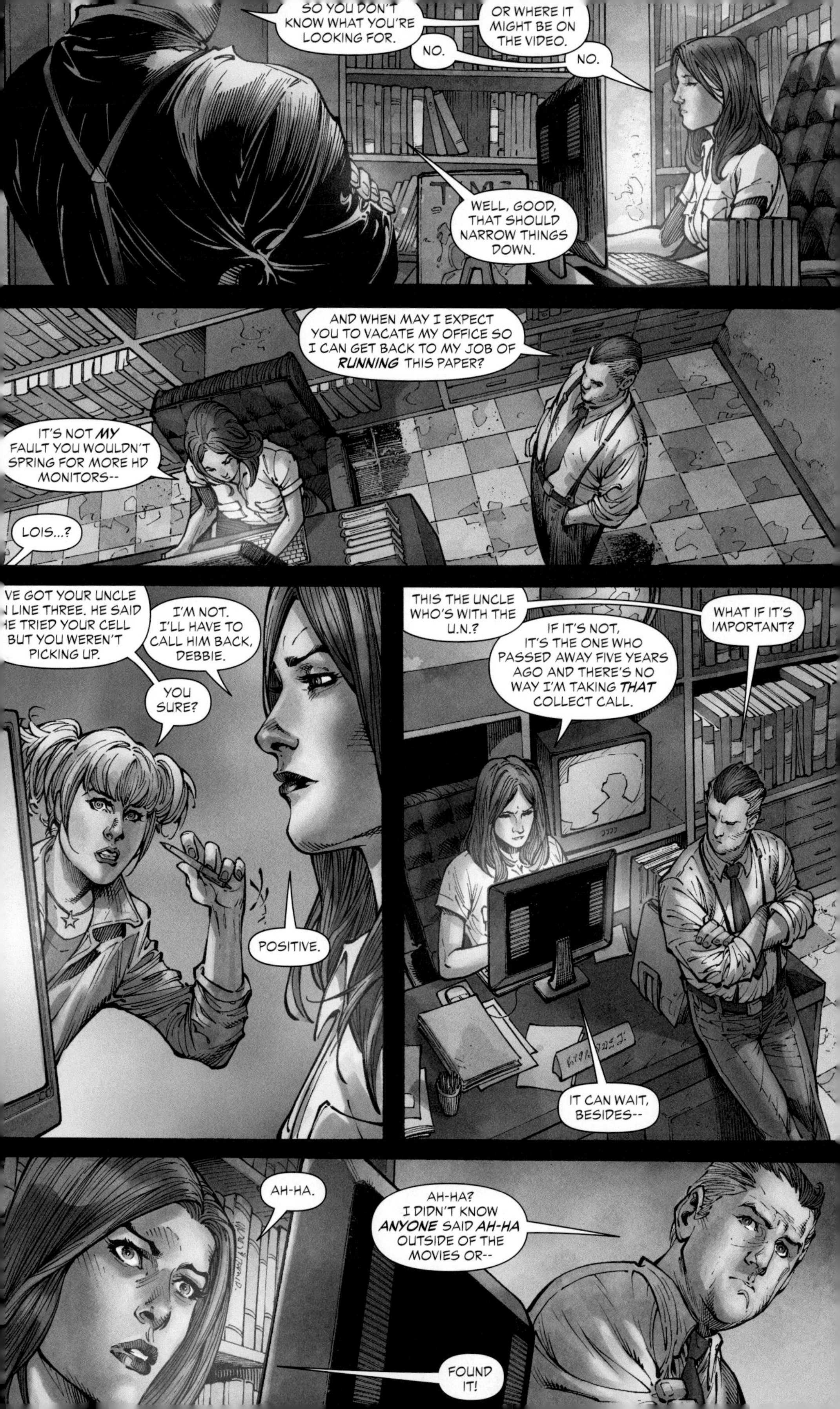
SO YOU DON'T KNOW WHAT YOU'RE LOOKING FOR.
NO.
OR WHERE IT MIGHT BE ON THE VIDEO.
NO.
WELL, GOOD, THAT SHOULD NARROW THINGS DOWN.
AND WHEN MAY I EXPECT YOU TO VACATE MY OFFICE SO I CAN GET BACK TO MY JOB OF RUNNING THIS PAPER?
IT'S NOT MY FAULT YOU WOULDN'T SPRING FOR MORE HD MONITORS--
LOIS...?
VE GOT YOUR UNCLE N LINE THREE. HE SAID HE TRIED YOUR CELL BUT YOU WEREN'T PICKING UP.
I'M NOT. I'LL HAVE TO CALL HIM BACK, DEBBIE.
YOU SURE?
POSITIVE.
THIS THE UNCLE WHO'S WITH THE U.N.?
IF IT'S NOT, IT'S THE ONE WHO PASSED AWAY FIVE YEARS AGO AND THERE'S NO WAY I'M TAKING THAT COLLECT CALL.
WHAT IF IT'S IMPORTANT?
IT CAN WAIT, BESIDES--
AH-HA.
AH-HA? I DIDN'T KNOW ANYONE SAID AH-HA OUTSIDE OF THE MOVIES OR--
FOUND IT!

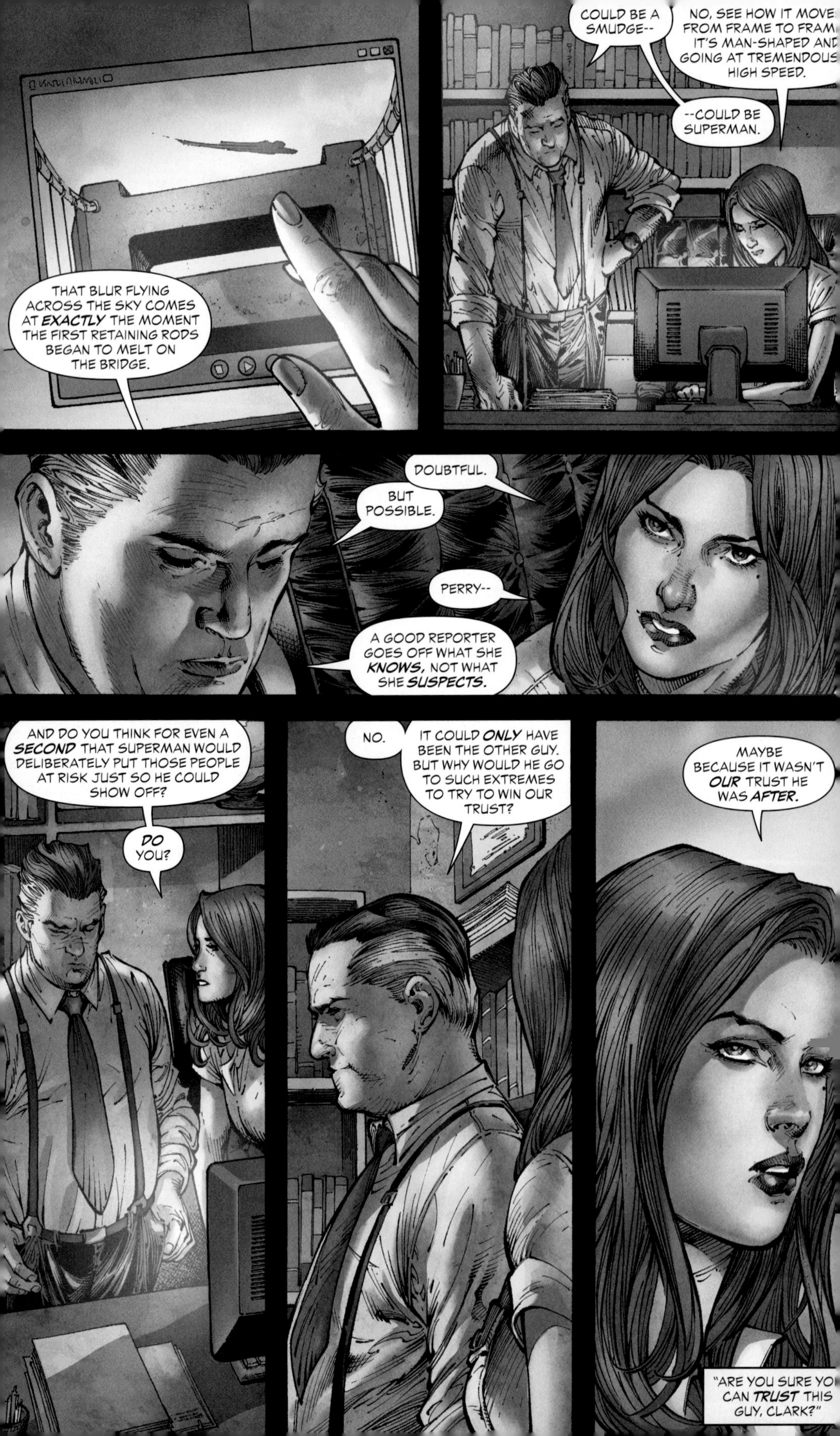
THAT BLUR FLYING ACROSS THE SKY COMES AT EXACTLY THE MOMENT THE FIRST RETAINING RODS BEGAN TO MELT ON THE BRIDGE.
COULD BE A SMUDGE--
--COULD BE SUPERMAN.
NO, SEE HOW IT MOVES FROM FRAME TO FRAME IT'S MAN-SHAPED AND GOING AT TREMENDOUS HIGH SPEED.
DOUBTFUL.
BUT POSSIBLE.
PERRY--
A GOOD REPORTER GOES OFF WHAT SHE KNOWS, NOT WHAT SHE SUSPECTS.
AND DO YOU THINK FOR EVEN A SECOND THAT SUPERMAN WOULD DELIBERATELY PUT THOSE PEOPLE AT RISK JUST SO HE COULD SHOW OFF?
DO YOU?
NO.
IT COULD ONLY HAVE BEEN THE OTHER GUY. BUT WHY WOULD HE GO TO SUCH EXTREMES TO TRY TO WIN OUR TRUST?
MAYBE BECAUSE IT WASN'T OUR TRUST HE WAS AFTER.
"ARE YOU SURE YOU CAN TRUST THIS GUY, CLARK?"

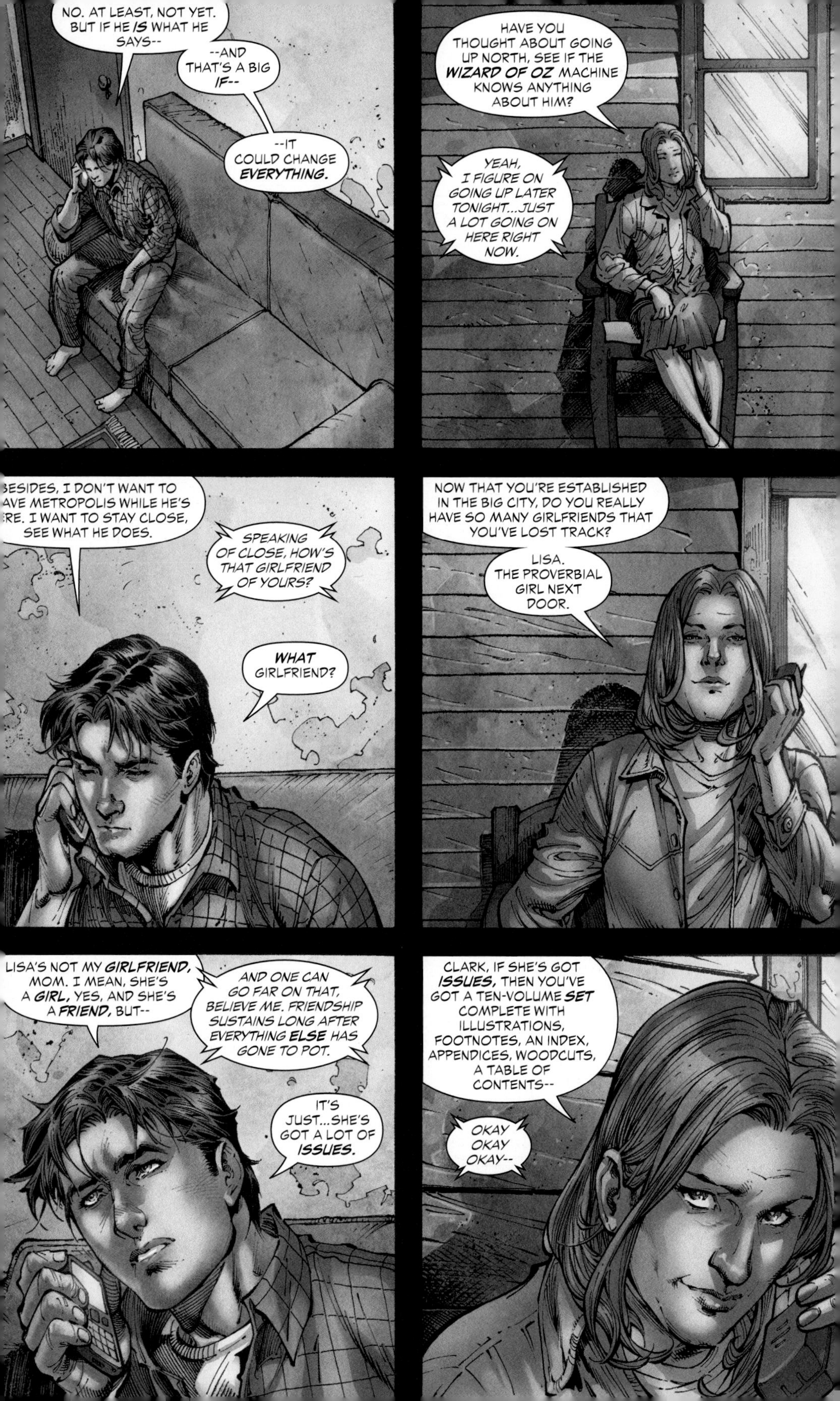
NO. AT LEAST, NOT YET. BUT IF HE IS WHAT HE SAYS--
--AND THAT'S A BIG IF--
--IT COULD CHANGE EVERYTHING.
HAVE YOU THOUGHT ABOUT GOING UP NORTH, SEE IF THE WIZARD OF OZ MACHINE KNOWS ANYTHING ABOUT HIM?
YEAH, I FIGURE ON GOING UP LATER TONIGHT...JUST A LOT GOING ON HERE RIGHT NOW.
ESIDES, I DON'T WANT TO AVE METROPOLIS WHILE HE'S RE. I WANT TO STAY CLOSE, SEE WHAT HE DOES.
SPEAKING OF CLOSE, HOW'S THAT GIRLFRIEND OF YOURS?
WHAT GIRLFRIEND?
NOW THAT YOU'RE ESTABLISHED IN THE BIG CITY, DO YOU REALLY HAVE SO MANY GIRLFRIENDS THAT YOU'VE LOST TRACK?
LISA. THE PROVERBIAL GIRL NEXT DOOR.
LISA'S NOT MY GIRLFRIEND, MOM. I MEAN, SHE'S A GIRL, YES, AND SHE'S A FRIEND, BUT--
AND ONE CAN GO FAR ON THAT, BELIEVE ME. FRIENDSHIP SUSTAINS LONG AFTER EVERYTHING ELSE HAS GONE TO POT.
IT'S JUST...SHE'S GOT A LOT OF ISSUES.
CLARK, IF SHE'S GOT ISSUES, THEN YOU'VE GOT A TEN-VOLUME SET COMPLETE WITH ILLUSTRATIONS, FOOTNOTES, AN INDEX, APPENDICES, WOODCUTS, A TABLE OF CONTENTS--
OKAY OKAY OKAY--

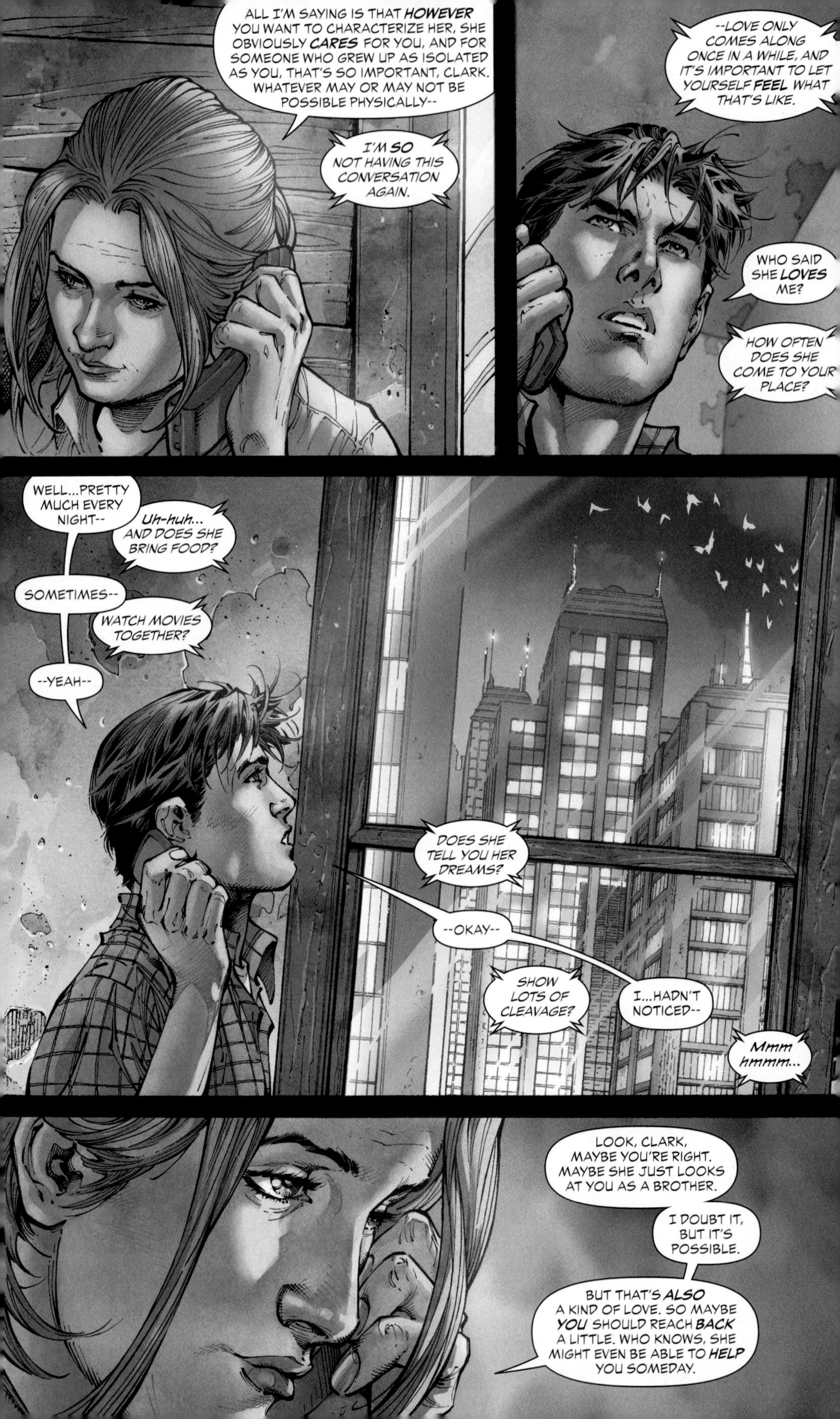
ALL I'M SAYING IS THAT *HOWEVER* YOU WANT TO CHARACTERIZE HER, SHE OBVIOUSLY *CARES* FOR YOU, AND FOR SOMEONE WHO GREW UP AS ISOLATED AS YOU, THAT'S SO IMPORTANT, CLARK. WHATEVER MAY OR MAY NOT BE POSSIBLE PHYSICALLY--
I'M *SO* NOT HAVING THIS CONVERSATION AGAIN.
--LOVE ONLY COMES ALONG ONCE IN A WHILE, AND IT'S IMPORTANT TO LET YOURSELF *FEEL* WHAT THAT'S LIKE.
WHO SAID SHE *LOVES* ME?
HOW OFTEN DOES SHE COME TO YOUR PLACE?
WELL...PRETTY MUCH EVERY NIGHT--
Uh-huh... AND DOES SHE BRING FOOD?
SOMETIMES--
WATCH MOVIES TOGETHER?
--YEAH--
DOES SHE TELL YOU HER DREAMS?
--OKAY--
SHOW LOTS OF CLEAVAGE?
I...HADN'T NOTICED--
Mmm hmmm...
LOOK, CLARK, MAYBE YOU'RE RIGHT. MAYBE SHE JUST LOOKS AT YOU AS A BROTHER.
I DOUBT IT, BUT IT'S POSSIBLE.
BUT THAT'S *ALSO* A KIND OF LOVE. SO MAYBE *YOU* SHOULD REACH *BACK* A LITTLE. WHO KNOWS, SHE MIGHT EVEN BE ABLE TO *HELP* YOU SOMEDAY.

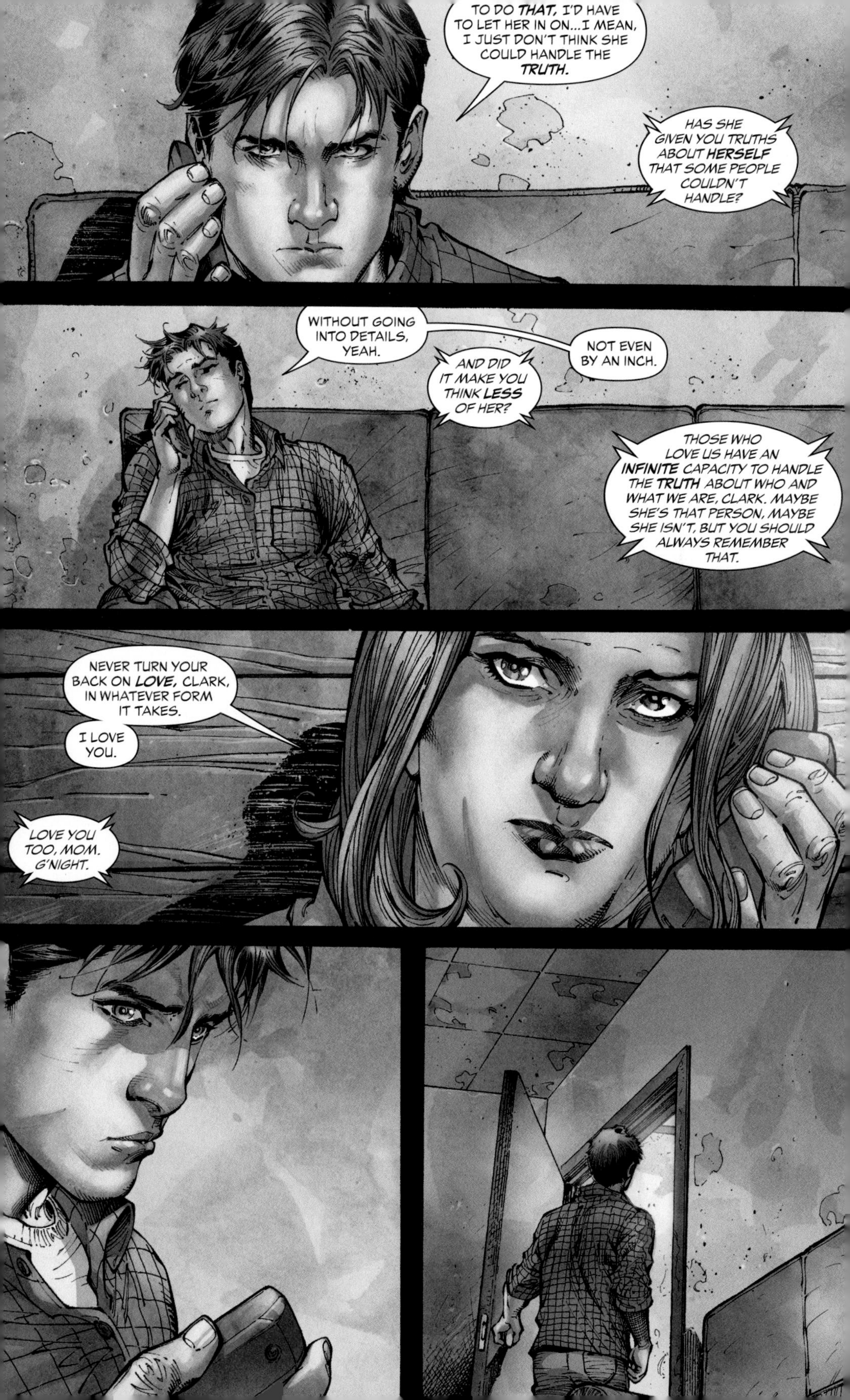
TO DO THAT, I'D HAVE TO LET HER IN ON...I MEAN, I JUST DON'T THINK SHE COULD HANDLE THE TRUTH.
HAS SHE GIVEN YOU TRUTHS ABOUT HERSELF THAT SOME PEOPLE COULDN'T HANDLE?
WITHOUT GOING INTO DETAILS, YEAH.
AND DID IT MAKE YOU THINK LESS OF HER?
NOT EVEN BY AN INCH.
THOSE WHO LOVE US HAVE AN INFINITE CAPACITY TO HANDLE THE TRUTH ABOUT WHO AND WHAT WE ARE, CLARK. MAYBE SHE'S THAT PERSON, MAYBE SHE ISN'T, BUT YOU SHOULD ALWAYS REMEMBER THAT.
NEVER TURN YOUR BACK ON LOVE, CLARK, IN WHATEVER FORM IT TAKES.
I LOVE YOU.
LOVE YOU TOO, MOM. G'NIGHT.

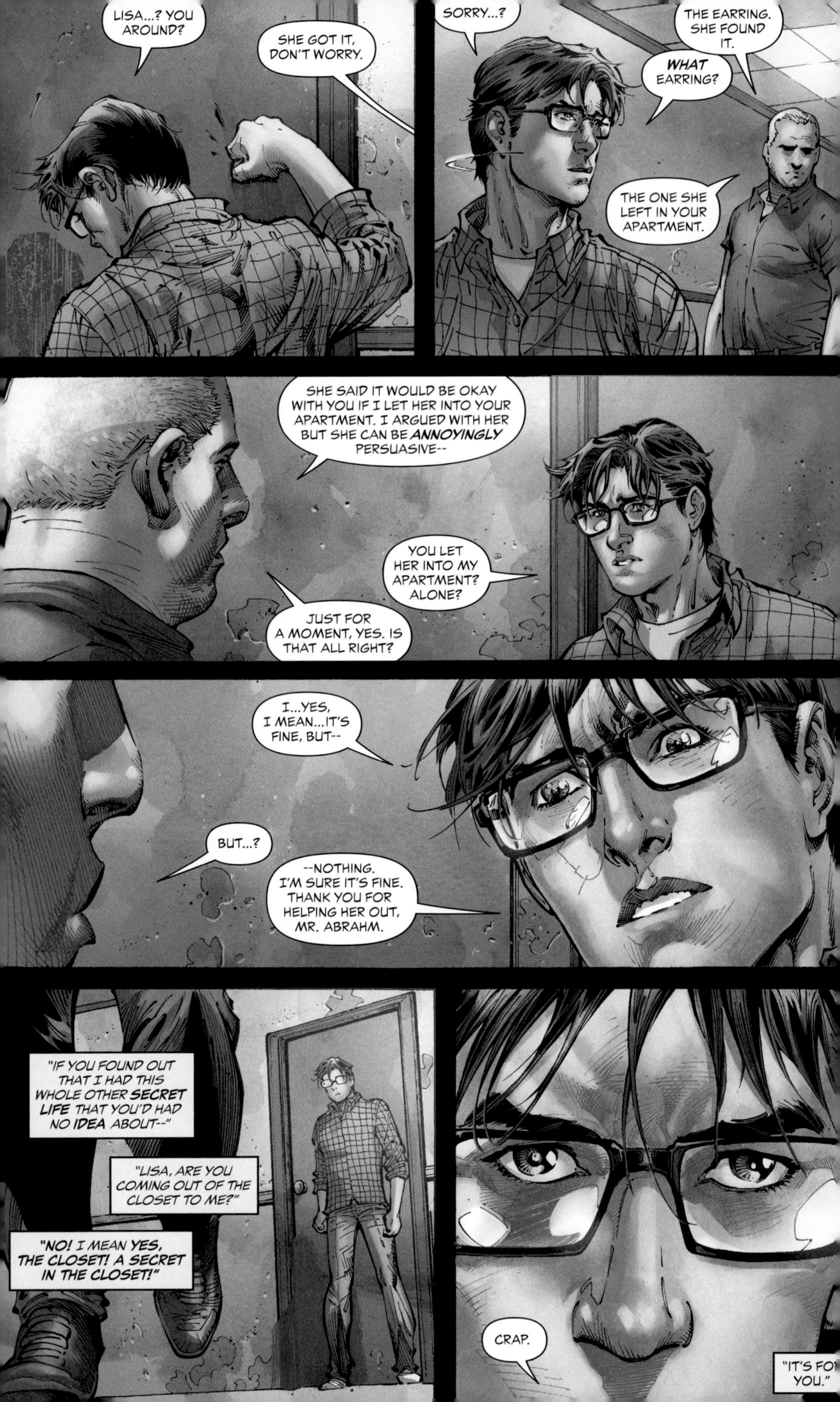
LISA...? YOU AROUND?
SHE GOT IT, DON'T WORRY.
SORRY...?
THE EARRING. SHE FOUND IT.
WHAT EARRING?
THE ONE SHE LEFT IN YOUR APARTMENT.
SHE SAID IT WOULD BE OKAY WITH YOU IF I LET HER INTO YOUR APARTMENT. I ARGUED WITH HER BUT SHE CAN BE ANNOYINGLY PERSUASIVE--
YOU LET HER INTO MY APARTMENT? ALONE?
JUST FOR A MOMENT, YES. IS THAT ALL RIGHT?
I...YES, I MEAN...IT'S FINE, BUT--
BUT...?
--NOTHING. I'M SURE IT'S FINE. THANK YOU FOR HELPING HER OUT, MR. ABRAHM.
"IF YOU FOUND OUT THAT I HAD THIS WHOLE OTHER SECRET LIFE THAT YOU'D HAD NO IDEA ABOUT--"
"LISA, ARE YOU COMING OUT OF THE CLOSET TO ME?"
"NO! I MEAN YES, THE CLOSET! A SECRET IN THE CLOSET!"
CRAP.
"IT'S FO
YOU."

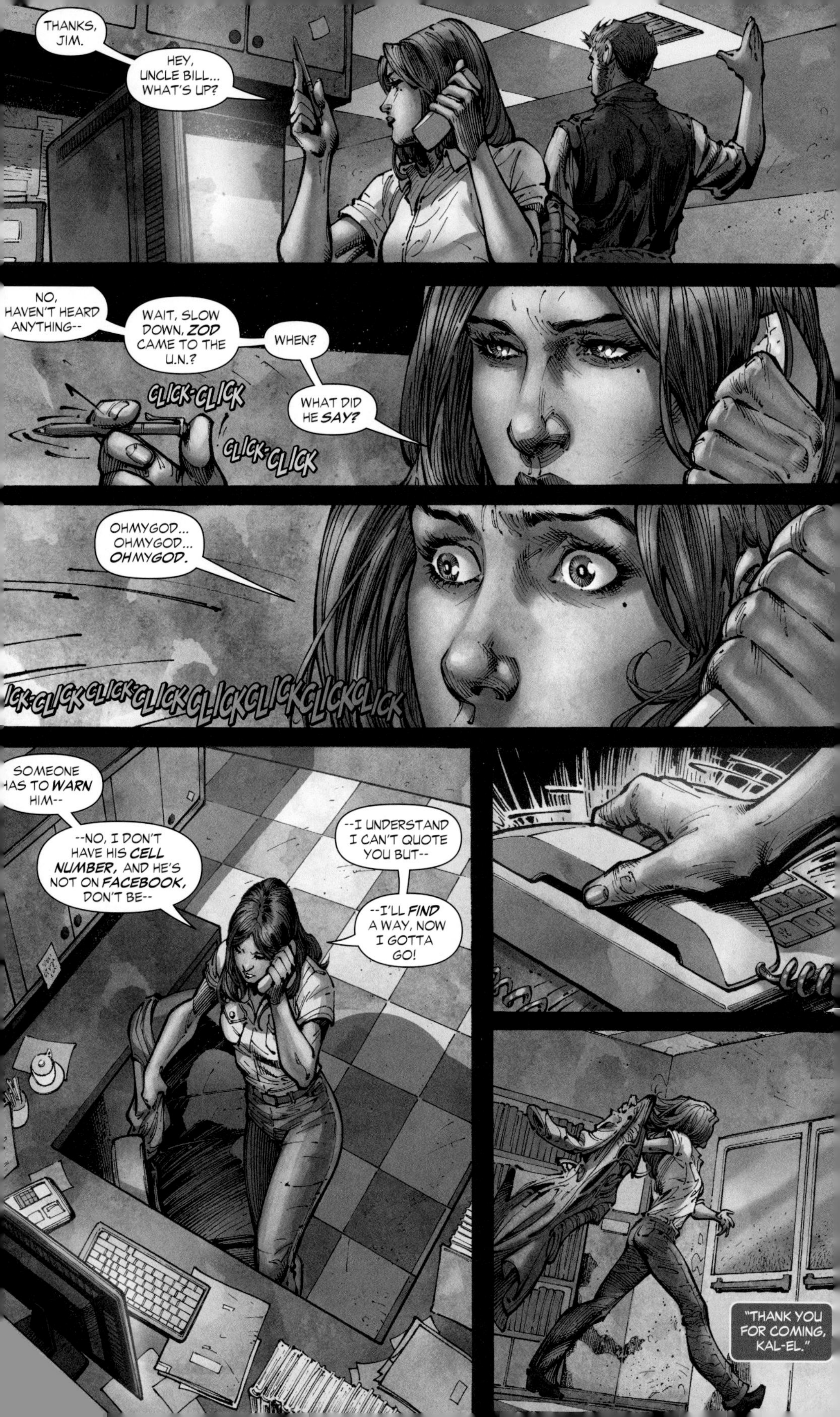
THANKS, JIM.
HEY, UNCLE BILL... WHAT'S UP?
NO, HAVEN'T HEARD ANYTHING--
WAIT, SLOW DOWN, ZOD CAME TO THE U.N.?
WHEN?
CLICK-CLICK
CLICK-CLICK
WHAT DID HE SAY?
OHMYGOD... OHMYGOD... OHMYGOD.
ICK-CLICK CLICK-CLICK CLICKCLICKCLICKCLICK
SOMEONE HAS TO WARN HIM--
--NO, I DON'T HAVE HIS CELL NUMBER, AND HE'S NOT ON FACEBOOK, DON'T BE--
--I UNDERSTAND I CAN'T QUOTE YOU BUT--
--I'LL FIND A WAY, NOW I GOTTA GO!
"THANK YOU FOR COMING, KAL-EL."

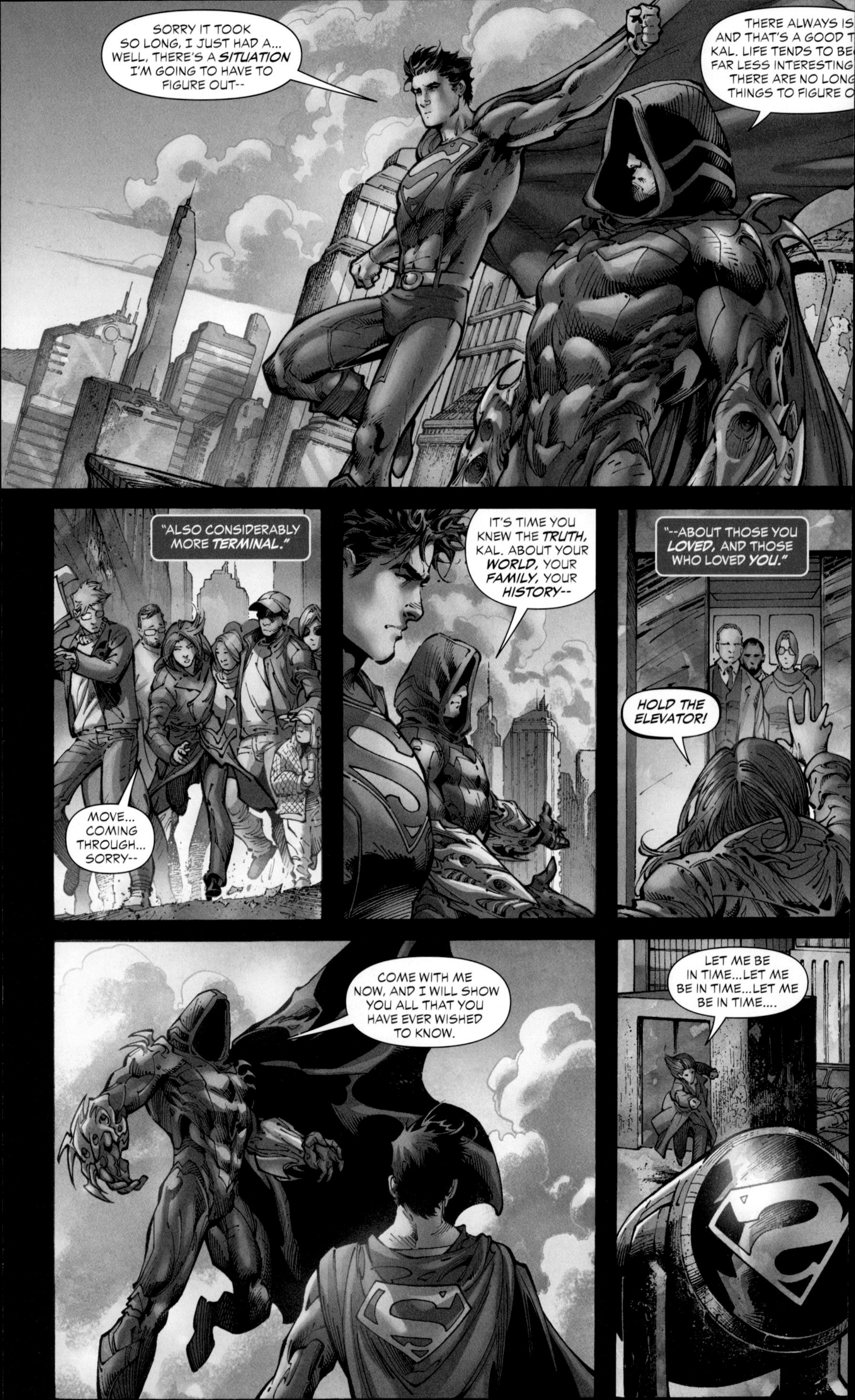

SORRY IT TOOK SO LONG, I JUST HAD A... WELL, THERE'S A SITUATION I'M GOING TO HAVE TO FIGURE OUT--
THERE ALWAYS IS AND THAT'S A GOOD T KAL. LIFE TENDS TO BE FAR LESS INTERESTING THERE ARE NO LONG THINGS TO FIGURE O
"ALSO CONSIDERABLY MORE TERMINAL."
MOVE... COMING THROUGH... SORRY--
IT'S TIME YOU KNEW THE TRUTH, KAL. ABOUT YOUR WORLD, YOUR FAMILY, YOUR HISTORY--
"--ABOUT THOSE YOU LOVED, AND THOSE WHO LOVED YOU."
HOLD THE ELEVATOR!
COME WITH ME NOW, AND I WILL SHOW YOU ALL THAT YOU HAVE EVER WISHED TO KNOW.
LET ME BE IN TIME...LET ME BE IN TIME...LET ME BE IN TIME....

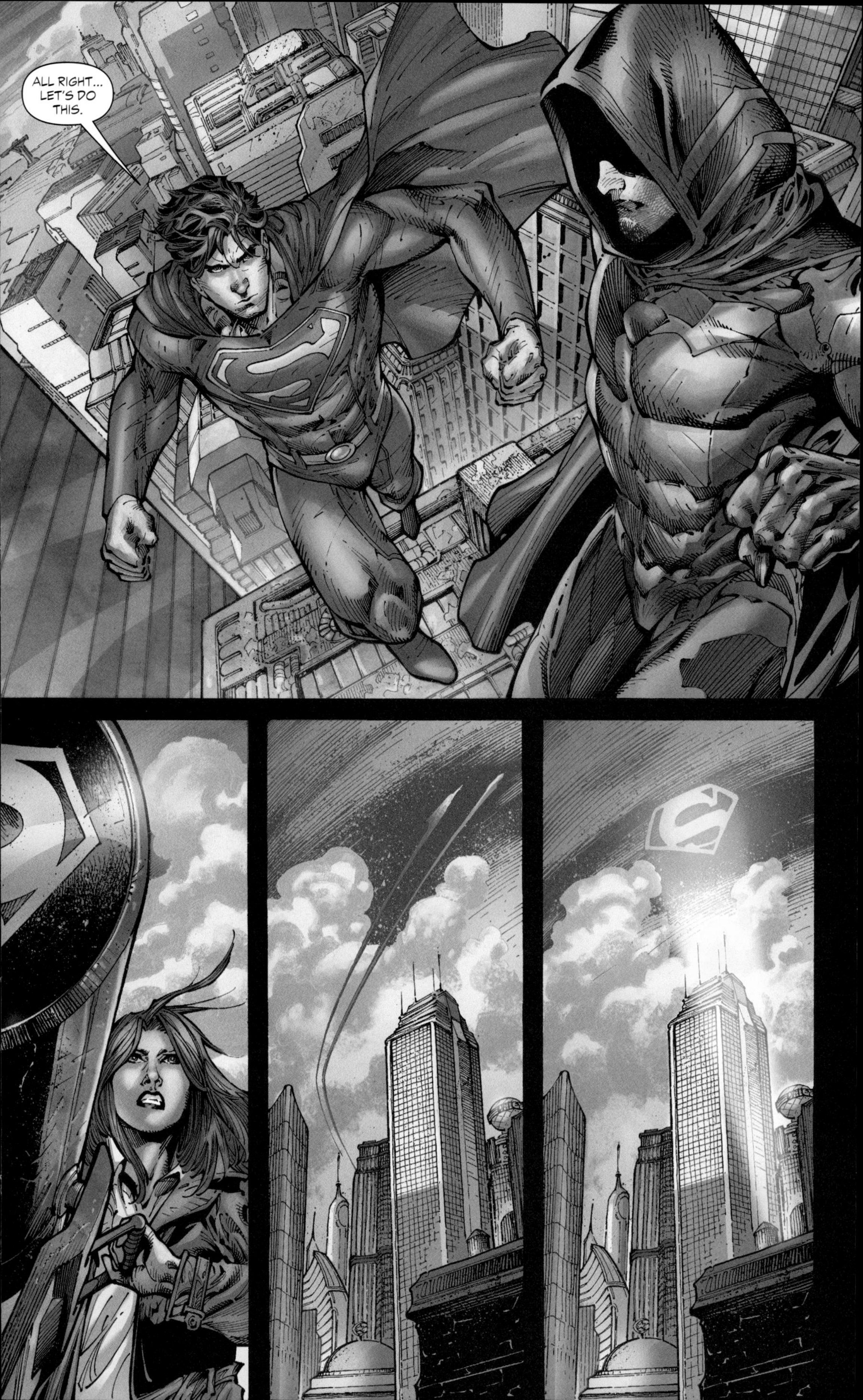
ALL RIGHT... LET'S DO THIS.

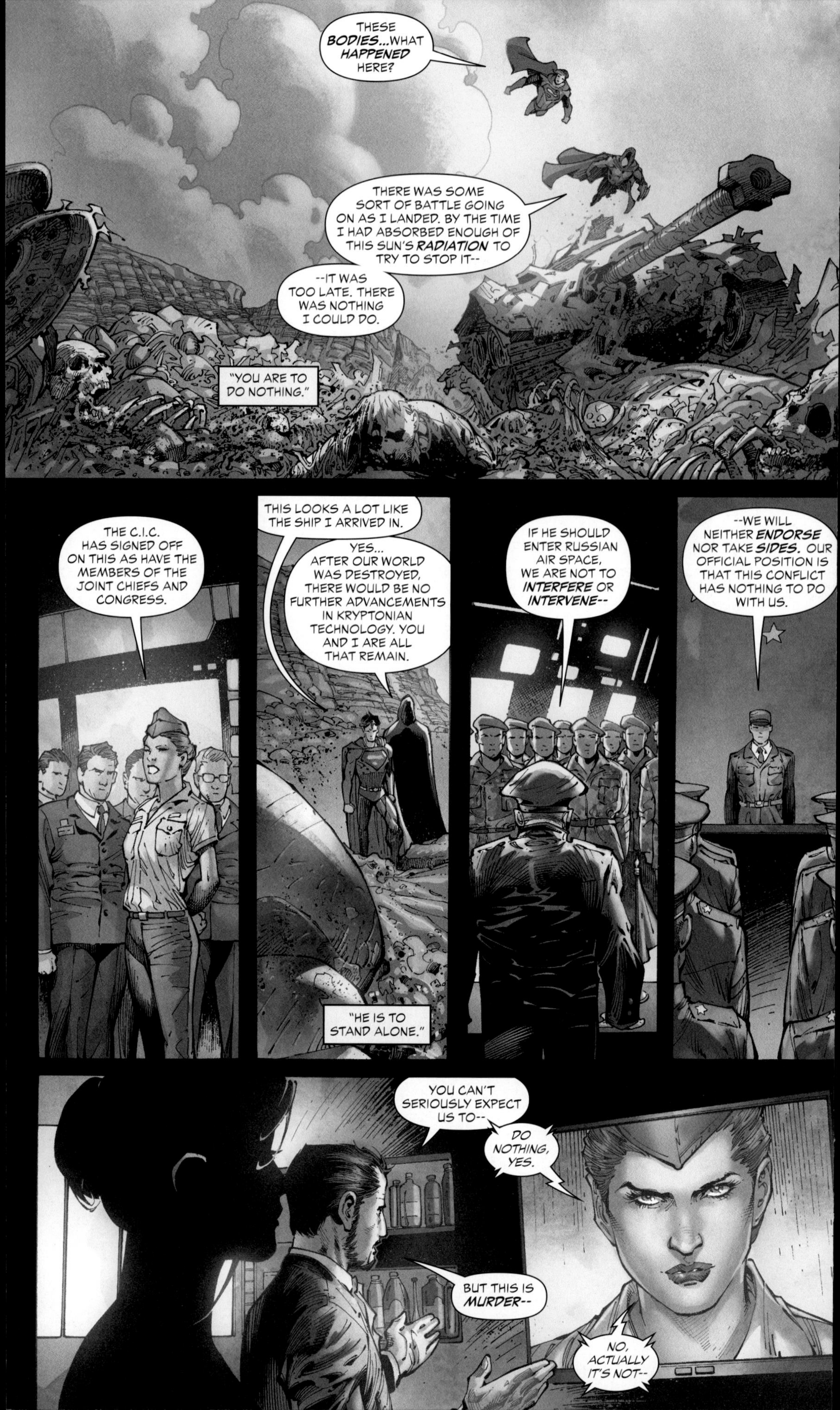
THESE BODIES...WHAT HAPPENED HERE?
THERE WAS SOME SORT OF BATTLE GOING ON AS I LANDED. BY THE TIME I HAD ABSORBED ENOUGH OF THIS SUN'S RADIATION TO TRY TO STOP IT--
--IT WAS TOO LATE. THERE WAS NOTHING I COULD DO.
"YOU ARE TO DO NOTHING."
THE C.I.C. HAS SIGNED OFF ON THIS AS HAVE THE MEMBERS OF THE JOINT CHIEFS AND CONGRESS.
THIS LOOKS A LOT LIKE THE SHIP I ARRIVED IN.
YES... AFTER OUR WORLD WAS DESTROYED, THERE WOULD BE NO FURTHER ADVANCEMENTS IN KRYPTONIAN TECHNOLOGY. YOU AND I ARE ALL THAT REMAIN.
"HE IS TO STAND ALONE."
IF HE SHOULD ENTER RUSSIAN AIR SPACE, WE ARE NOT TO INTERFERE OR INTERVENE--
--WE WILL NEITHER ENDORSE NOR TAKE SIDES. OUR OFFICIAL POSITION IS THAT THIS CONFLICT HAS NOTHING TO DO WITH US.
YOU CAN'T SERIOUSLY EXPECT US TO--
DO NOTHING, YES.
BUT THIS IS MURDER--
NO, ACTUALLY IT'S NOT--

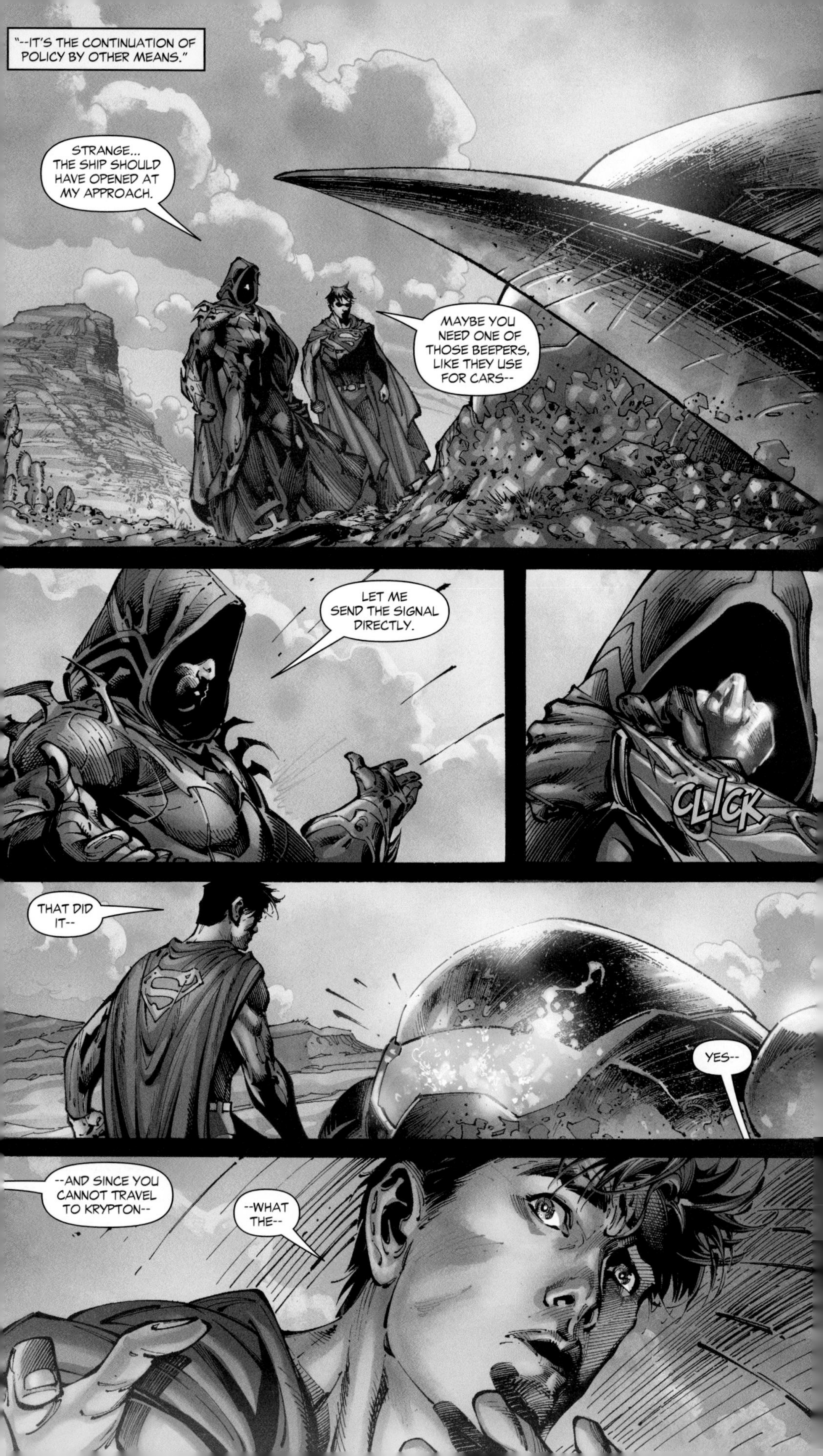
"--IT'S THE CONTINUATION OF POLICY BY OTHER MEANS."
STRANGE... THE SHIP SHOULD HAVE OPENED AT MY APPROACH.
MAYBE YOU NEED ONE OF THOSE BEEPERS, LIKE THEY USE FOR CARS--
LET ME SEND THE SIGNAL DIRECTLY.
CLICK
THAT DID IT--
YES--
--AND SINCE YOU CANNOT TRAVEL TO KRYPTON--
--WHAT THE--

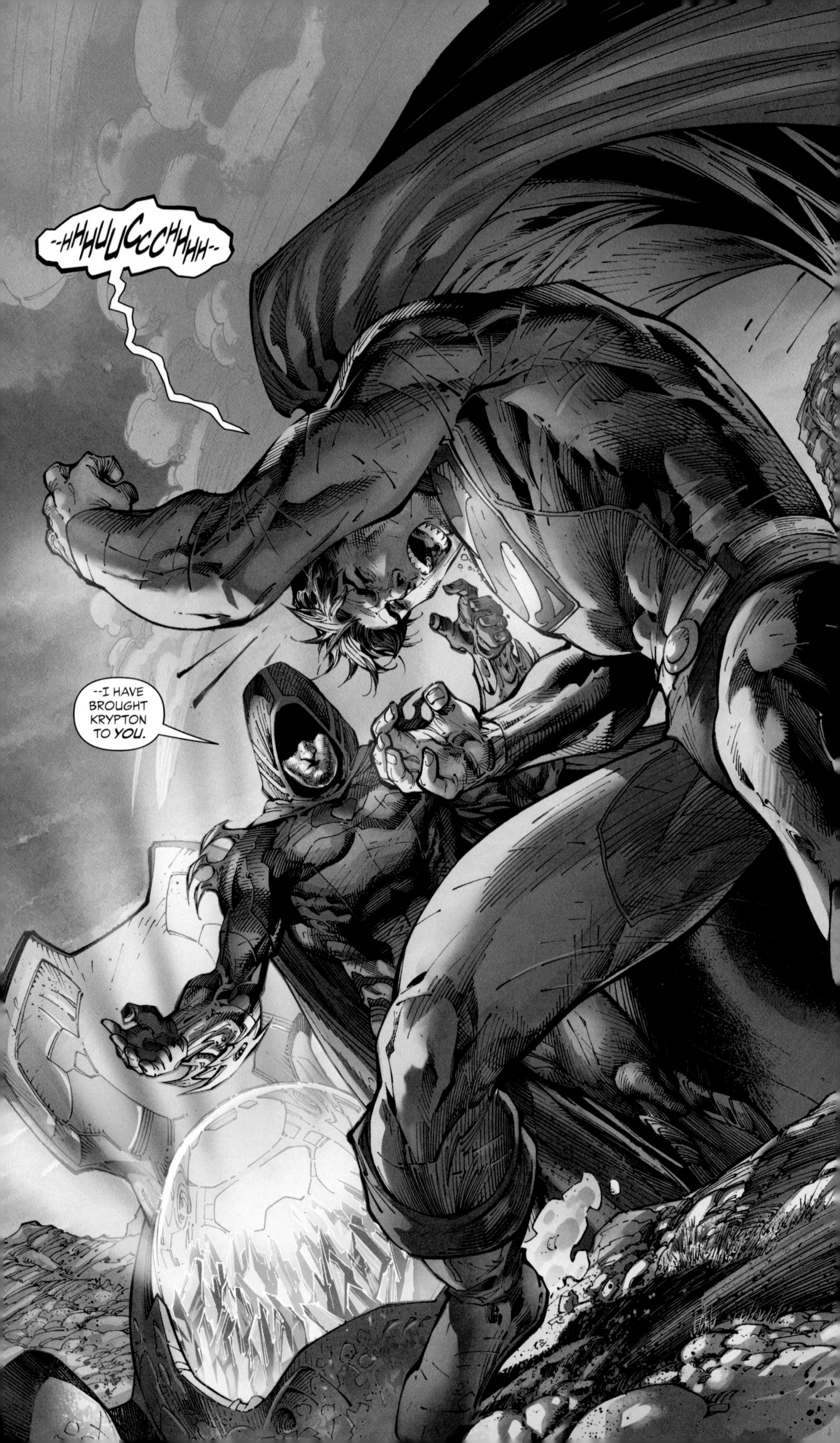
--HHHUUCCCHHHH--
--I HAVE BROUGHT KRYPTON TO *YOU*.

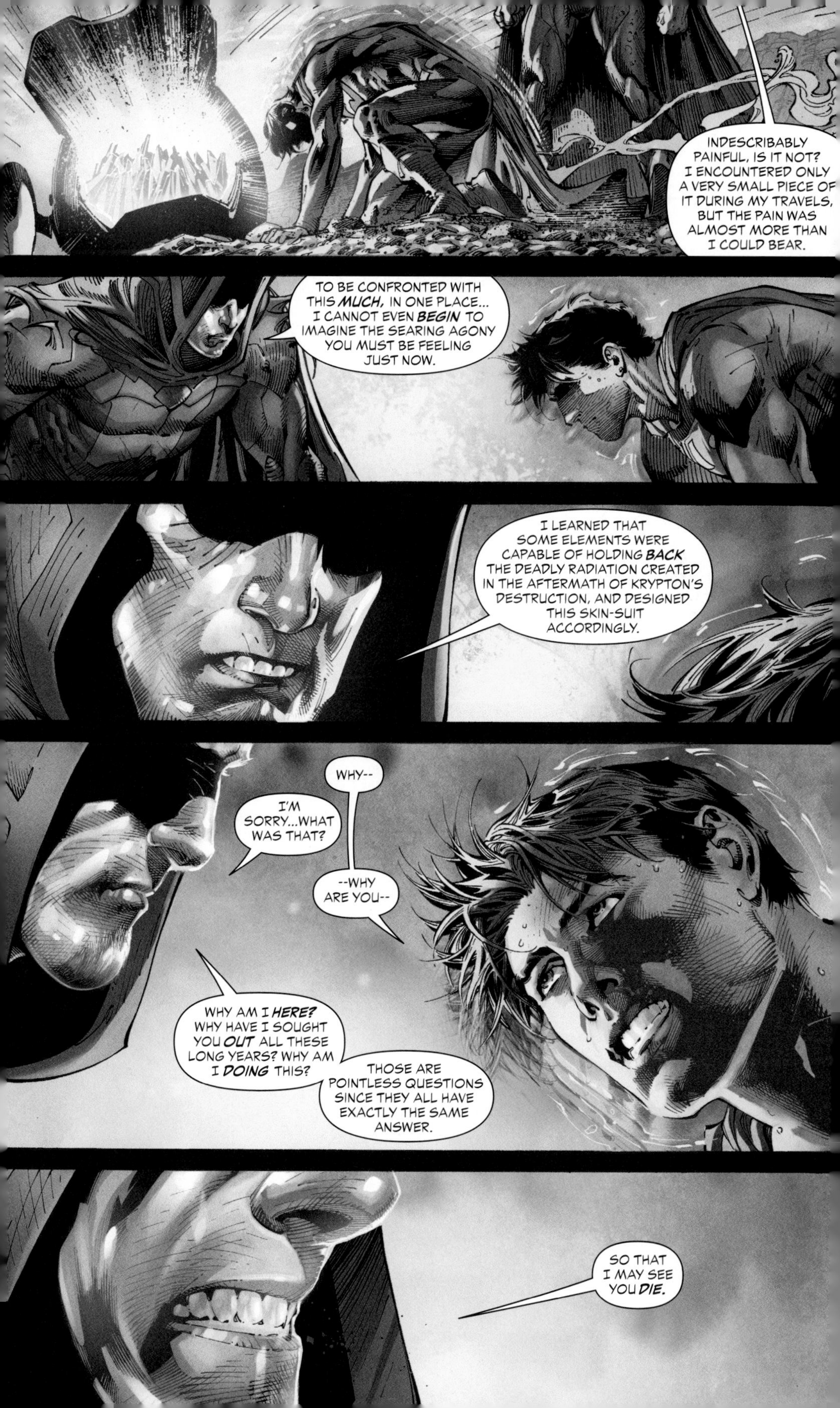
INDESCRIBABLY PAINFUL, IS IT NOT? I ENCOUNTERED ONLY A VERY SMALL PIECE OF IT DURING MY TRAVELS, BUT THE PAIN WAS ALMOST MORE THAN I COULD BEAR.
TO BE CONFRONTED WITH THIS *MUCH,* IN ONE PLACE... I CANNOT EVEN *BEGIN* TO IMAGINE THE SEARING AGONY YOU MUST BE FEELING JUST NOW.
I LEARNED THAT SOME ELEMENTS WERE CAPABLE OF HOLDING *BACK* THE DEADLY RADIATION CREATED IN THE AFTERMATH OF KRYPTON'S DESTRUCTION, AND DESIGNED THIS SKIN-SUIT ACCORDINGLY.
WHY--
I'M SORRY...WHAT WAS THAT?
--WHY ARE YOU--
WHY AM I *HERE?* WHY HAVE I SOUGHT YOU *OUT* ALL THESE LONG YEARS? WHY AM I *DOING* THIS?
THOSE ARE POINTLESS QUESTIONS SINCE THEY ALL HAVE EXACTLY THE SAME ANSWER.
SO THAT I MAY SEE YOU *DIE.*

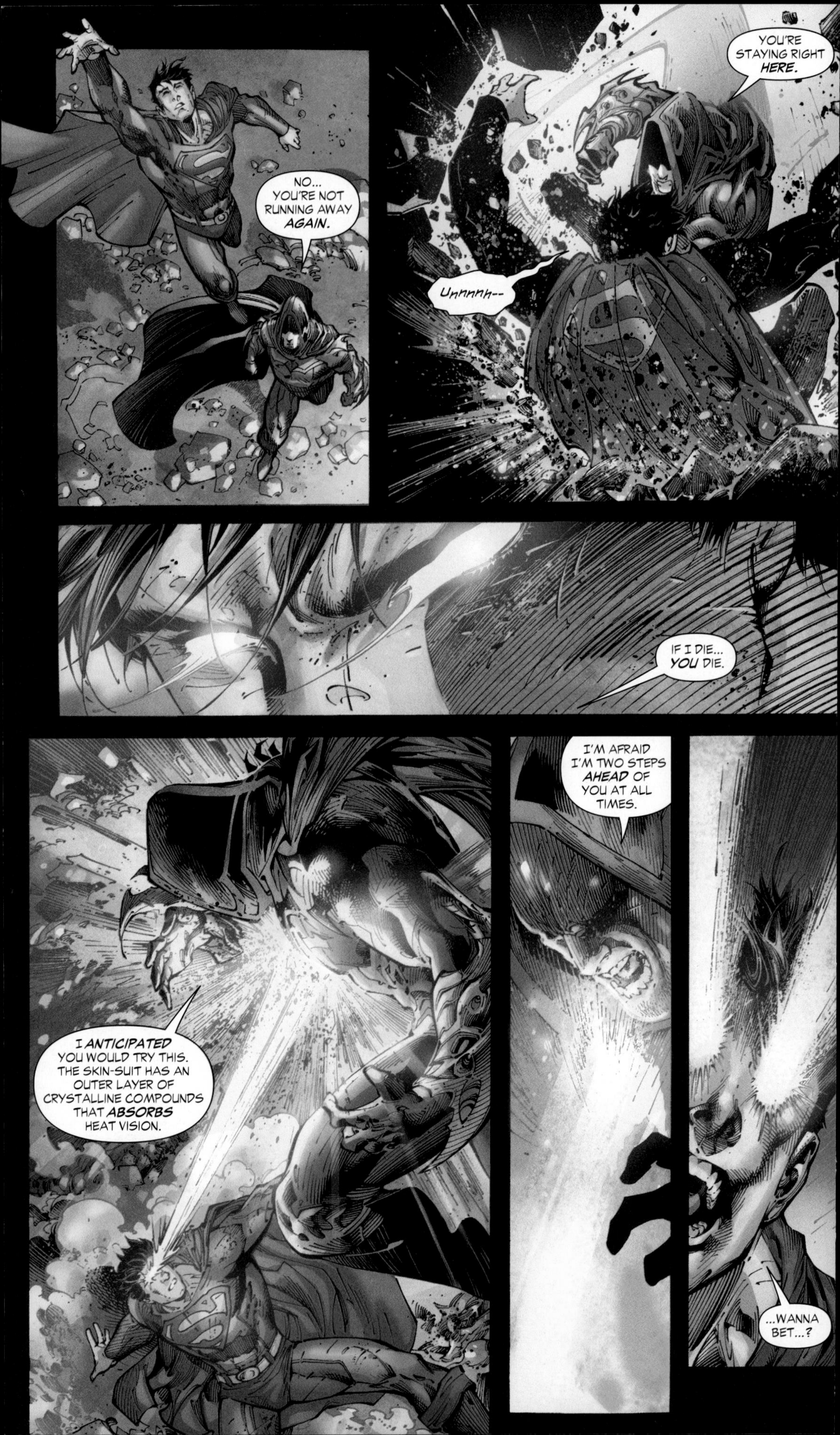
NO... YOU'RE NOT RUNNING AWAY AGAIN.
YOU'RE STAYING RIGHT HERE.
Unnnnh--
IF I DIE... YOU DIE.
I ANTICIPATED YOU WOULD TRY THIS. THE SKIN-SUIT HAS AN OUTER LAYER OF CRYSTALLINE COMPOUNDS THAT ABSORBS HEAT VISION.
I'M AFRAID I'M TWO STEPS AHEAD OF YOU AT ALL TIMES.
...WANNA BET...?

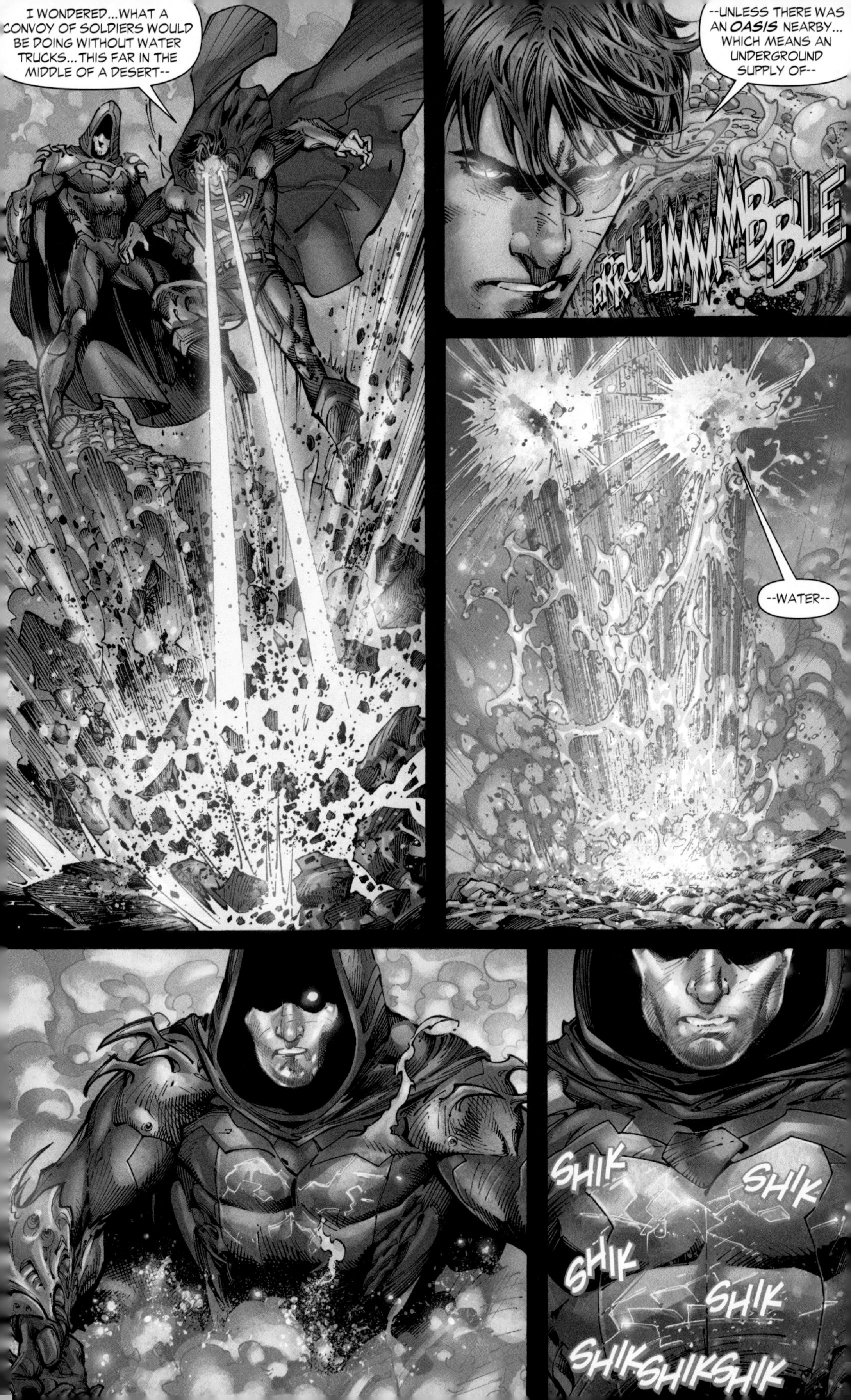
I WONDERED...WHAT A CONVOY OF SOLDIERS WOULD BE DOING WITHOUT WATER TRUCKS...THIS FAR IN THE MIDDLE OF A DESERT--
--UNLESS THERE WAS AN OASIS NEARBY... WHICH MEANS AN UNDERGROUND SUPPLY OF--
BRRUUMMBBLE
--WATER--
SHIK
SHIK
SHIK
SHIK
SHIKSHIKSHIK

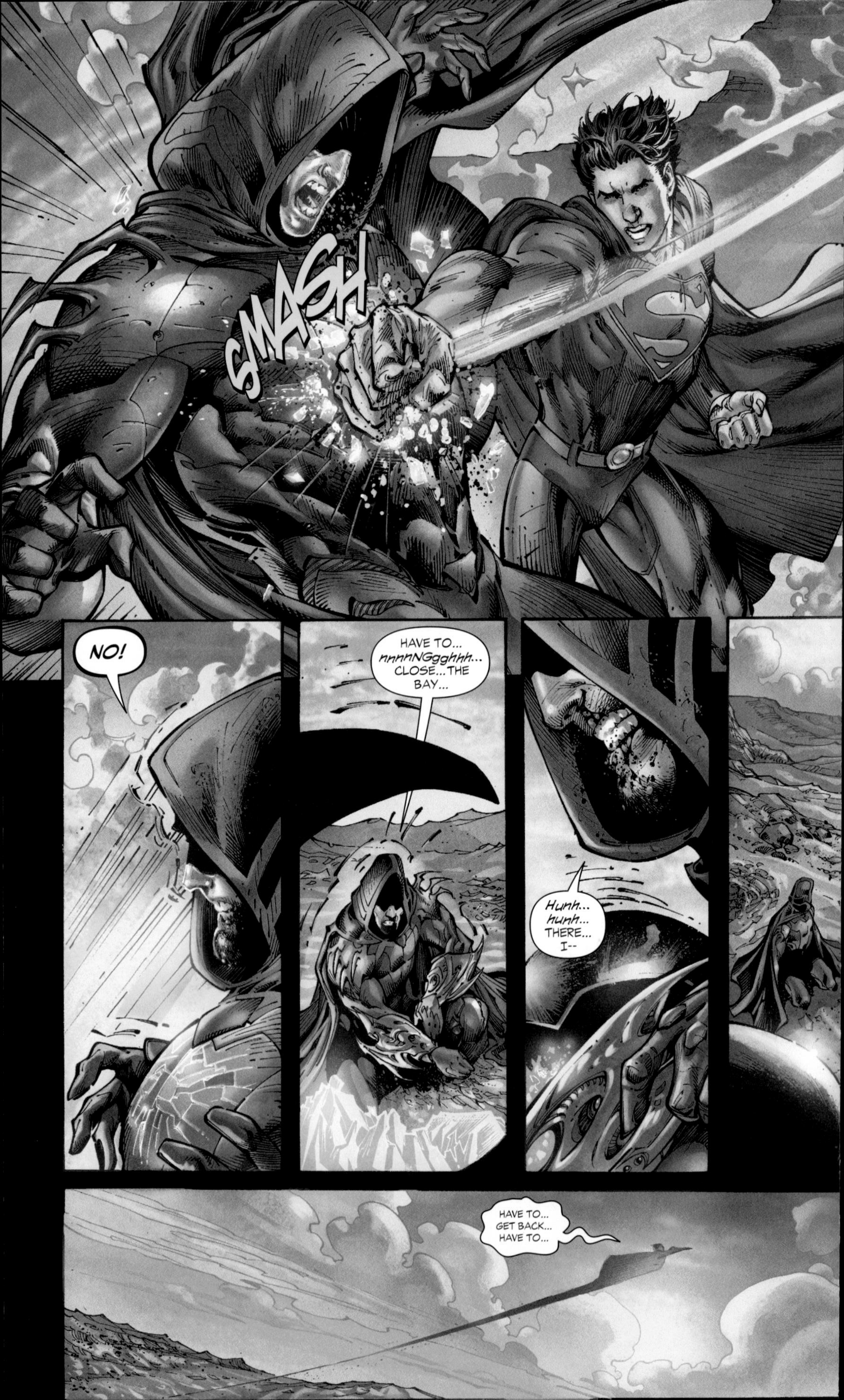
SMASH
NO!
HAVE TO... nnnnNGgghhh... CLOSE... THE BAY...
Hunh... hunh... THERE... I--
HAVE TO... GET BACK... HAVE TO...

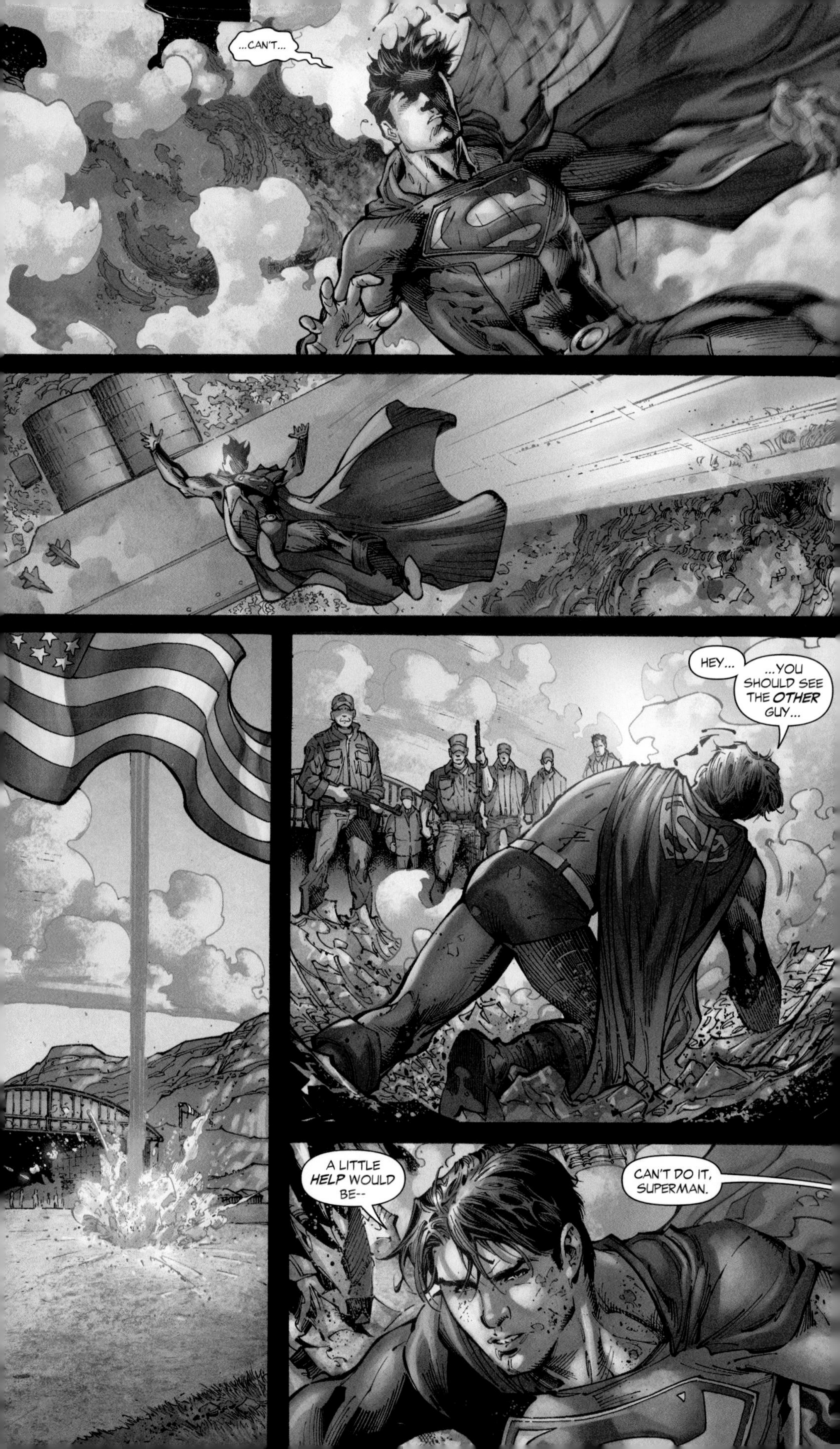
...CAN'T...
HEY...
...YOU SHOULD SEE THE OTHER GUY...
A LITTLE HELP WOULD BE--
CAN'T DO IT, SUPERMAN.

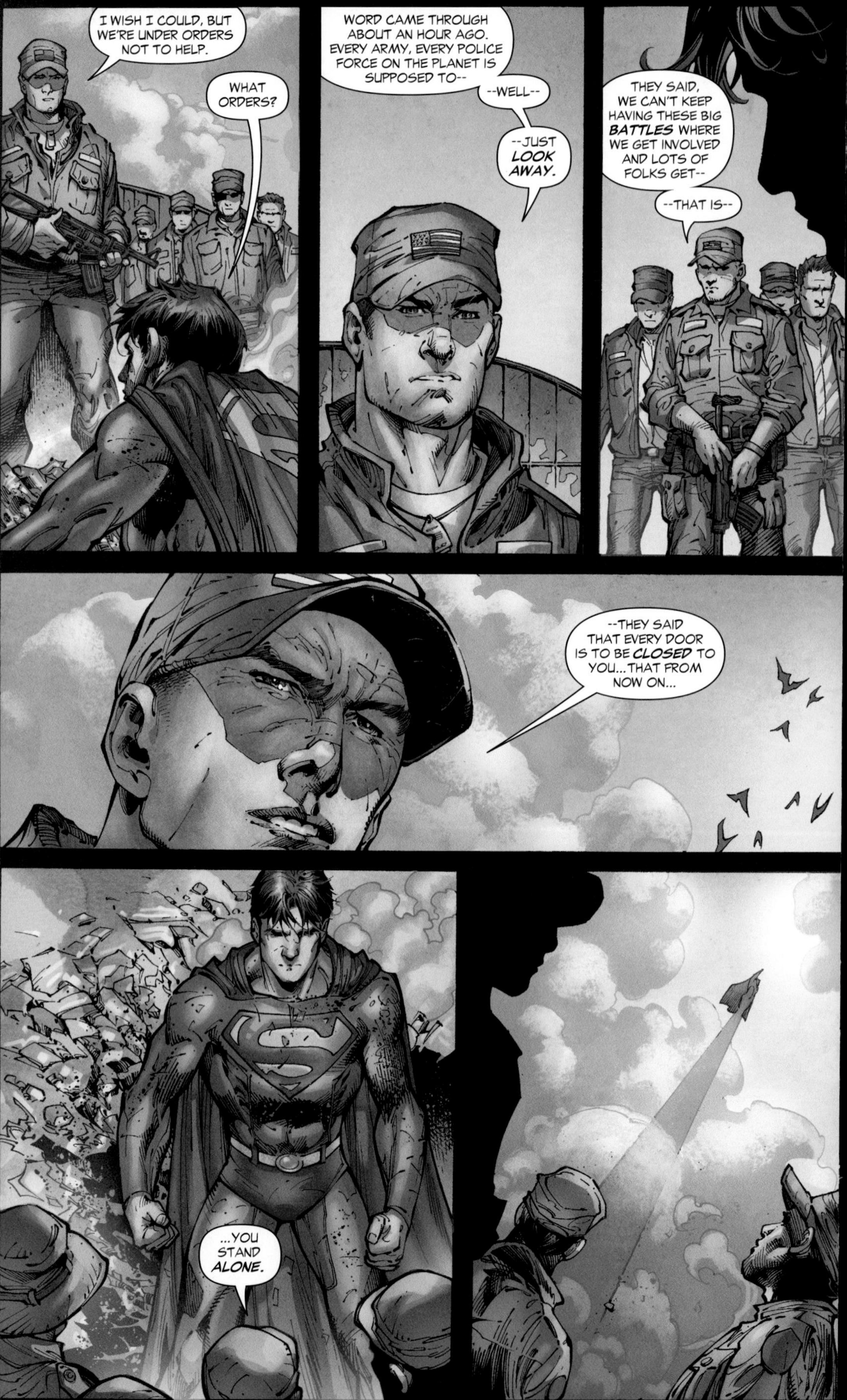
I WISH I COULD, BUT WE'RE UNDER ORDERS NOT TO HELP.
WHAT ORDERS?
WORD CAME THROUGH ABOUT AN HOUR AGO. EVERY ARMY, EVERY POLICE FORCE ON THE PLANET IS SUPPOSED TO--
--WELL--
--JUST LOOK AWAY.
THEY SAID, WE CAN'T KEEP HAVING THESE BIG BATTLES WHERE WE GET INVOLVED AND LOTS OF FOLKS GET--
--THAT IS--
--THEY SAID THAT EVERY DOOR IS TO BE CLOSED TO YOU...THAT FROM NOW ON...
...YOU STAND ALONE.

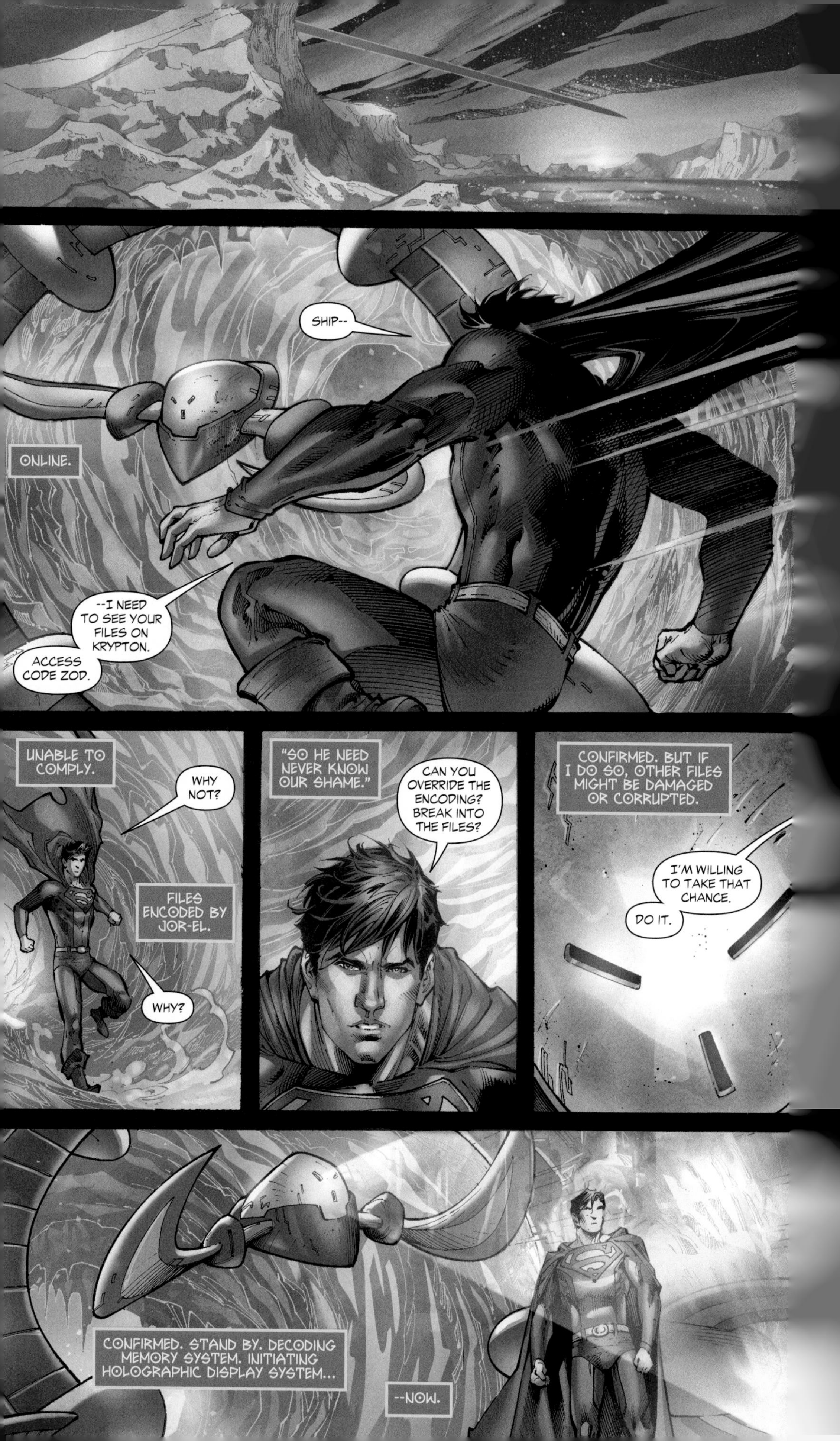
SHIP--
ONLINE.
ACCESS CODE ZOD.
--I NEED TO SEE YOUR FILES ON KRYPTON.
UNABLE TO COMPLY.
WHY NOT?
FILES ENCODED BY JOR-EL.
WHY?
"SO HE NEED NEVER KNOW OUR SHAME."
CAN YOU OVERRIDE THE ENCODING? BREAK INTO THE FILES?
CONFIRMED. BUT IF I DO SO, OTHER FILES MIGHT BE DAMAGED OR CORRUPTED.
I'M WILLING TO TAKE THAT CHANCE.
DO IT.
CONFIRMED. STAND BY. DECODING MEMORY SYSTEM. INITIATING HOLOGRAPHIC DISPLAY SYSTEM...
--NOW.

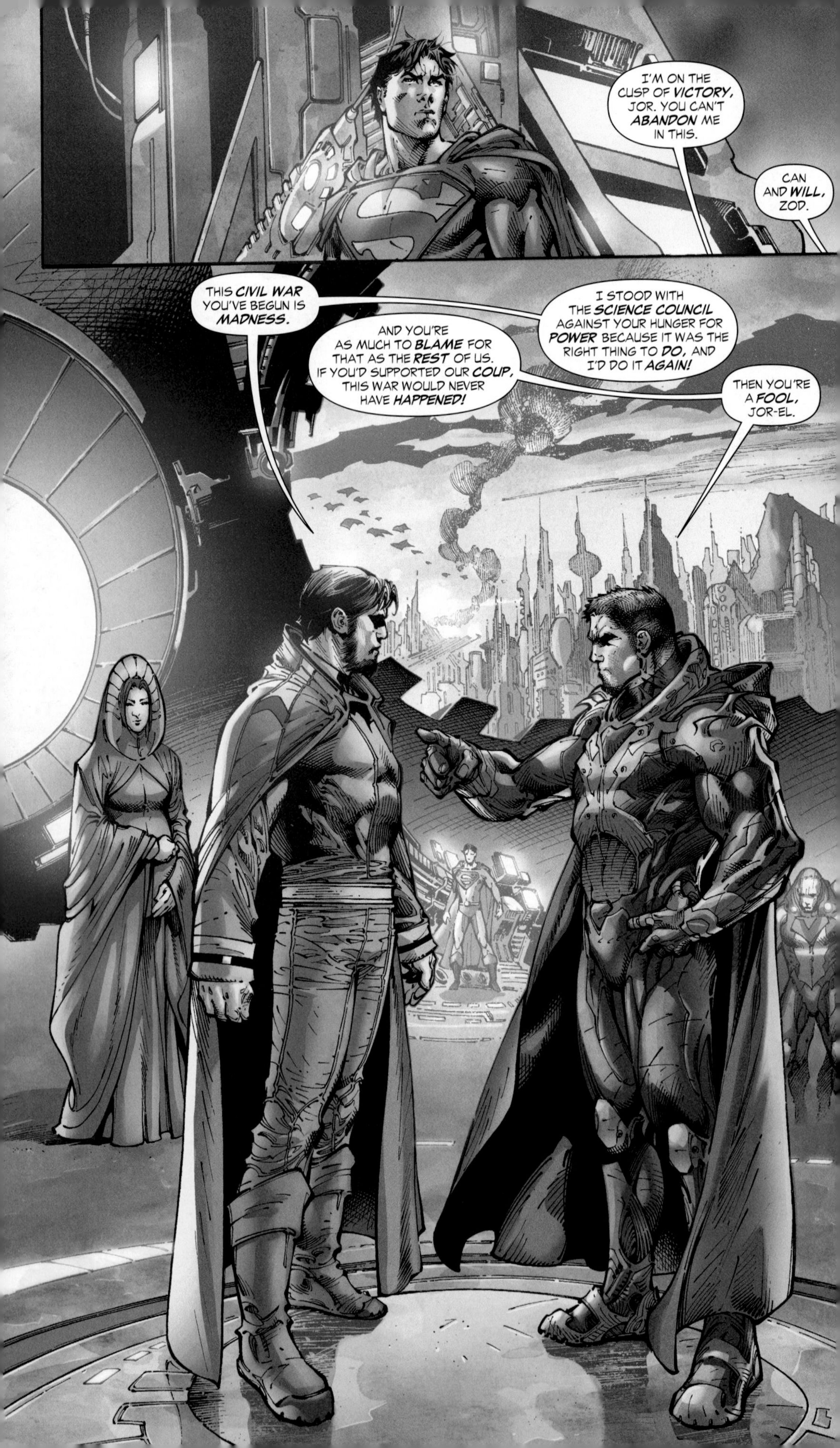
I'M ON THE CUSP OF VICTORY, JOR. YOU CAN'T ABANDON ME IN THIS.
CAN AND WILL, ZOD.
THIS CIVIL WAR YOU'VE BEGUN IS MADNESS.
I STOOD WITH THE SCIENCE COUNCIL AGAINST YOUR HUNGER FOR POWER BECAUSE IT WAS THE RIGHT THING TO DO, AND I'D DO IT AGAIN!
AND YOU'RE AS MUCH TO BLAME FOR THAT AS THE REST OF US. IF YOU'D SUPPORTED OUR COUP, THIS WAR WOULD NEVER HAVE HAPPENED!
THEN YOU'RE A FOOL, JOR-EL.

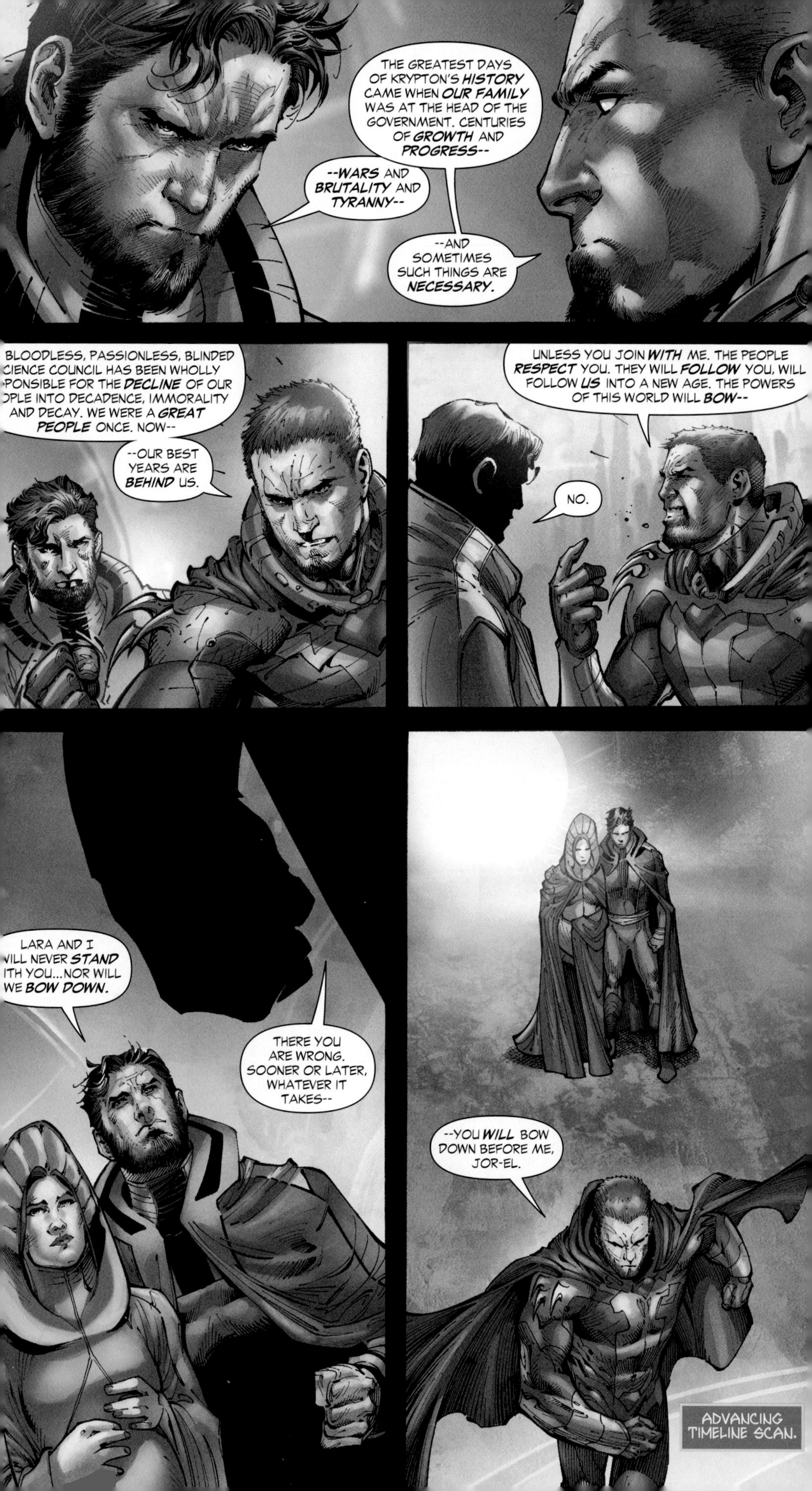
THE GREATEST DAYS OF KRYPTON'S HISTORY CAME WHEN OUR FAMILY WAS AT THE HEAD OF THE GOVERNMENT. CENTURIES OF GROWTH AND PROGRESS--
--WARS AND BRUTALITY AND TYRANNY--
--AND SOMETIMES SUCH THINGS ARE NECESSARY.
BLOODLESS, PASSIONLESS, BLINDED CIENCE COUNCIL HAS BEEN WHOLLY PONSIBLE FOR THE DECLINE OF OUR PLE INTO DECADENCE, IMMORALITY AND DECAY. WE WERE A GREAT PEOPLE ONCE. NOW--
--OUR BEST YEARS ARE BEHIND US.
UNLESS YOU JOIN WITH ME. THE PEOPLE RESPECT YOU. THEY WILL FOLLOW YOU, WILL FOLLOW US INTO A NEW AGE. THE POWERS OF THIS WORLD WILL BOW--
NO.
LARA AND I VILL NEVER STAND ITH YOU...NOR WILL WE BOW DOWN.
THERE YOU ARE WRONG. SOONER OR LATER, WHATEVER IT TAKES--
--YOU WILL BOW DOWN BEFORE ME, JOR-EL.
ADVANCING TIMELINE SCAN.

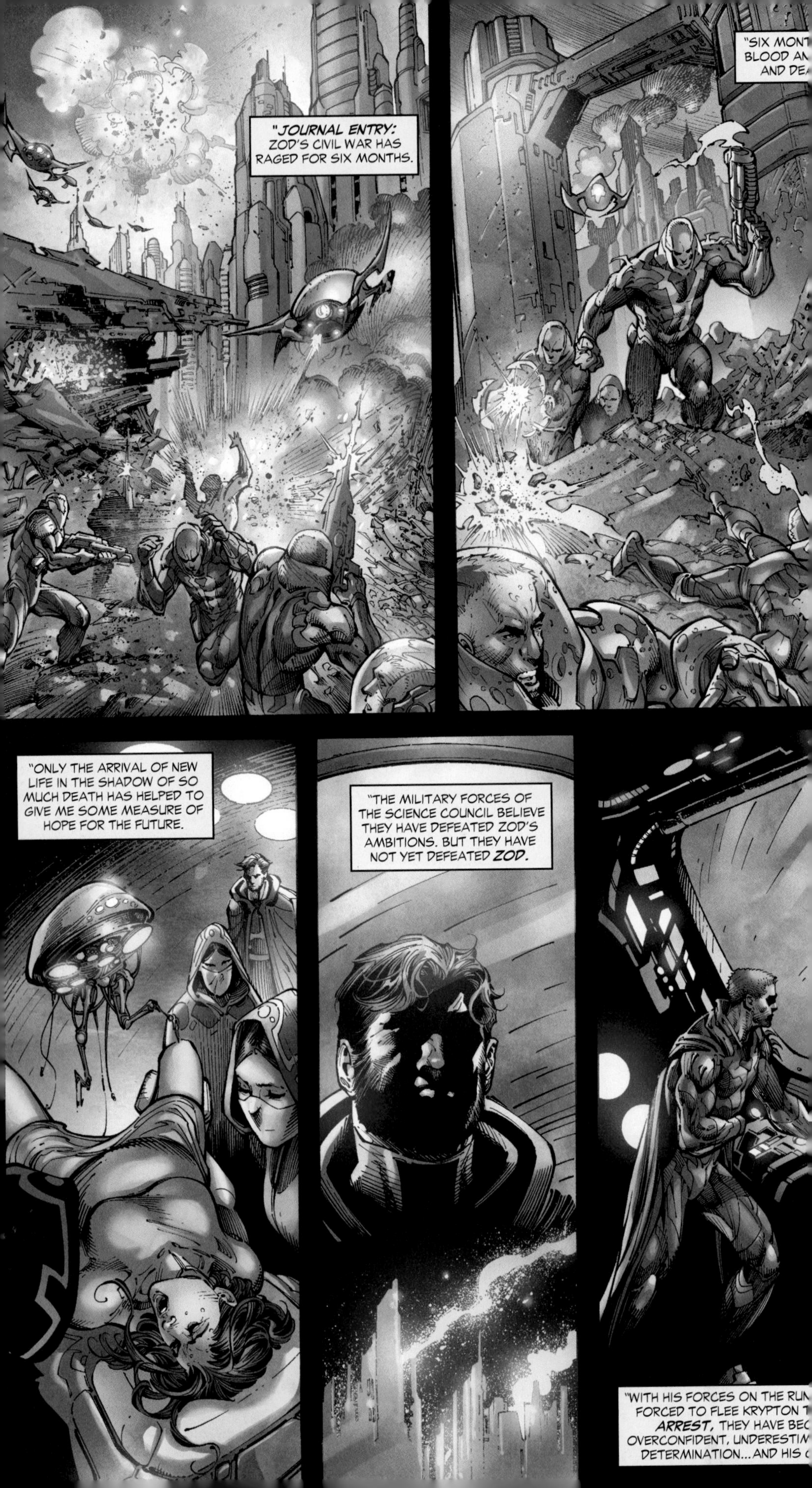
"JOURNAL ENTRY: ZOD'S CIVIL WAR HAS RAGED FOR SIX MONTHS.
"SIX MONT BLOOD AN AND DE
"ONLY THE ARRIVAL OF NEW LIFE IN THE SHADOW OF SO MUCH DEATH HAS HELPED TO GIVE ME SOME MEASURE OF HOPE FOR THE FUTURE.
"THE MILITARY FORCES OF THE SCIENCE COUNCIL BELIEVE THEY HAVE DEFEATED ZOD'S AMBITIONS. BUT THEY HAVE NOT YET DEFEATED ZOD.
"WITH HIS FORCES ON THE RUN FORCED TO FLEE KRYPTON T ARREST, THEY HAVE BEC OVERCONFIDENT, UNDERESTIM DETERMINATION... AND HIS

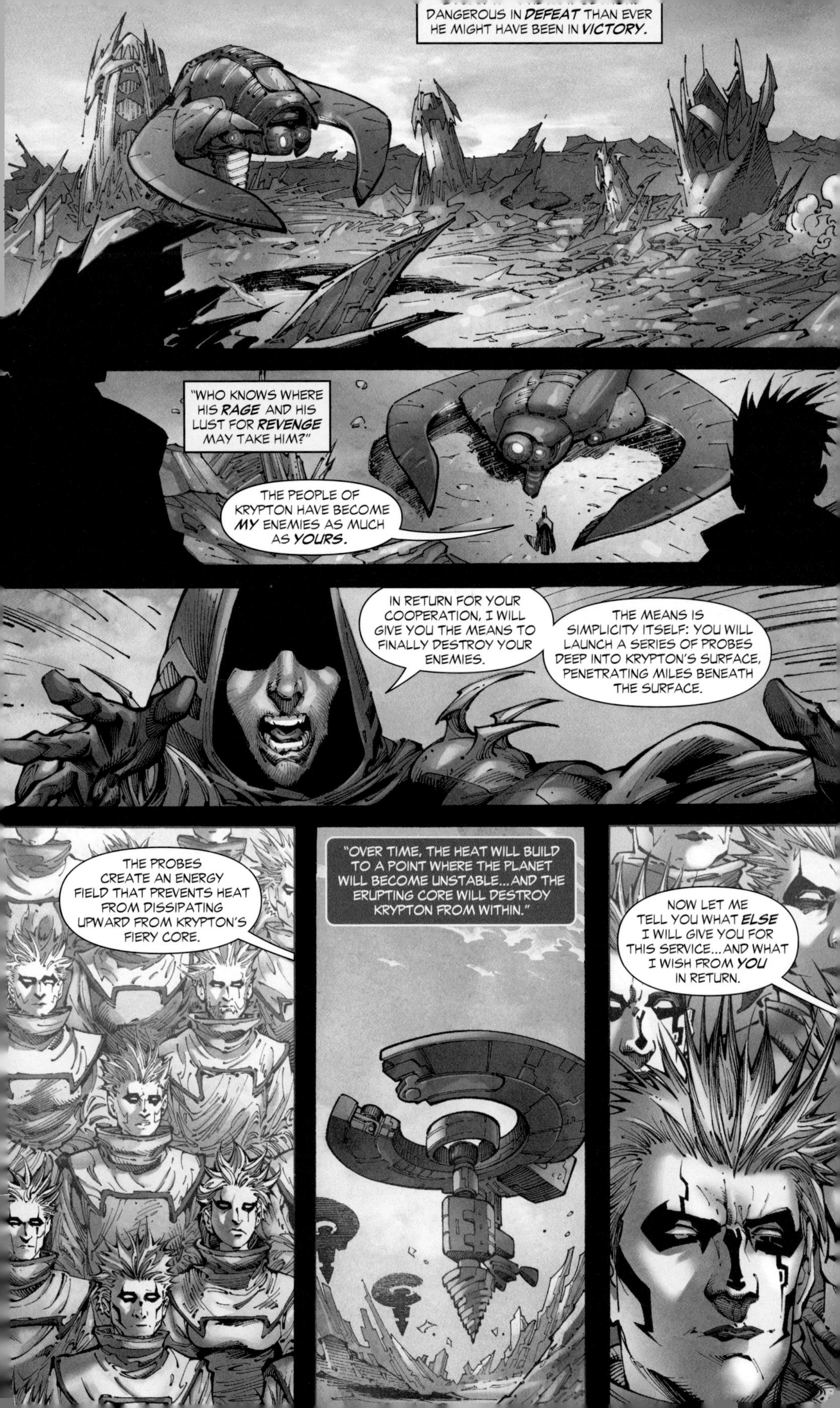
DANGEROUS IN DEFEAT THAN EVER HE MIGHT HAVE BEEN IN VICTORY.
"WHO KNOWS WHERE HIS RAGE AND HIS LUST FOR REVENGE MAY TAKE HIM?"
THE PEOPLE OF KRYPTON HAVE BECOME MY ENEMIES AS MUCH AS YOURS.
IN RETURN FOR YOUR COOPERATION, I WILL GIVE YOU THE MEANS TO FINALLY DESTROY YOUR ENEMIES.
THE MEANS IS SIMPLICITY ITSELF: YOU WILL LAUNCH A SERIES OF PROBES DEEP INTO KRYPTON'S SURFACE, PENETRATING MILES BENEATH THE SURFACE.
THE PROBES CREATE AN ENERGY FIELD THAT PREVENTS HEAT FROM DISSIPATING UPWARD FROM KRYPTON'S FIERY CORE.
"OVER TIME, THE HEAT WILL BUILD TO A POINT WHERE THE PLANET WILL BECOME UNSTABLE...AND THE ERUPTING CORE WILL DESTROY KRYPTON FROM WITHIN."
NOW LET ME TELL YOU WHAT ELSE I WILL GIVE YOU FOR THIS SERVICE...AND WHAT I WISH FROM YOU IN RETURN.

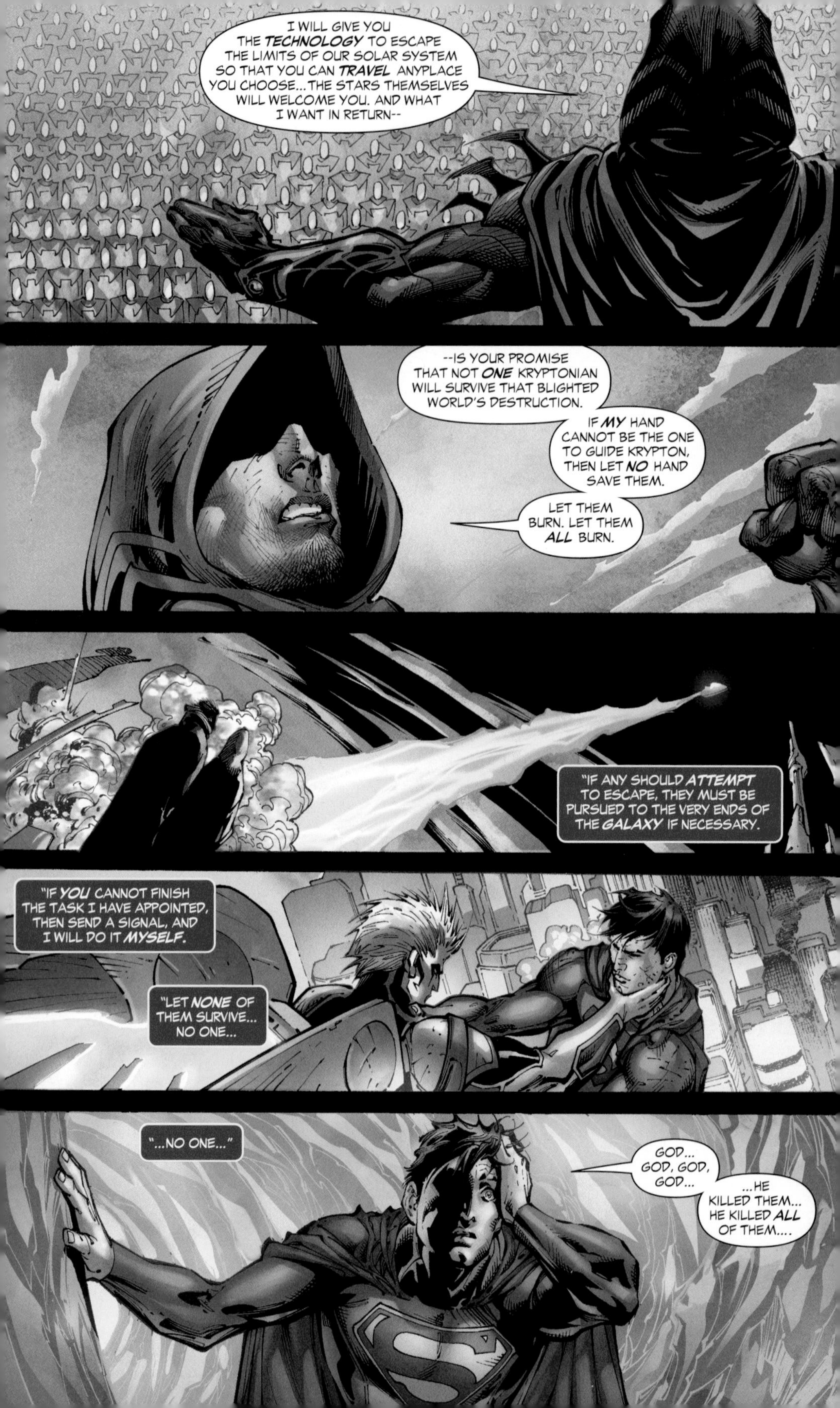
I WILL GIVE YOU THE TECHNOLOGY TO ESCAPE THE LIMITS OF OUR SOLAR SYSTEM SO THAT YOU CAN TRAVEL ANYPLACE YOU CHOOSE...THE STARS THEMSELVES WILL WELCOME YOU. AND WHAT I WANT IN RETURN--
--IS YOUR PROMISE THAT NOT ONE KRYPTONIAN WILL SURVIVE THAT BLIGHTED WORLD'S DESTRUCTION.
IF MY HAND CANNOT BE THE ONE TO GUIDE KRYPTON, THEN LET NO HAND SAVE THEM.
LET THEM BURN. LET THEM ALL BURN.
"IF ANY SHOULD ATTEMPT TO ESCAPE, THEY MUST BE PURSUED TO THE VERY ENDS OF THE GALAXY IF NECESSARY.
"IF YOU CANNOT FINISH THE TASK I HAVE APPOINTED, THEN SEND A SIGNAL, AND I WILL DO IT MYSELF.
"LET NONE OF THEM SURVIVE... NO ONE...
"...NO ONE..."
GOD... GOD, GOD, GOD...
...HE KILLED THEM... HE KILLED ALL OF THEM....

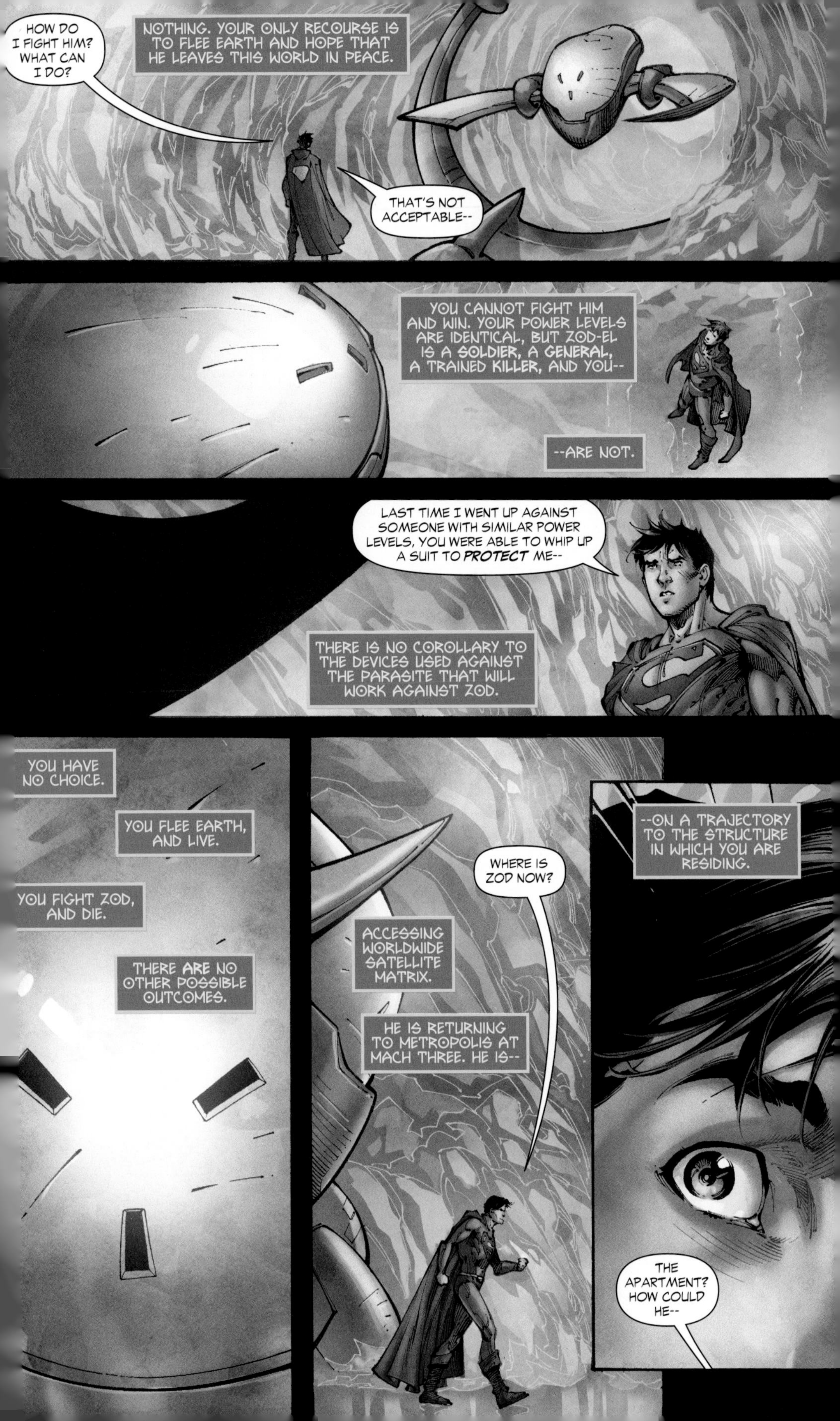
HOW DO I FIGHT HIM? WHAT CAN I DO?
NOTHING. YOUR ONLY RECOURSE IS TO FLEE EARTH AND HOPE THAT HE LEAVES THIS WORLD IN PEACE.
THAT'S NOT ACCEPTABLE--
YOU CANNOT FIGHT HIM AND WIN. YOUR POWER LEVELS ARE IDENTICAL, BUT ZOD-EL IS A SOLDIER, A GENERAL, A TRAINED KILLER, AND YOU--
--ARE NOT.
LAST TIME I WENT UP AGAINST SOMEONE WITH SIMILAR POWER LEVELS, YOU WERE ABLE TO WHIP UP A SUIT TO PROTECT ME--
THERE IS NO COROLLARY TO THE DEVICES USED AGAINST THE PARASITE THAT WILL WORK AGAINST ZOD.
YOU HAVE NO CHOICE.
YOU FLEE EARTH, AND LIVE.
YOU FIGHT ZOD, AND DIE.
THERE ARE NO OTHER POSSIBLE OUTCOMES.
WHERE IS ZOD NOW?
ACCESSING WORLDWIDE SATELLITE MATRIX.
HE IS RETURNING TO METROPOLIS AT MACH THREE. HE IS--
--ON A TRAJECTORY TO THE STRUCTURE IN WHICH YOU ARE RESIDING.
THE APARTMENT? HOW COULD HE--

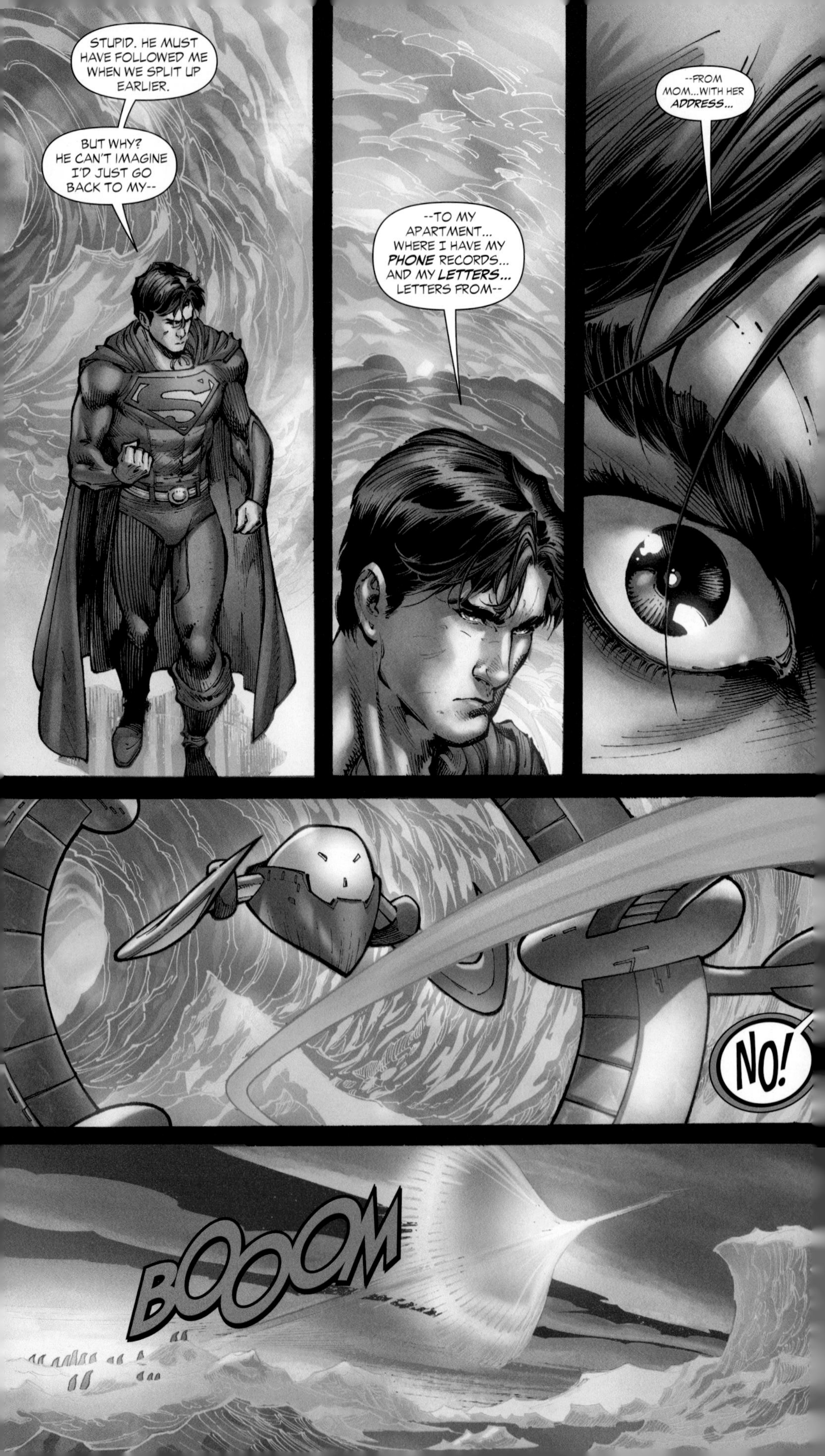
STUPID. HE MUST HAVE FOLLOWED ME WHEN WE SPLIT UP EARLIER.
BUT WHY? HE CAN'T IMAGINE I'D JUST GO BACK TO MY--
--TO MY APARTMENT... WHERE I HAVE MY PHONE RECORDS... AND MY LETTERS... LETTERS FROM--
--FROM MOM...WITH HER ADDRESS...
NO!
BOOOM

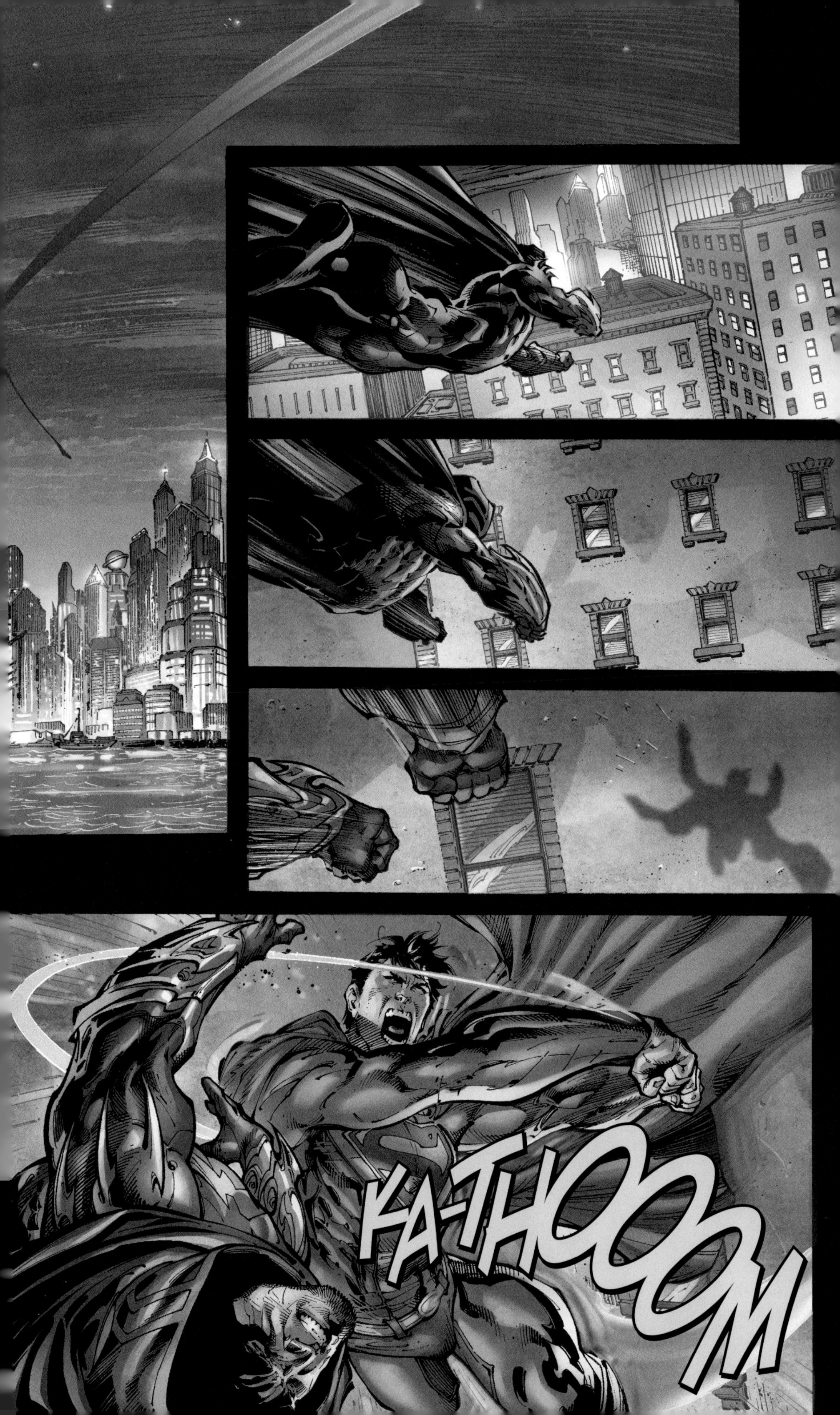
KA-THOOOOM

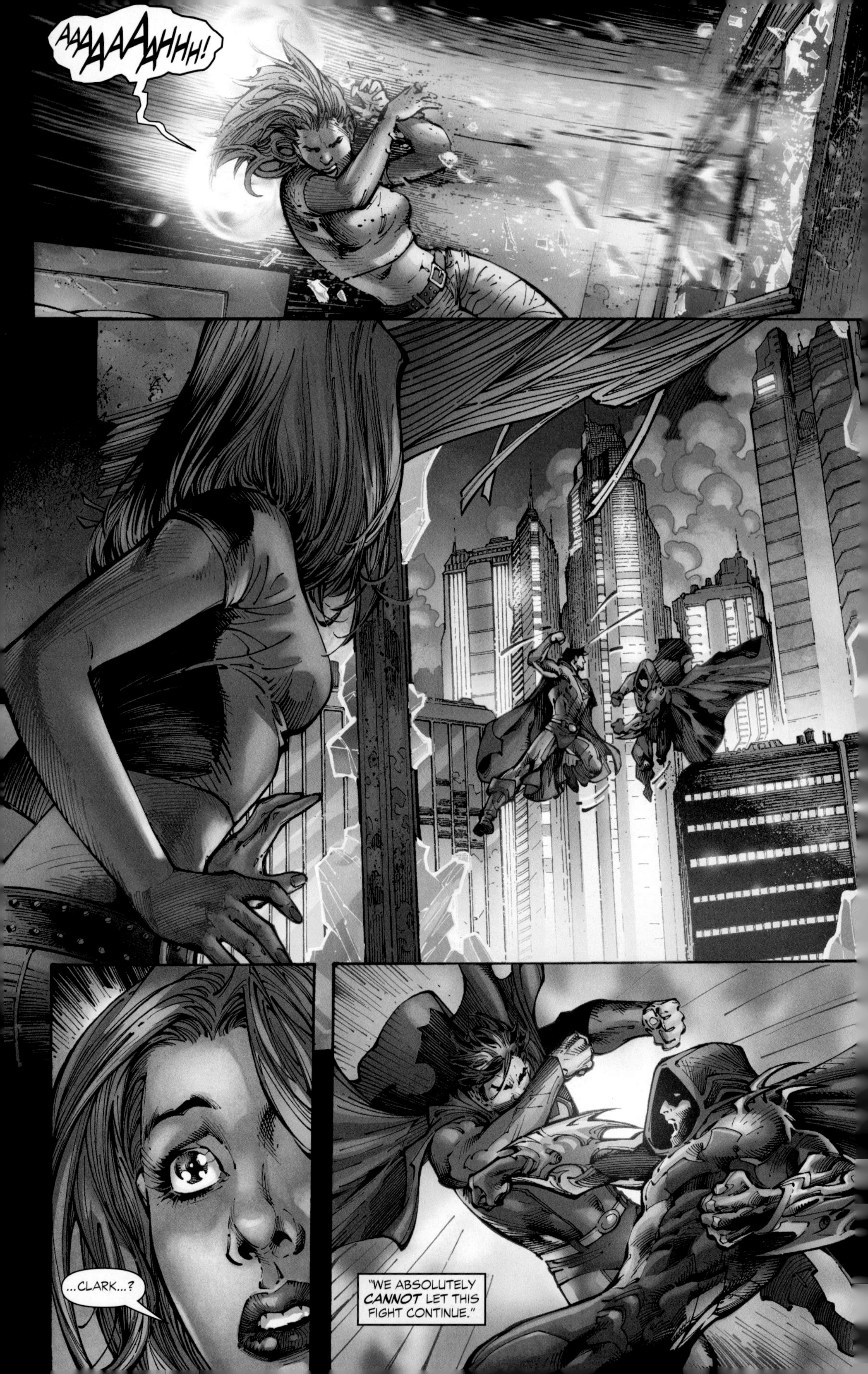
AAAAAAHHH!
...CLARK...?
"WE ABSOLUTELY CANNOT LET THIS FIGHT CONTINUE."

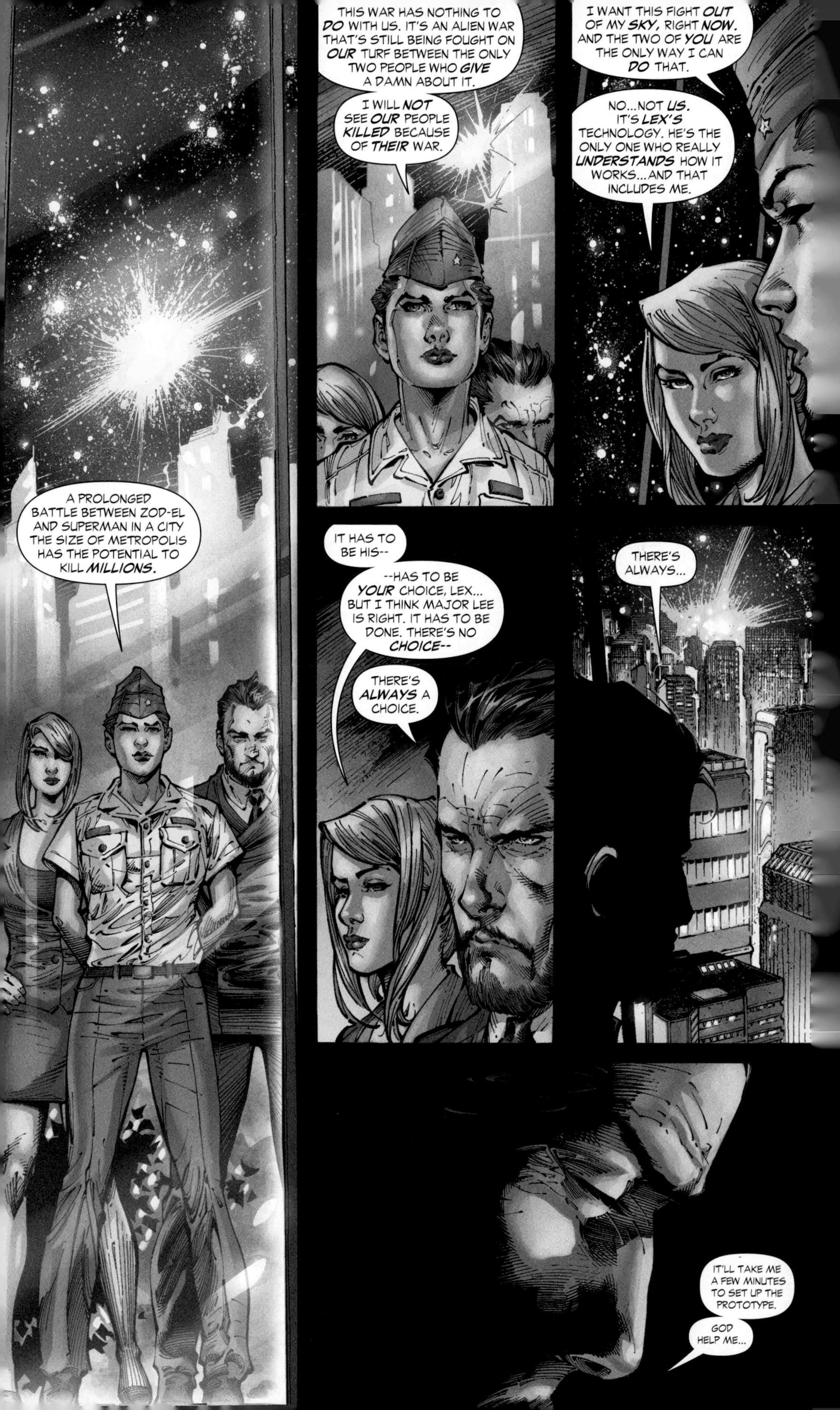

A PROLONGED BATTLE BETWEEN ZOD-EL AND SUPERMAN IN A CITY THE SIZE OF METROPOLIS HAS THE POTENTIAL TO KILL MILLIONS.
THIS WAR HAS NOTHING TO DO WITH US. IT'S AN ALIEN WAR THAT'S STILL BEING FOUGHT ON OUR TURF BETWEEN THE ONLY TWO PEOPLE WHO GIVE A DAMN ABOUT IT.
I WILL NOT SEE OUR PEOPLE KILLED BECAUSE OF THEIR WAR.
I WANT THIS FIGHT OUT OF MY SKY, RIGHT NOW. AND THE TWO OF YOU ARE THE ONLY WAY I CAN DO THAT.
NO...NOT US. IT'S LEX'S TECHNOLOGY. HE'S THE ONLY ONE WHO REALLY UNDERSTANDS HOW IT WORKS...AND THAT INCLUDES ME.
IT HAS TO BE HIS--
--HAS TO BE YOUR CHOICE, LEX... BUT I THINK MAJOR LEE IS RIGHT. IT HAS TO BE DONE. THERE'S NO CHOICE--
THERE'S ALWAYS A CHOICE.
THERE'S ALWAYS...
IT'LL TAKE ME A FEW MINUTES TO SET UP THE PROTOTYPE.
GOD HELP ME...

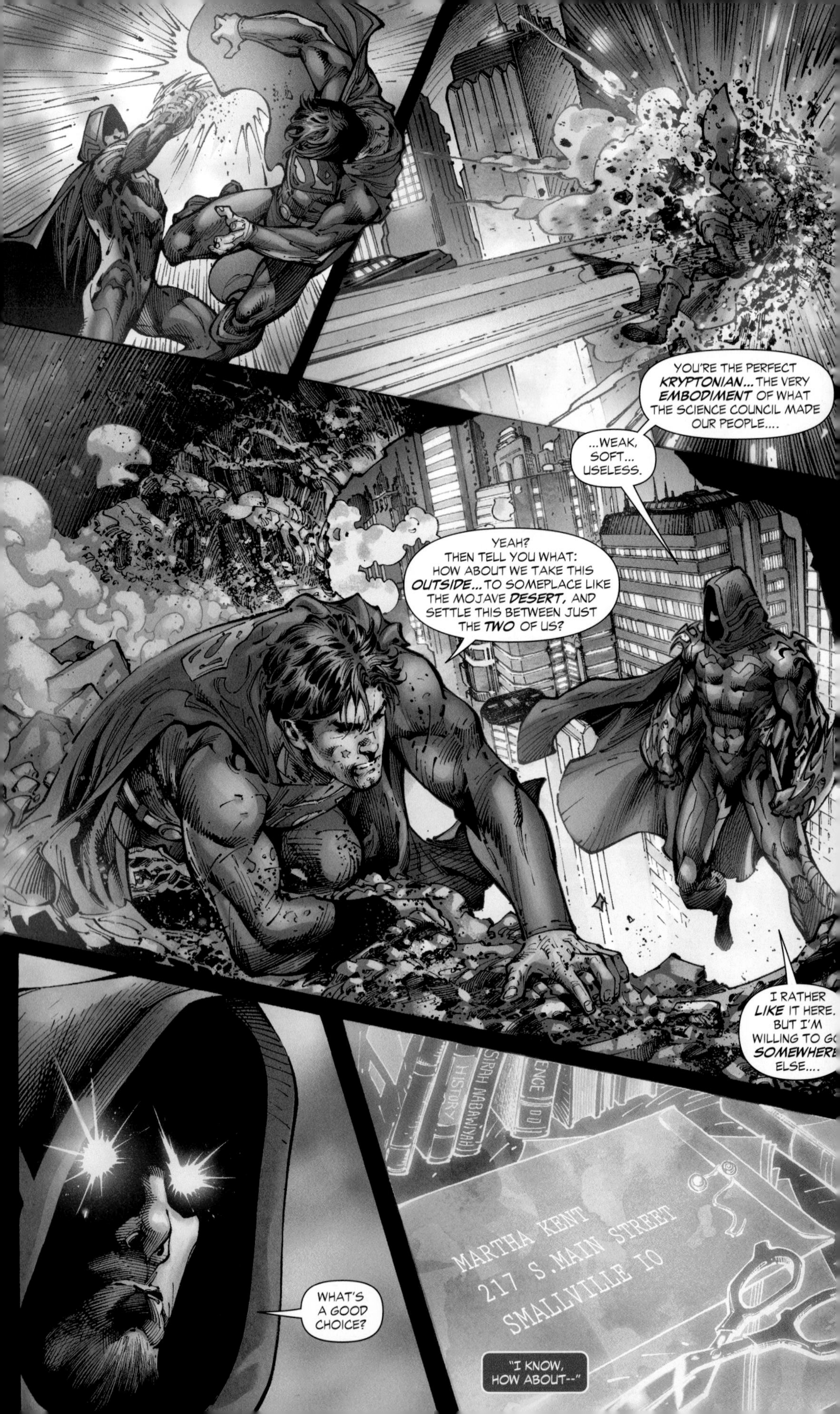
YOU'RE THE PERFECT KRYPTONIAN... THE VERY EMBODIMENT OF WHAT THE SCIENCE COUNCIL MADE OUR PEOPLE....
...WEAK, SOFT... USELESS.
YEAH? THEN TELL YOU WHAT: HOW ABOUT WE TAKE THIS OUTSIDE... TO SOMEPLACE LIKE THE MOJAVE DESERT, AND SETTLE THIS BETWEEN JUST THE TWO OF US?
I RATHER LIKE IT HERE. BUT I'M WILLING TO GO SOMEWHERE ELSE....
WHAT'S A GOOD CHOICE?
HISTORY
MARTHA KENT
217 S.MAIN STREET
SMALLVILLE IO
"I KNOW, HOW ABOUT--"

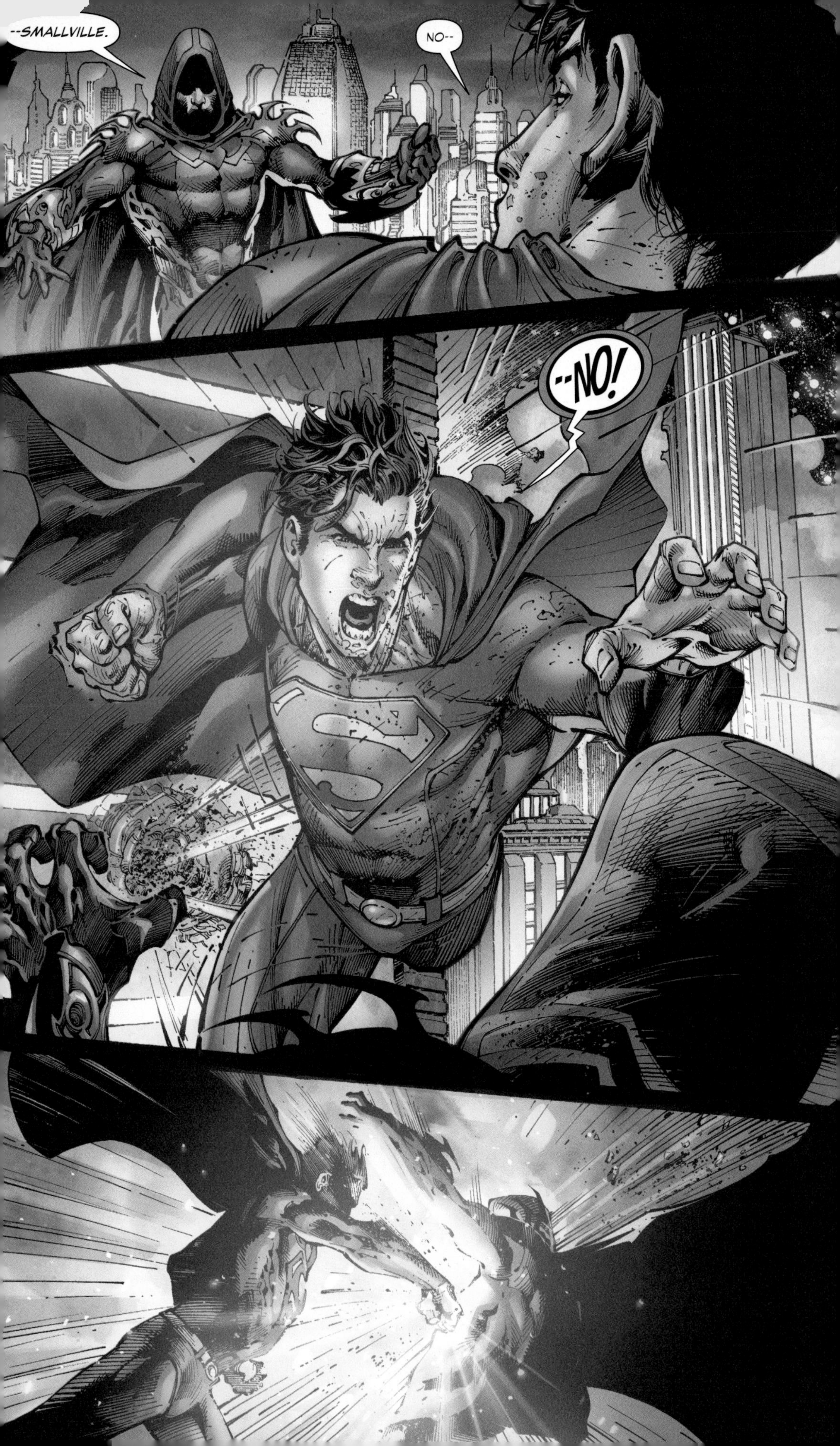
--SMALLVILLE.
NO--
--NO!

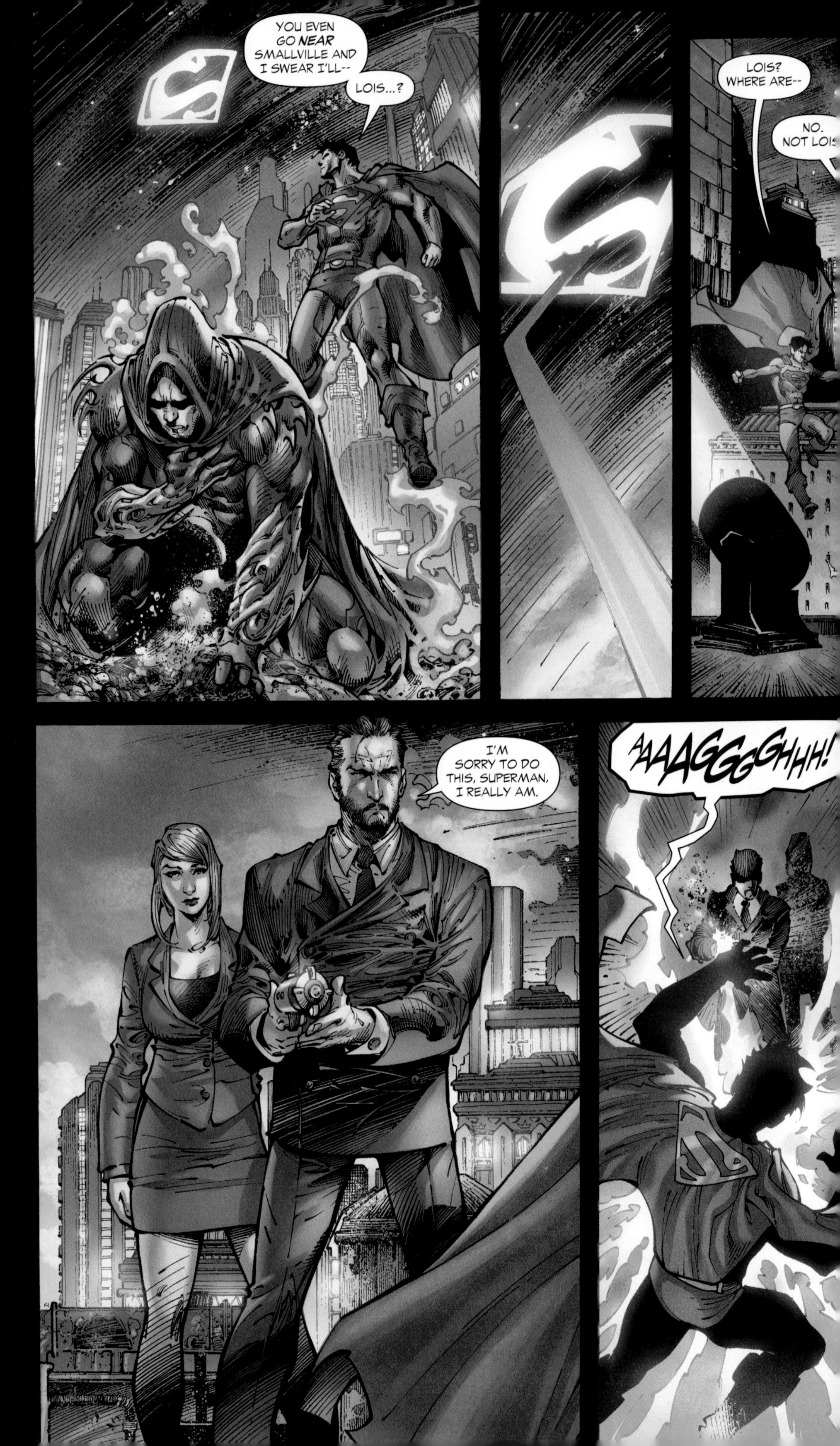
YOU EVEN GO NEAR SMALLVILLE AND I SWEAR I'LL--
LOIS...?
LOIS? WHERE ARE--
NO. NOT LOIS
I'M SORRY TO DO THIS, SUPERMAN, I REALLY AM.
AAAAGGGGHHH!

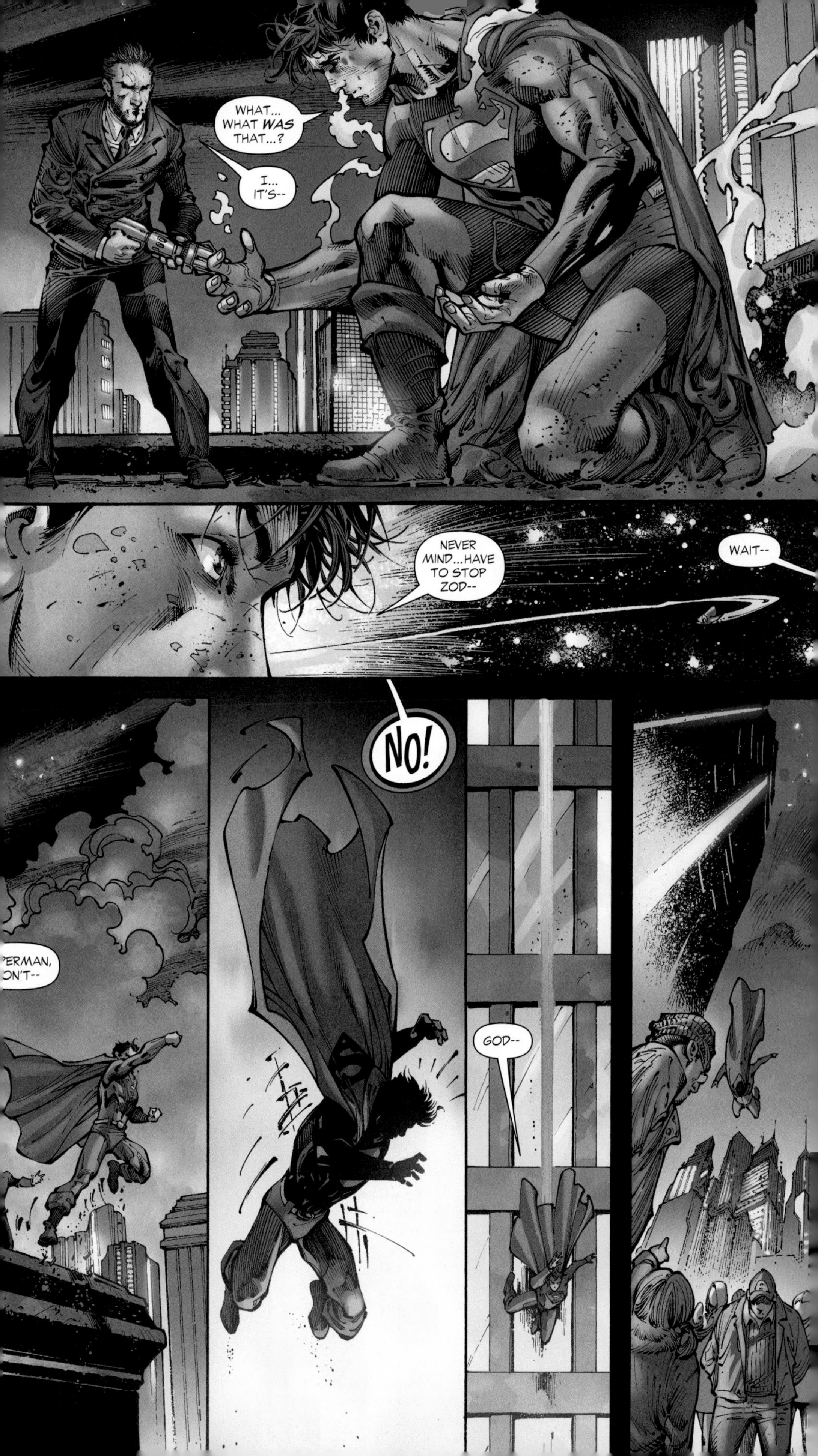
WHAT... WHAT **WAS** THAT...?
I... IT'S--
NEVER MIND...HAVE TO STOP ZOD--
WAIT--
PERMAN, ON'T--
NO!
GOD--

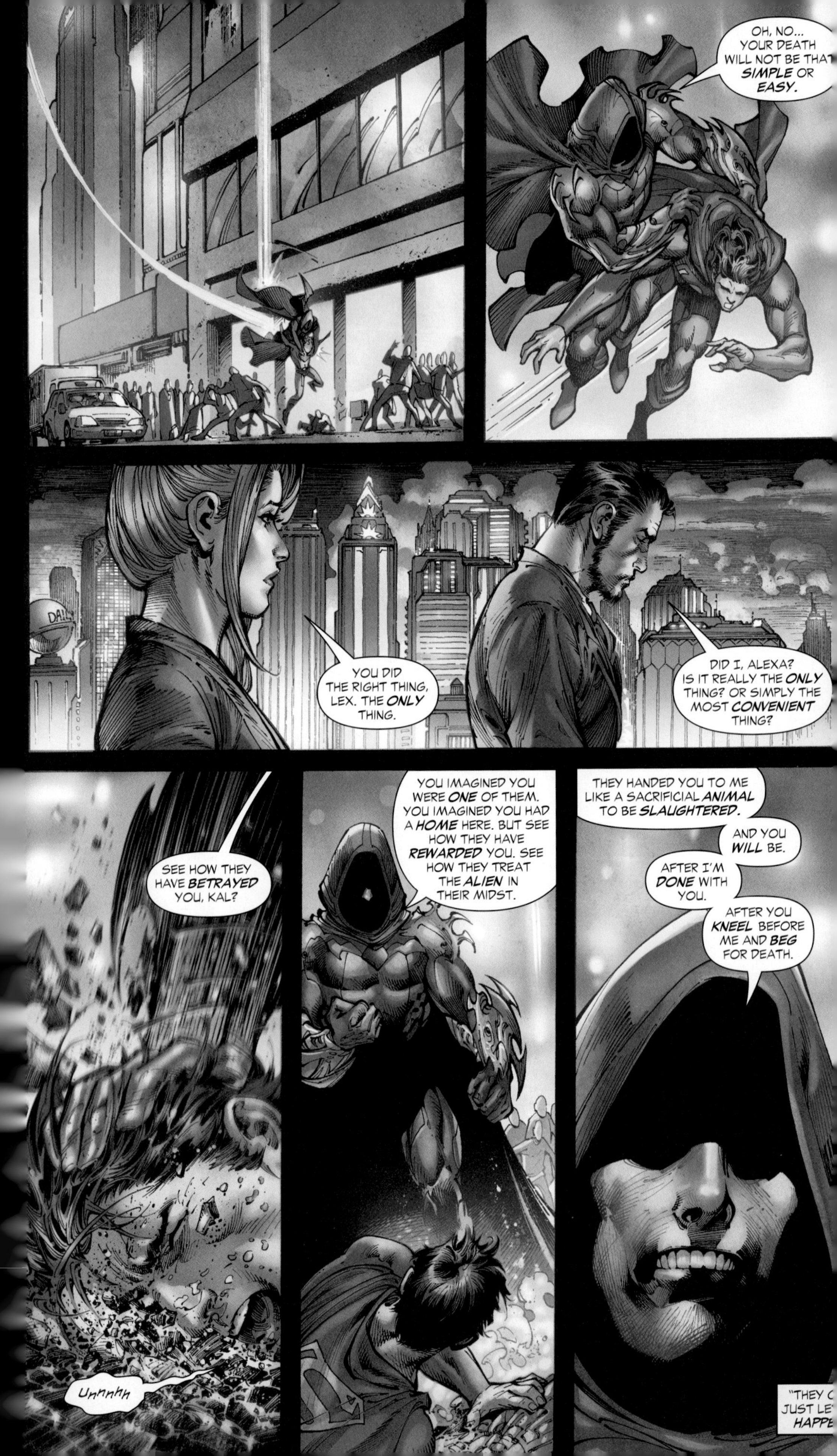
OH, NO... YOUR DEATH WILL NOT BE THAT SIMPLE OR EASY.
YOU DID THE RIGHT THING, LEX. THE ONLY THING.
DID I, ALEXA? IS IT REALLY THE ONLY THING? OR SIMPLY THE MOST CONVENIENT THING?
SEE HOW THEY HAVE BETRAYED YOU, KAL?
Unnnhh
YOU IMAGINED YOU WERE ONE OF THEM. YOU IMAGINED YOU HAD A HOME HERE. BUT SEE HOW THEY HAVE REWARDED YOU. SEE HOW THEY TREAT THE ALIEN IN THEIR MIDST.
THEY HANDED YOU TO ME LIKE A SACRIFICIAL ANIMAL TO BE SLAUGHTERED.
AND YOU WILL BE.
AFTER I'M DONE WITH YOU.
AFTER YOU KNEEL BEFORE ME AND BEG FOR DEATH.

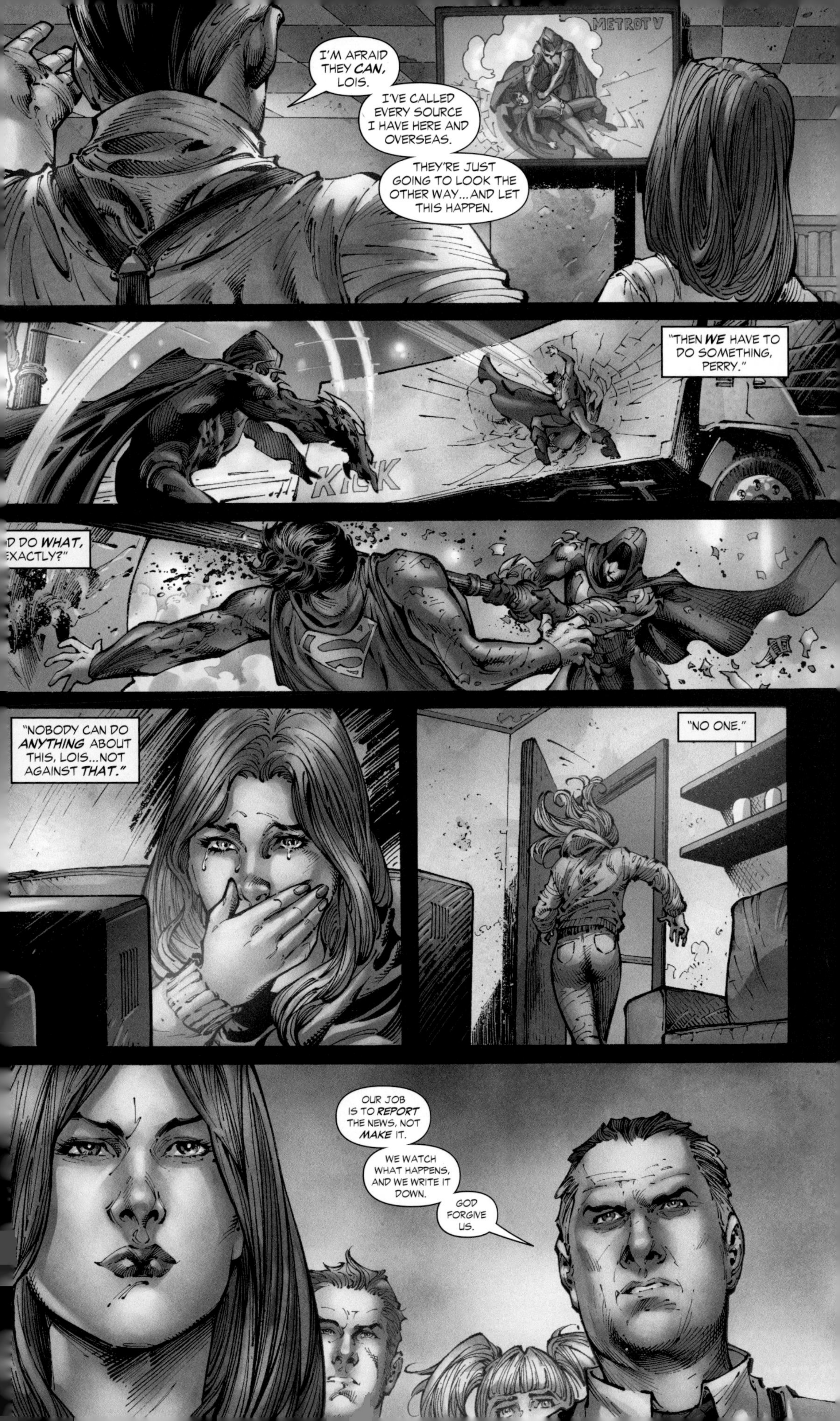
METROTV
I'M AFRAID THEY *CAN,* LOIS.
I'VE CALLED EVERY SOURCE I HAVE HERE AND OVERSEAS.
THEY'RE JUST GOING TO LOOK THE OTHER WAY...AND LET THIS HAPPEN.
"THEN *WE* HAVE TO DO SOMETHING, PERRY."
KLLK
D DO *WHAT,* EXACTLY?"
"NOBODY CAN DO *ANYTHING* ABOUT THIS, LOIS...NOT AGAINST *THAT.*"
"NO ONE."
OUR JOB IS TO *REPORT* THE NEWS, NOT *MAKE* IT.
WE WATCH WHAT HAPPENS, AND WE WRITE IT DOWN.
GOD FORGIVE US.

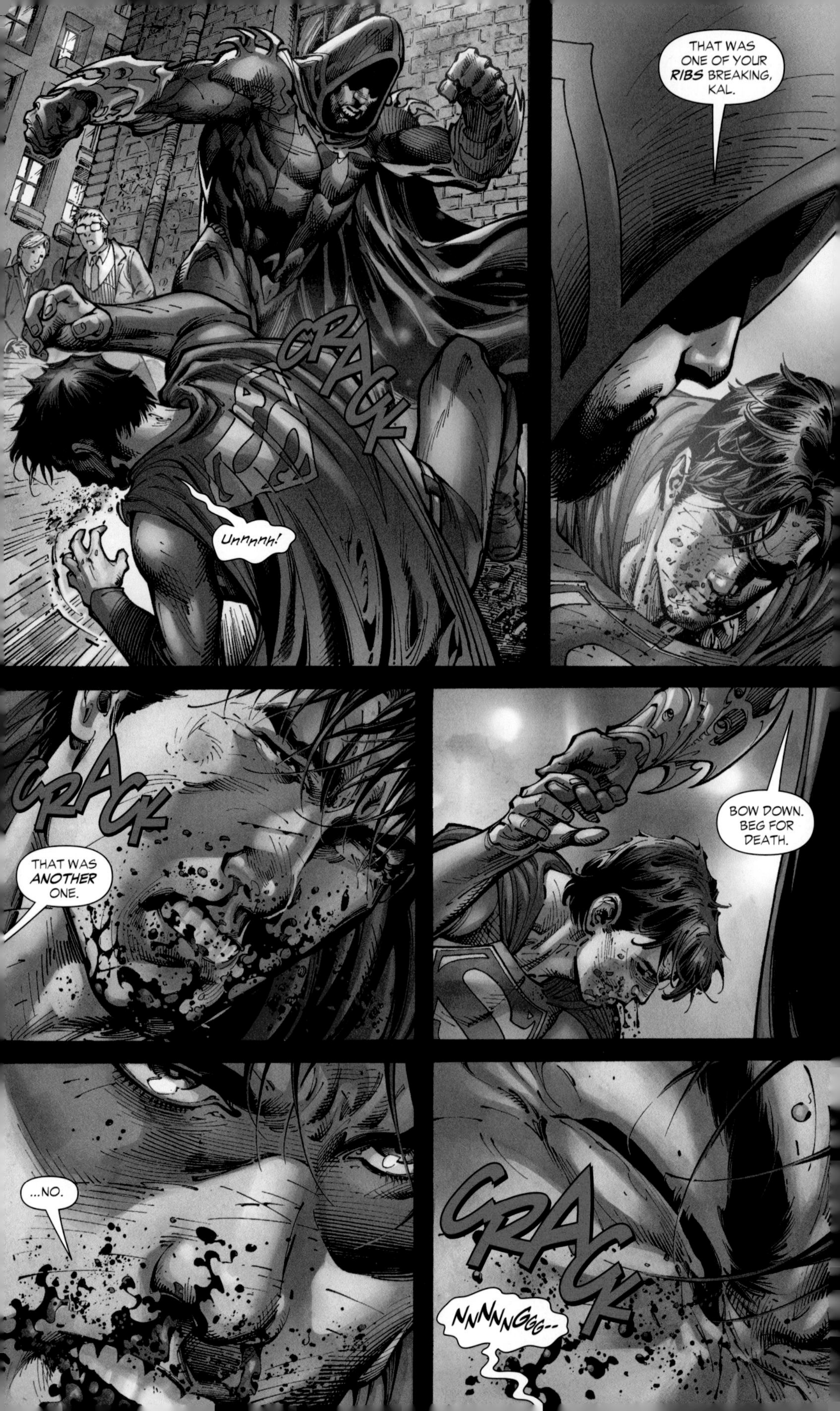

CRACK
Unnnnh!
THAT WAS ONE OF YOUR RIBS BREAKING, KAL.
CRACK
THAT WAS ANOTHER ONE.
BOW DOWN. BEG FOR DEATH.
...NO.
CRACK
NNNNNGGG--

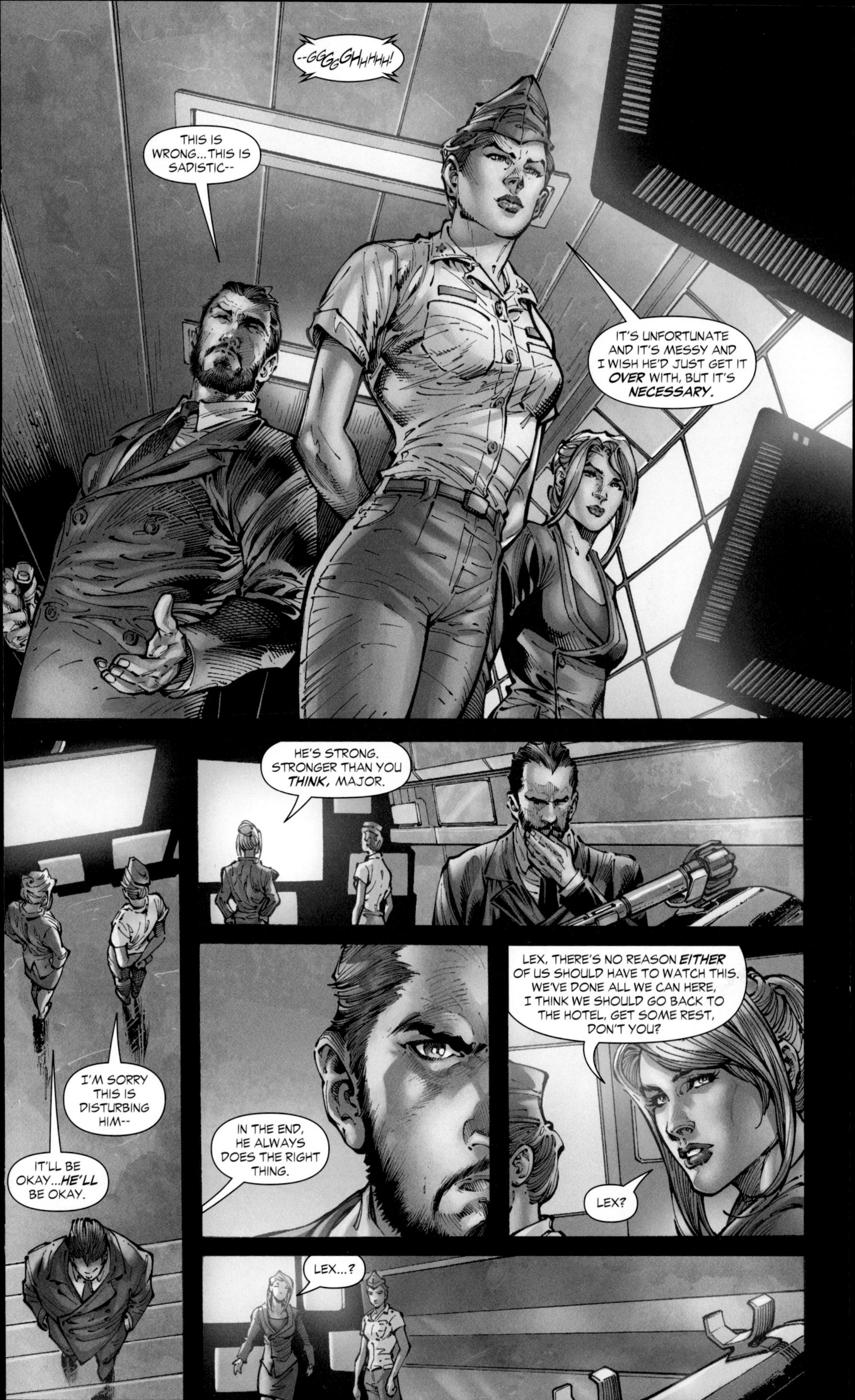
--GGGGGHHHHH!
THIS IS WRONG...THIS IS SADISTIC--
IT'S UNFORTUNATE AND IT'S MESSY AND I WISH HE'D JUST GET IT OVER WITH, BUT IT'S NECESSARY.
HE'S STRONG. STRONGER THAN YOU THINK, MAJOR.
I'M SORRY THIS IS DISTURBING HIM--
IT'LL BE OKAY...HE'LL BE OKAY.
IN THE END, HE ALWAYS DOES THE RIGHT THING.
LEX, THERE'S NO REASON EITHER OF US SHOULD HAVE TO WATCH THIS. WE'VE DONE ALL WE CAN HERE, I THINK WE SHOULD GO BACK TO THE HOTEL, GET SOME REST, DON'T YOU?
LEX?
LEX...?

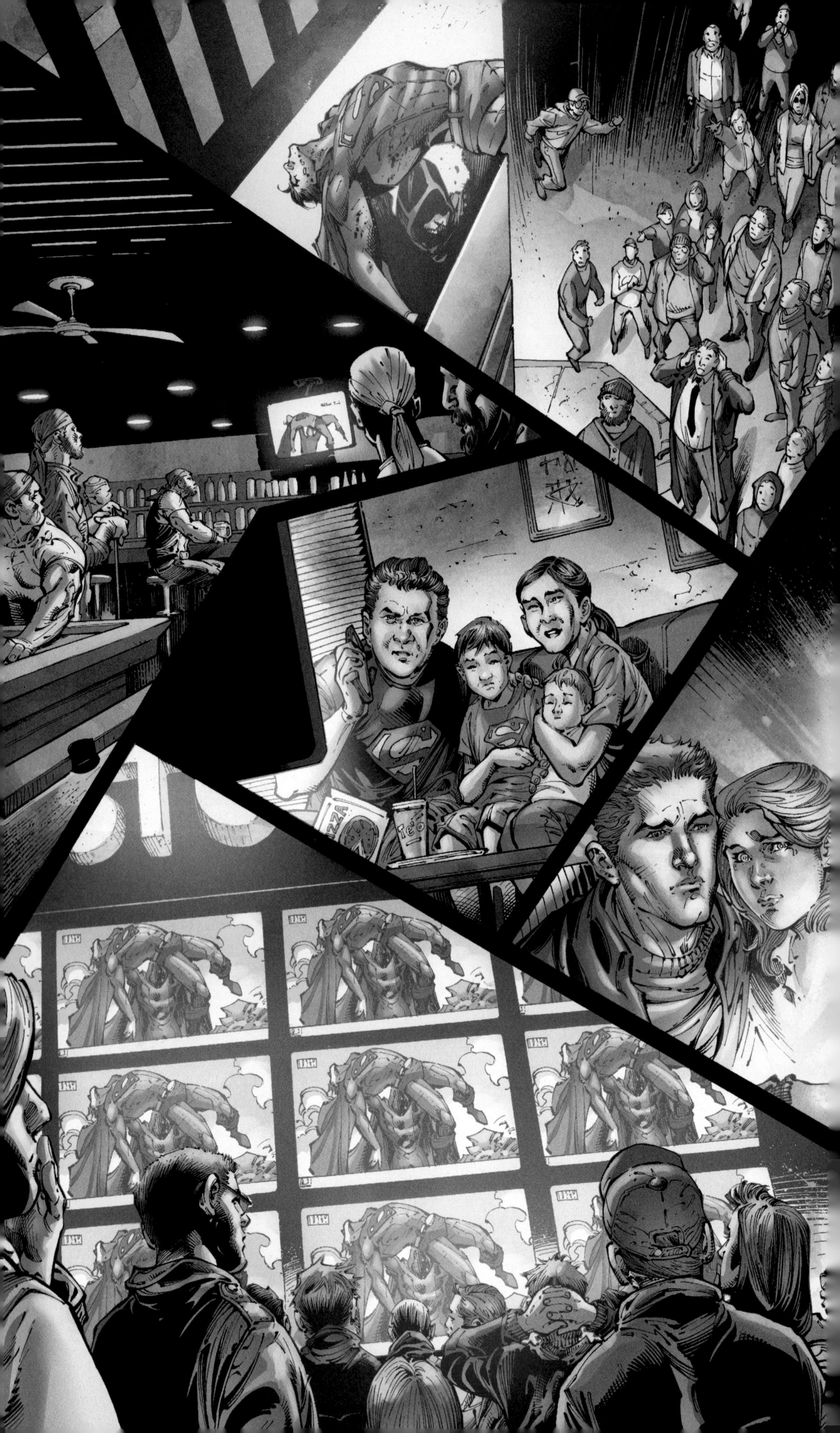

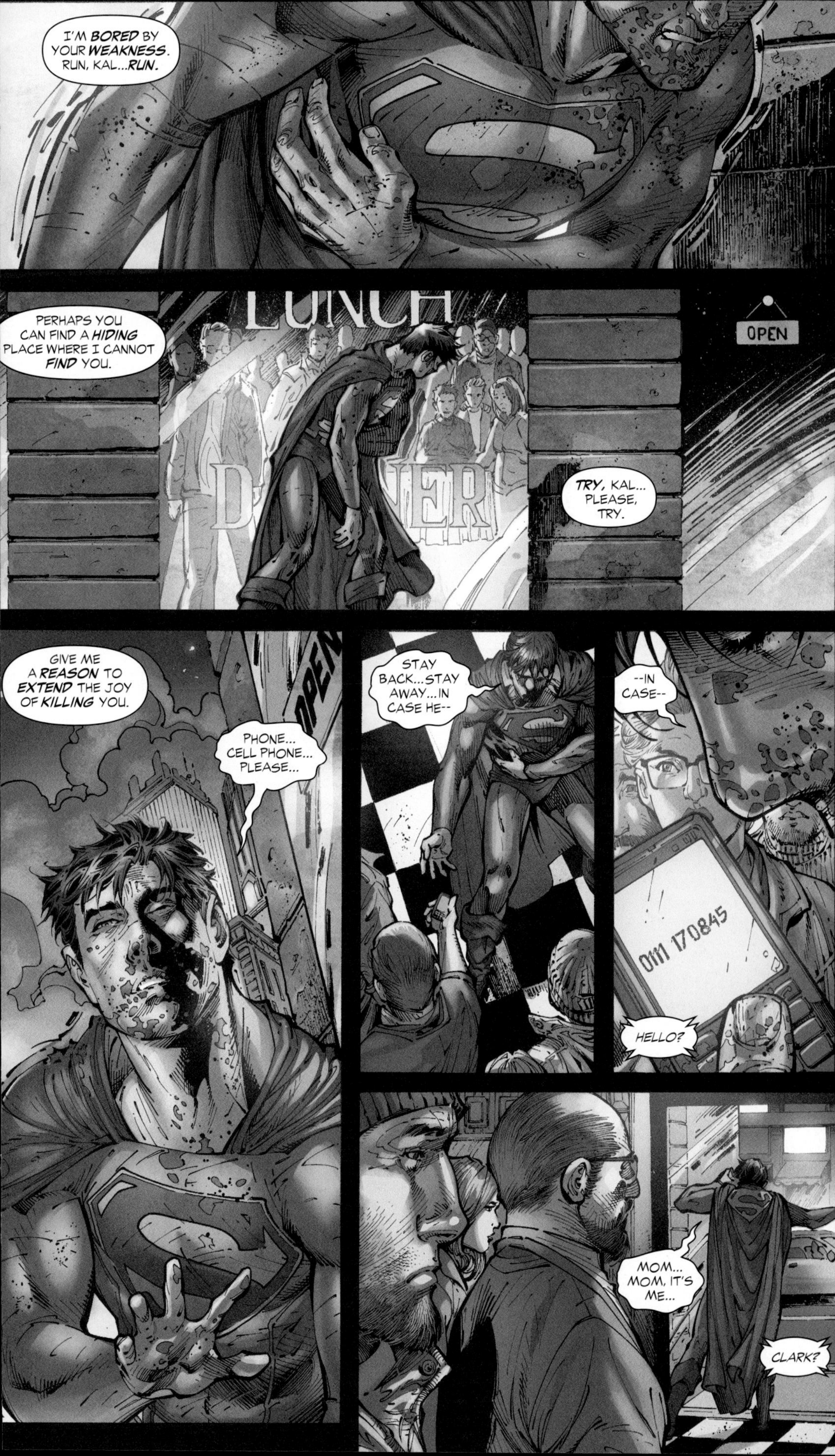
I'M BORED BY YOUR WEAKNESS. RUN, KAL...RUN.
LUNCH
PERHAPS YOU CAN FIND A HIDING PLACE WHERE I CANNOT FIND YOU.
OPEN
TRY, KAL... PLEASE, TRY.
GIVE ME A REASON TO EXTEND THE JOY OF KILLING YOU.
PHONE... CELL PHONE... PLEASE...
STAY BACK...STAY AWAY...IN CASE HE--
--IN CASE--
011 170845
HELLO?
MOM... MOM, IT'S ME...
CLARK?

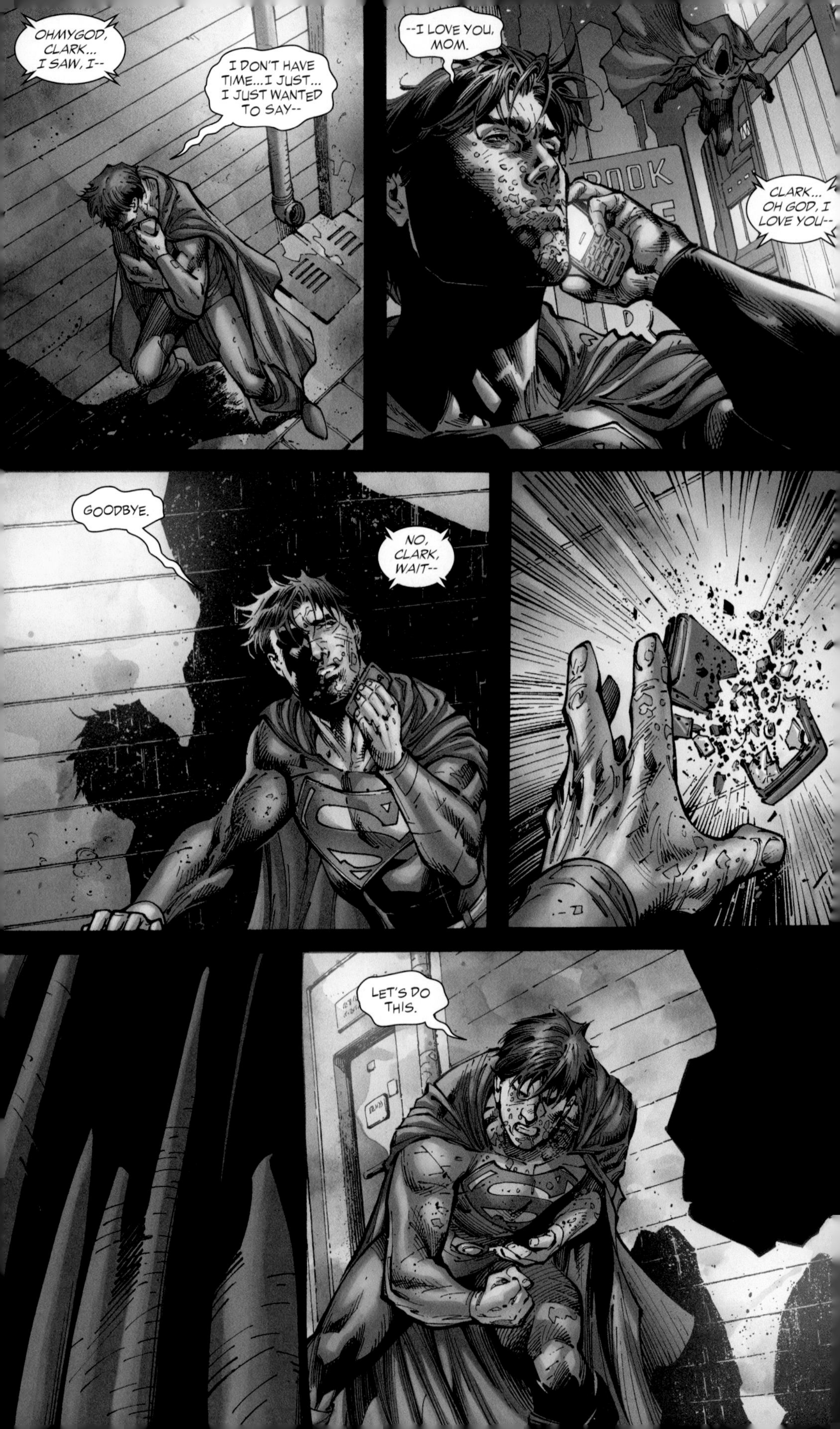
OHMYGOD, CLARK... I SAW, I--
I DON'T HAVE TIME...I JUST... I JUST WANTED TO SAY--
--I LOVE YOU, MOM.
CLARK... OH GOD, I LOVE YOU--
GOODBYE.
NO, CLARK, WAIT--
LET'S DO THIS.

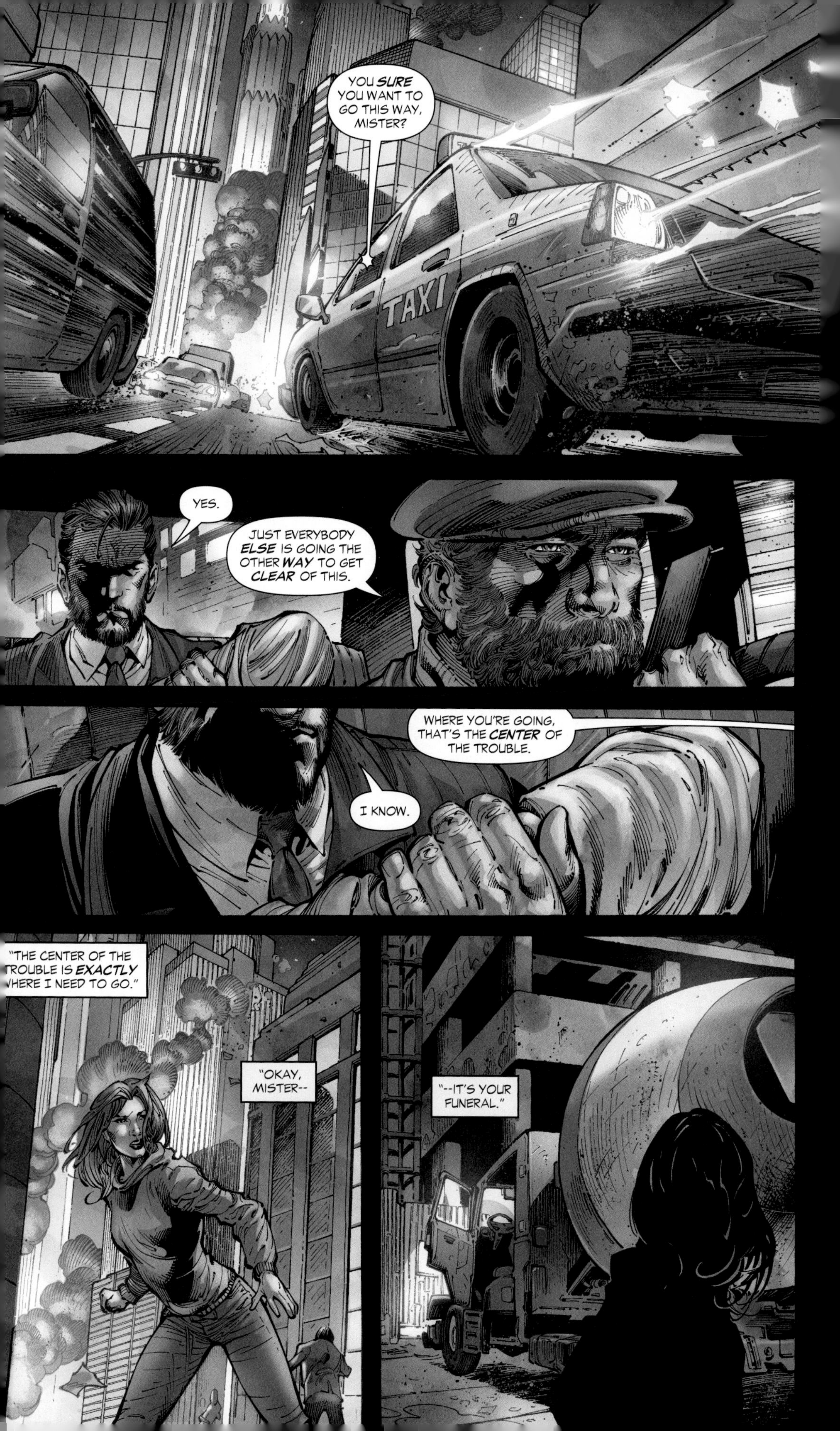
YOU SURE YOU WANT TO GO THIS WAY, MISTER?
TAXI
YES.
JUST EVERYBODY ELSE IS GOING THE OTHER WAY TO GET CLEAR OF THIS.
WHERE YOU'RE GOING, THAT'S THE CENTER OF THE TROUBLE.
I KNOW.
"THE CENTER OF THE TROUBLE IS EXACTLY WHERE I NEED TO GO."
"OKAY, MISTER--
"--IT'S YOUR FUNERAL."

BANK

YOU REALIZE, OF COURSE, THAT THE ONLY REASON I HAVEN'T *PULVERIZED* YOUR LEG IS SO THAT YOU WILL HAVE SOMETHING TO *KNEEL* ON.

UnnnNHhh

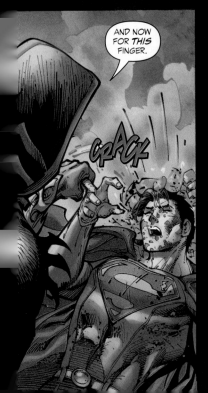

AND NOW FOR *THIS* FINGER.

CRACK

INTERESTING... TOOK THE BAREST FLICKER OF ADDITIONAL *STRENGTH* TO BREAK *THAT* ONE. LOOKS LIKE THE EFFECT WAS ONLY *TEMPORARY.*

SO AS MUCH AS I'VE *ENJOYED* THIS, IT LOOKS LIKE I'LL HAVE TO *FINISH* THIS BEFORE YOUR *POWERS* COME BACK.

THIS IS YOUR LAST... YOUR *VERY LAST* CHANCE, KAL.

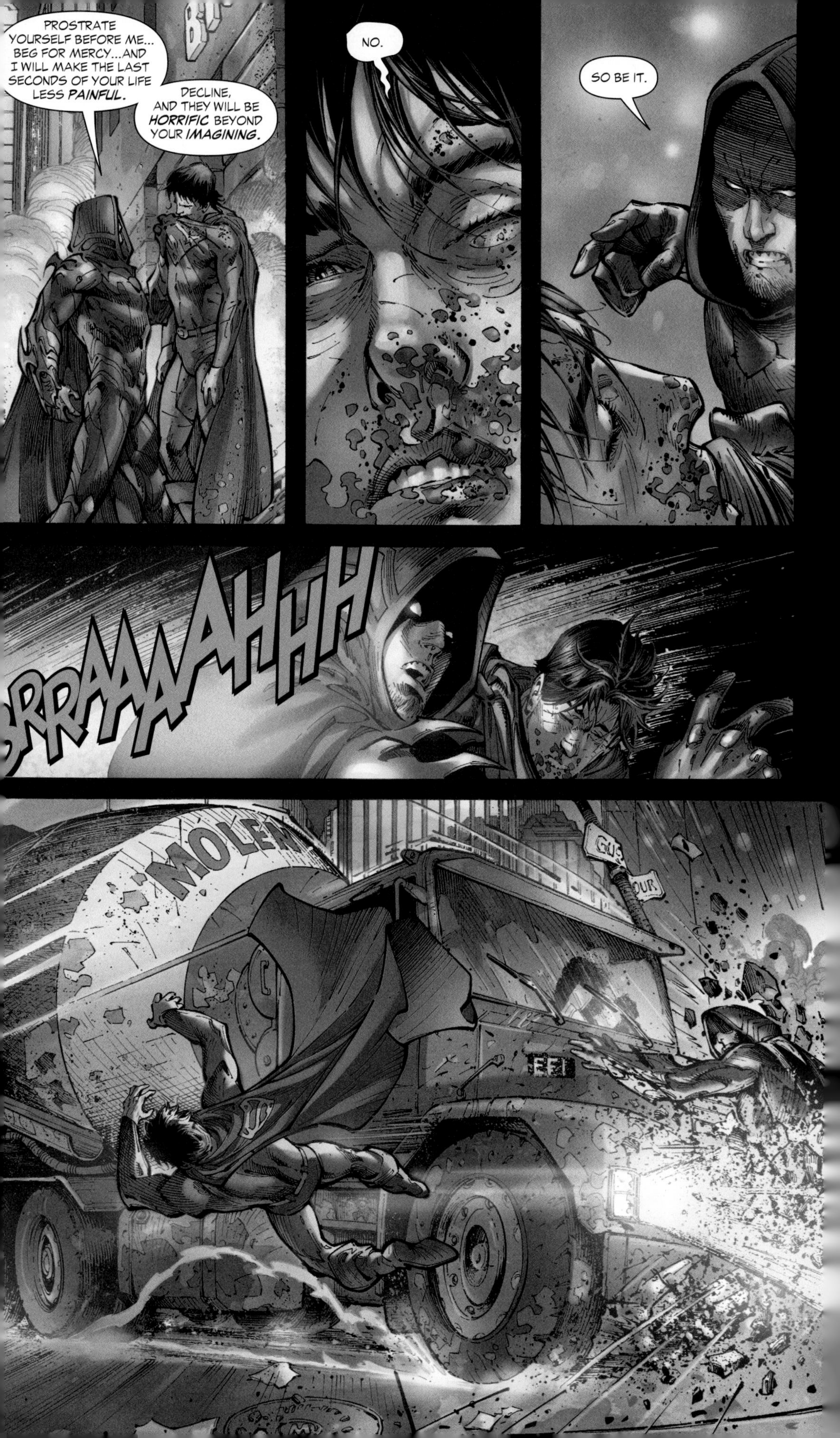
PROSTRATE YOURSELF BEFORE ME... BEG FOR MERCY...AND I WILL MAKE THE LAST SECONDS OF YOUR LIFE LESS PAINFUL.
DECLINE, AND THEY WILL BE HORRIFIC BEYOND YOUR IMAGINING.
NO.
SO BE IT.
RRAAAAHHH
MOLE

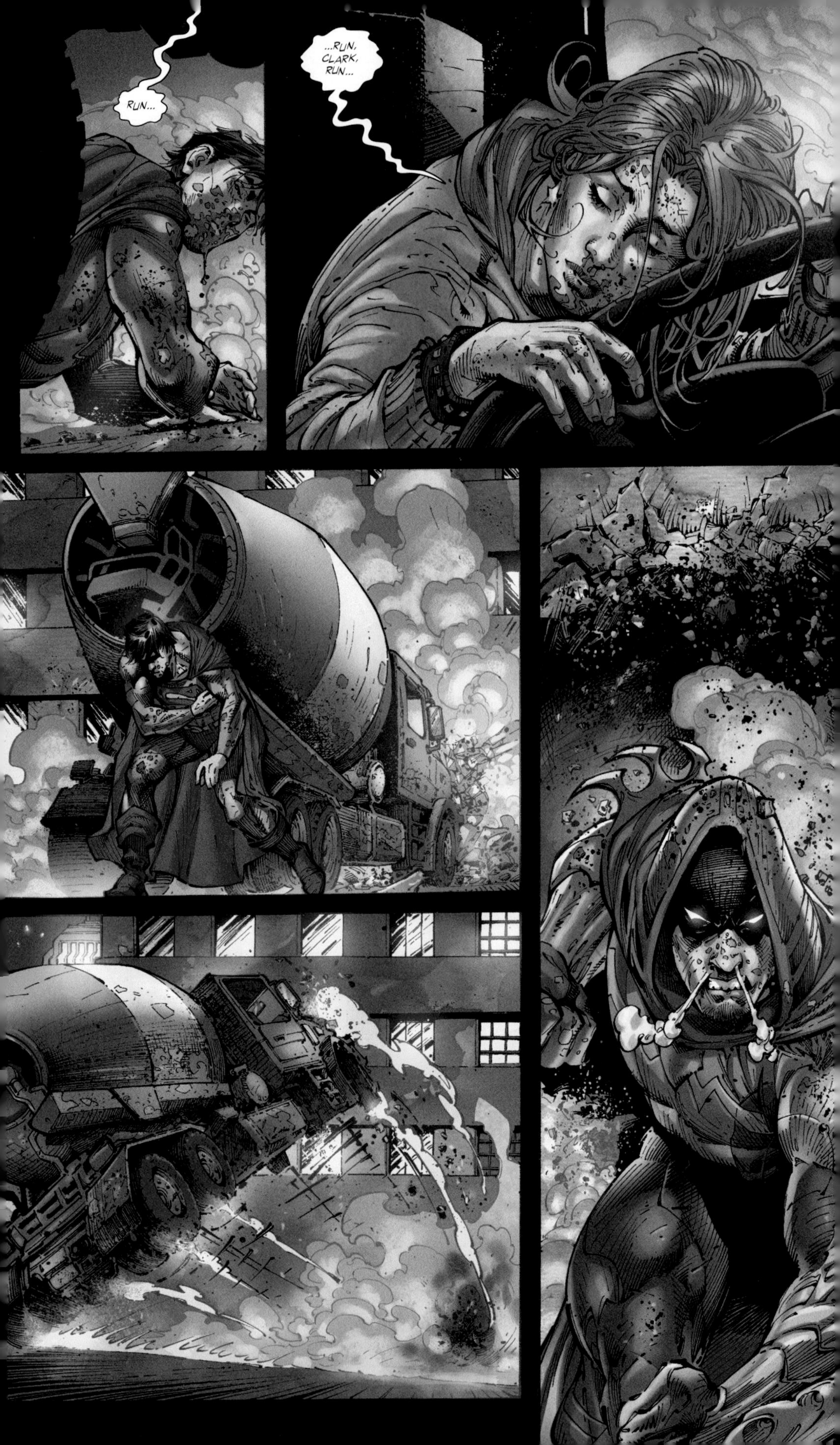
RUN...
...RUN, CLARK, RUN...

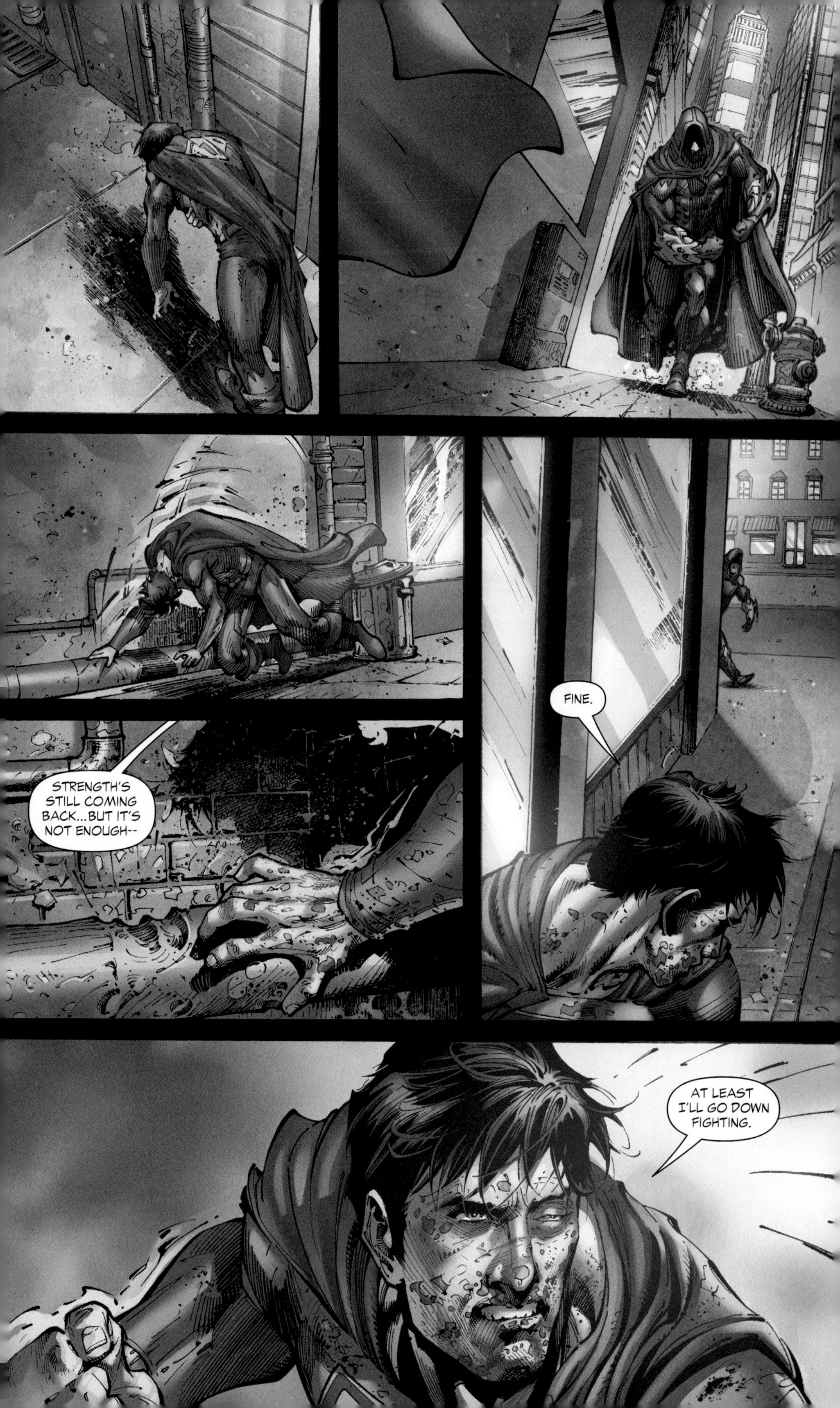
STRENGTH'S STILL COMING BACK...BUT IT'S NOT ENOUGH--
FINE.
AT LEAST I'LL GO DOWN FIGHTING.

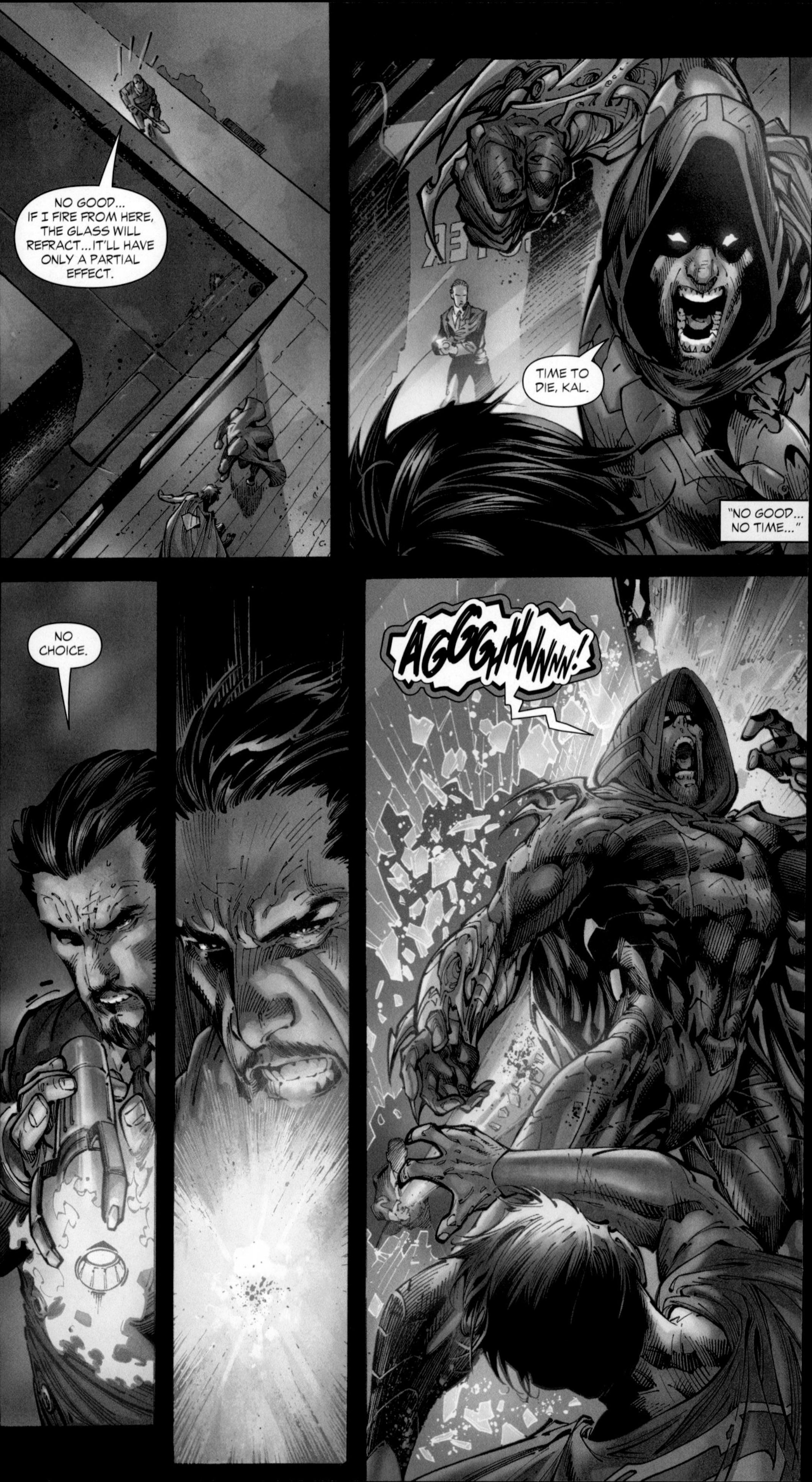
NO GOOD... IF I FIRE FROM HERE, THE GLASS WILL REFRACT...IT'LL HAVE ONLY A PARTIAL EFFECT.
TIME TO DIE, KAL.
"NO GOOD... NO TIME..."
NO CHOICE.
AGGGHNNNN!

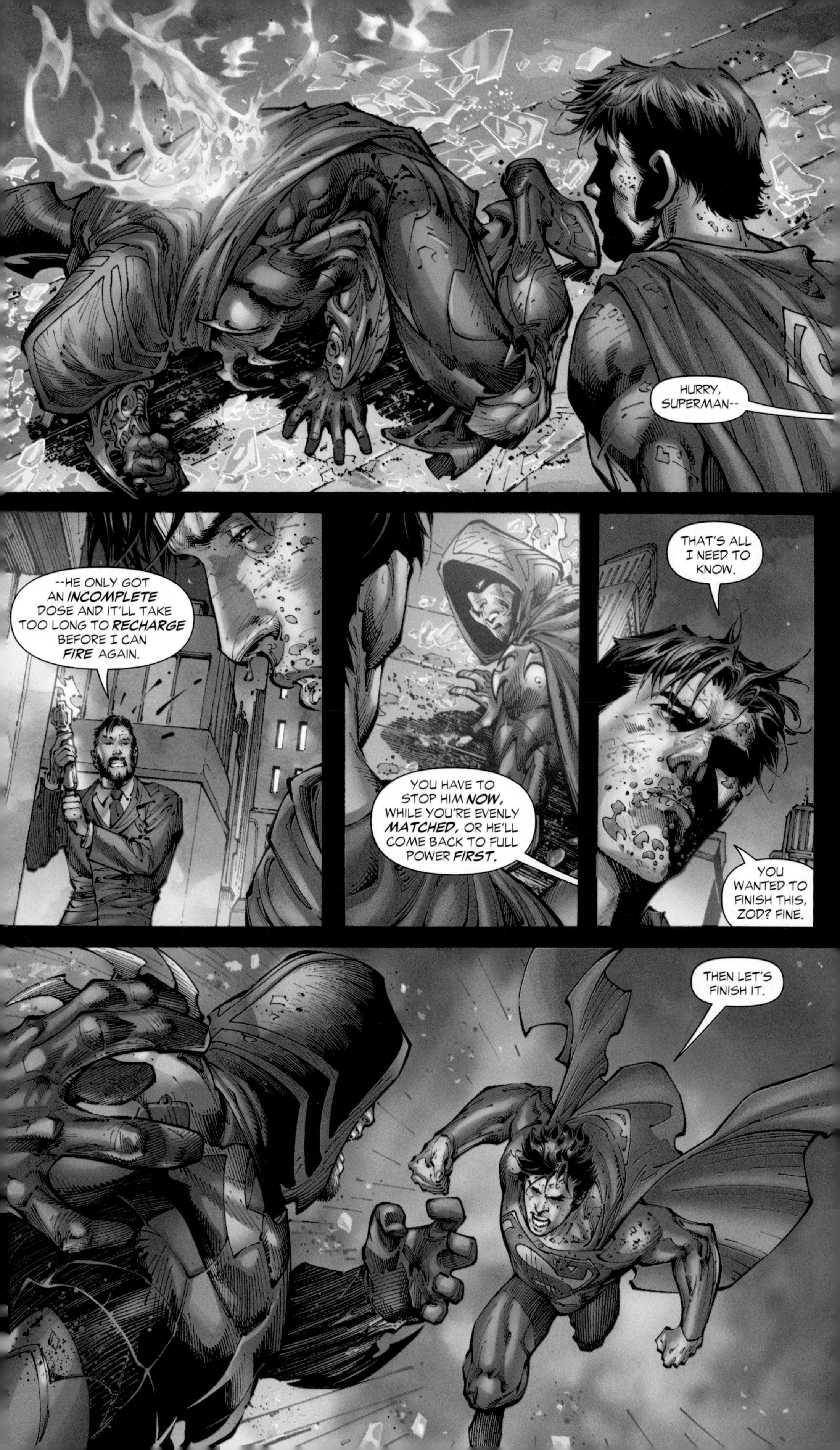
HURRY, SUPERMAN--
--HE ONLY GOT AN *INCOMPLETE* DOSE AND IT'LL TAKE TOO LONG TO *RECHARGE* BEFORE I CAN *FIRE* AGAIN.
YOU HAVE TO STOP HIM *NOW,* WHILE YOU'RE EVENLY *MATCHED,* OR HE'LL COME BACK TO FULL POWER *FIRST.*
THAT'S ALL I NEED TO KNOW.
YOU WANTED TO FINISH THIS, ZOD? FINE.
THEN LET'S FINISH IT.

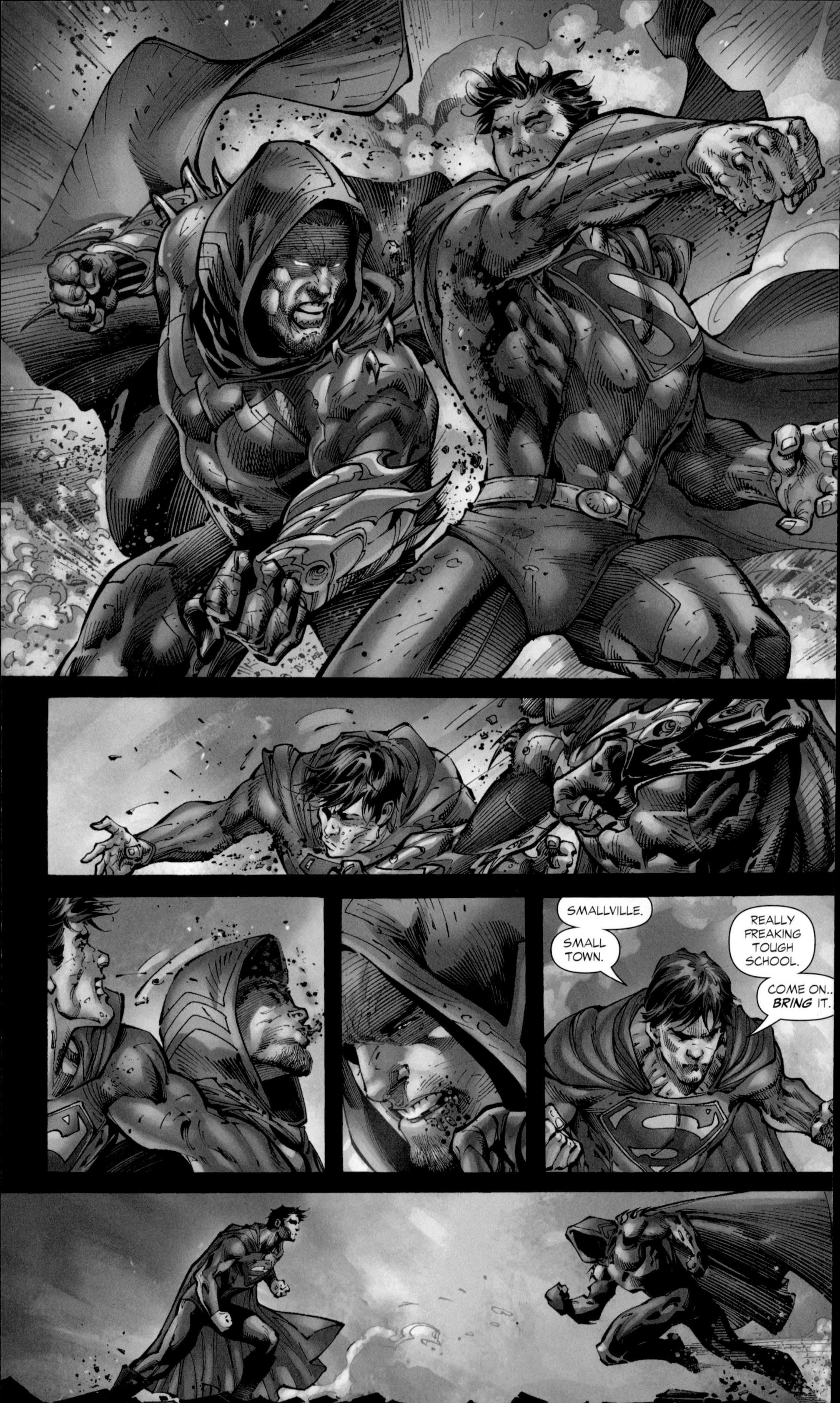
SMALLVILLE.
SMALL TOWN.
REALLY FREAKING TOUGH SCHOOL.
COME ON.. BRING IT.

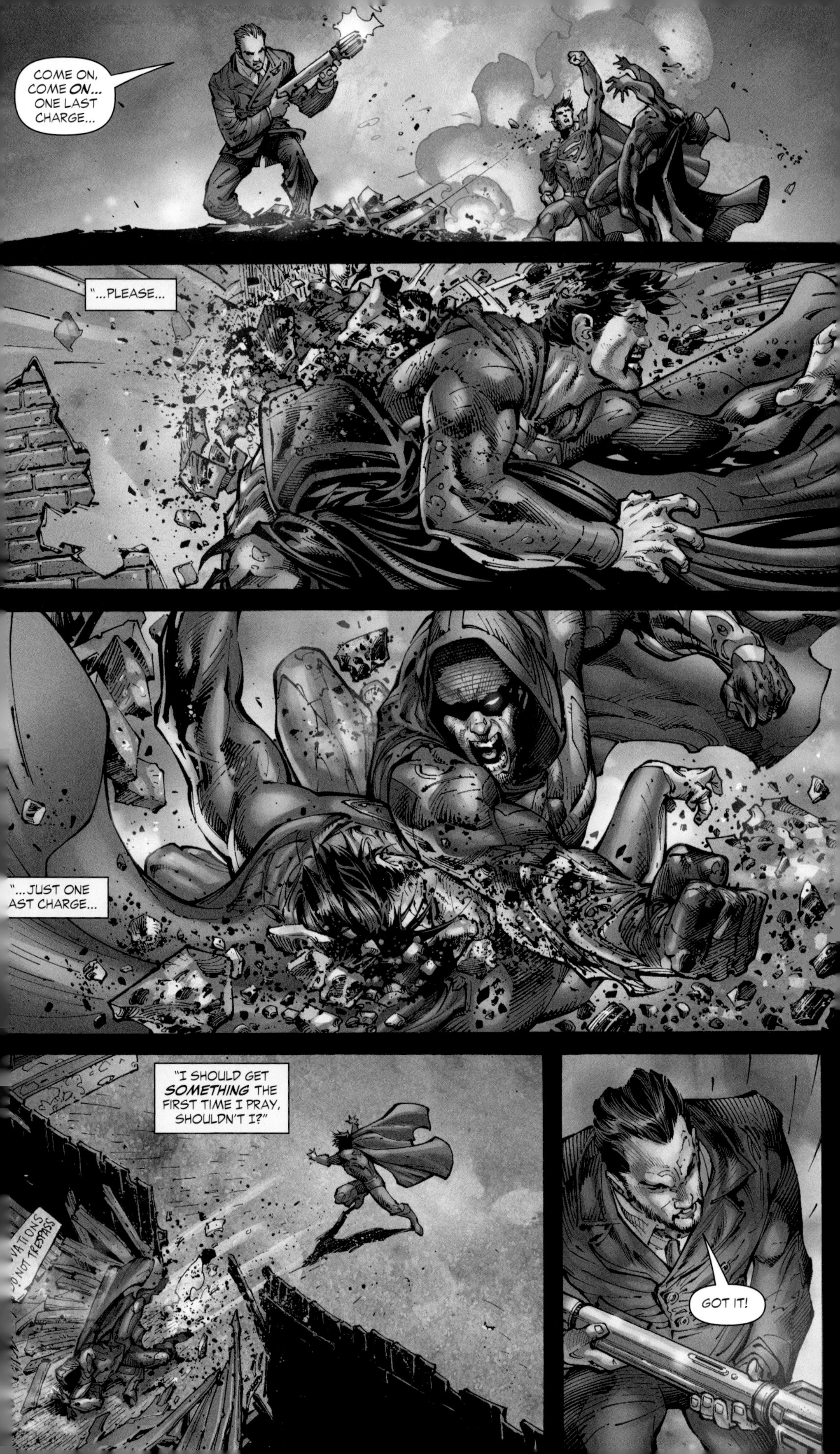
COME ON, COME ON... ONE LAST CHARGE...
"...PLEASE...
"...JUST ONE LAST CHARGE...
"I SHOULD GET SOMETHING THE FIRST TIME I PRAY, SHOULDN'T I?"
DO NOT TRESPASS
GOT IT!

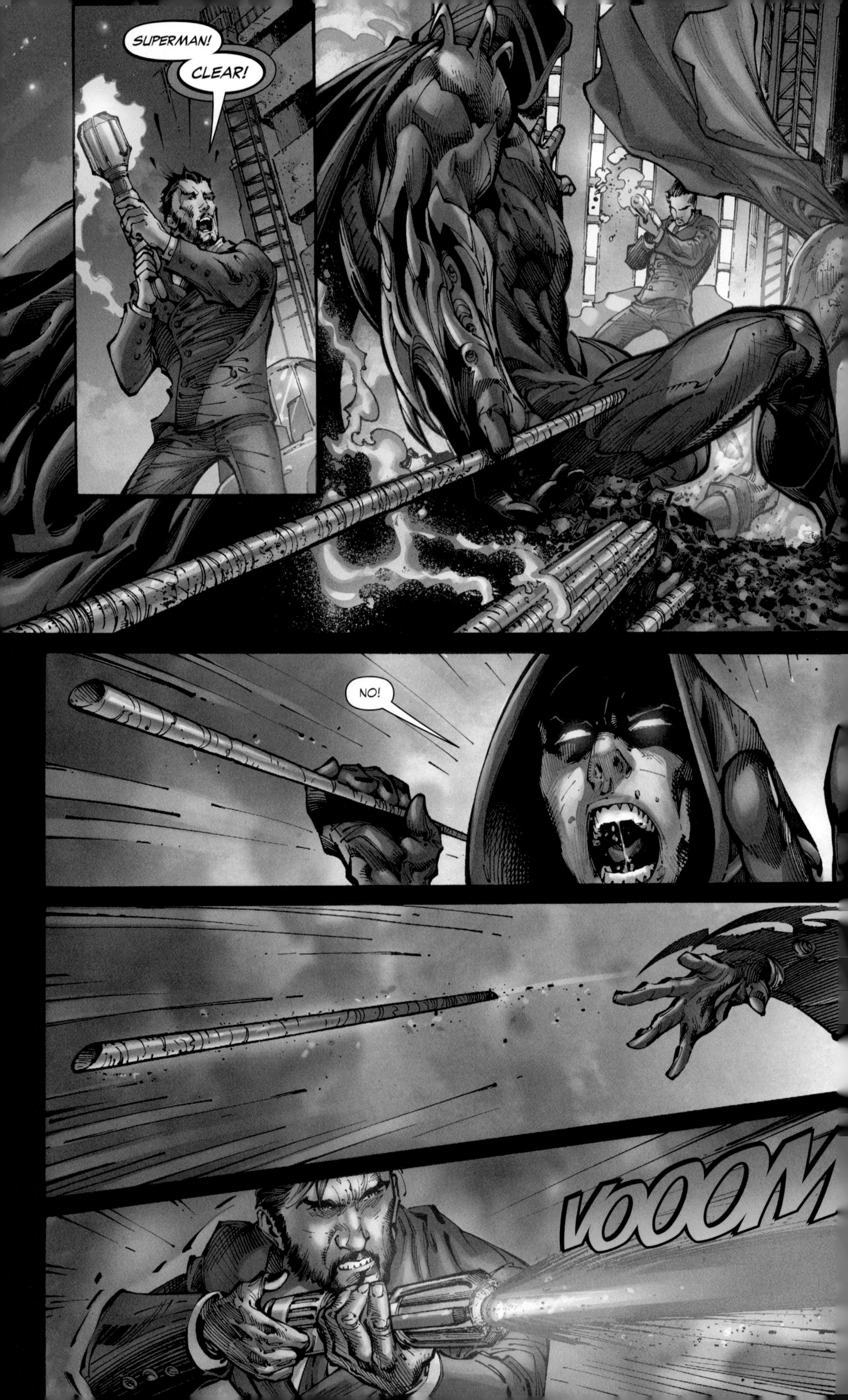
SUPERMAN!
CLEAR!
NO!
VOOOM

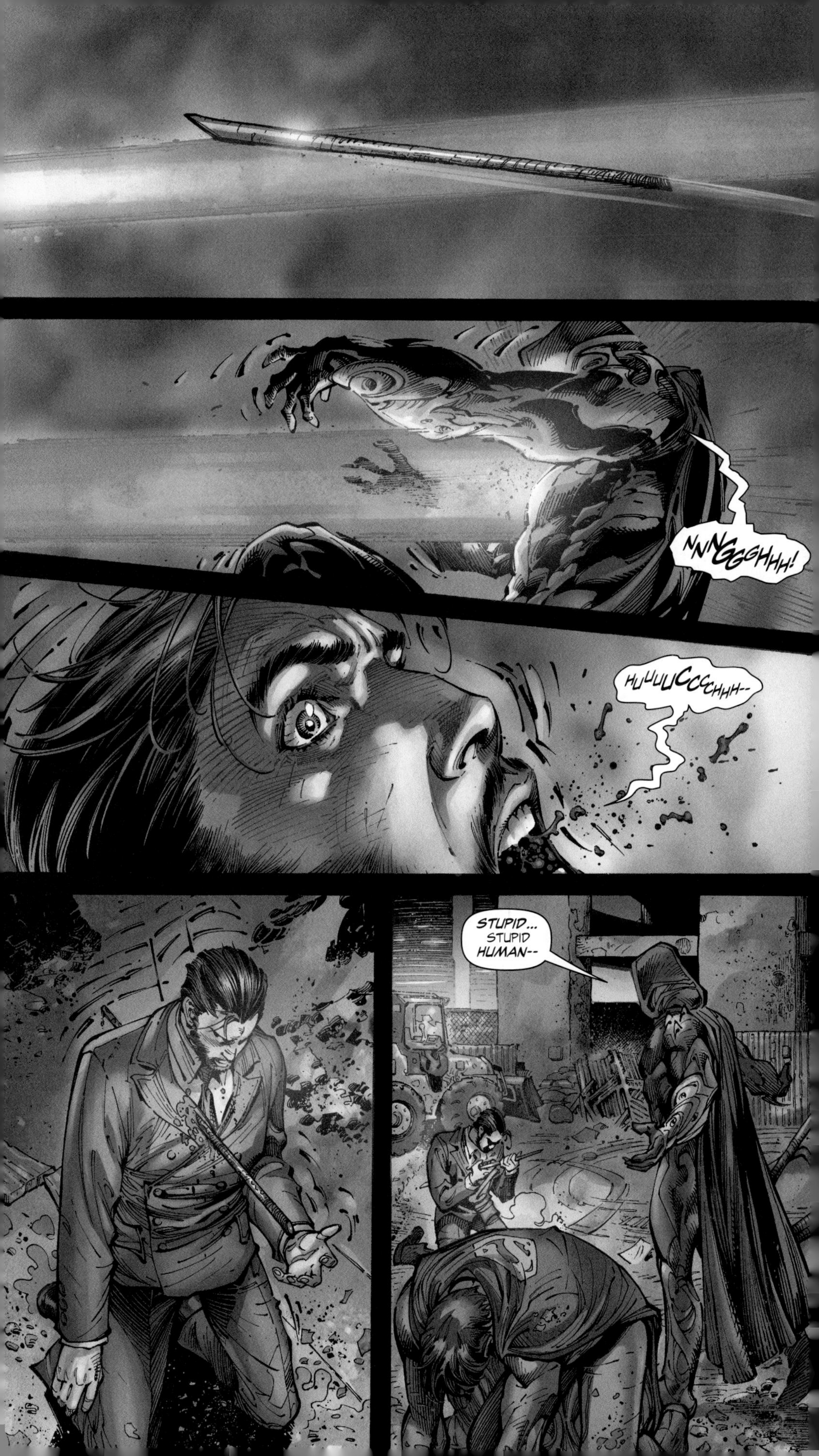
NNNGGGHHH!
HUUUUCCCCHHH--
STUPID... STUPID HUMAN--

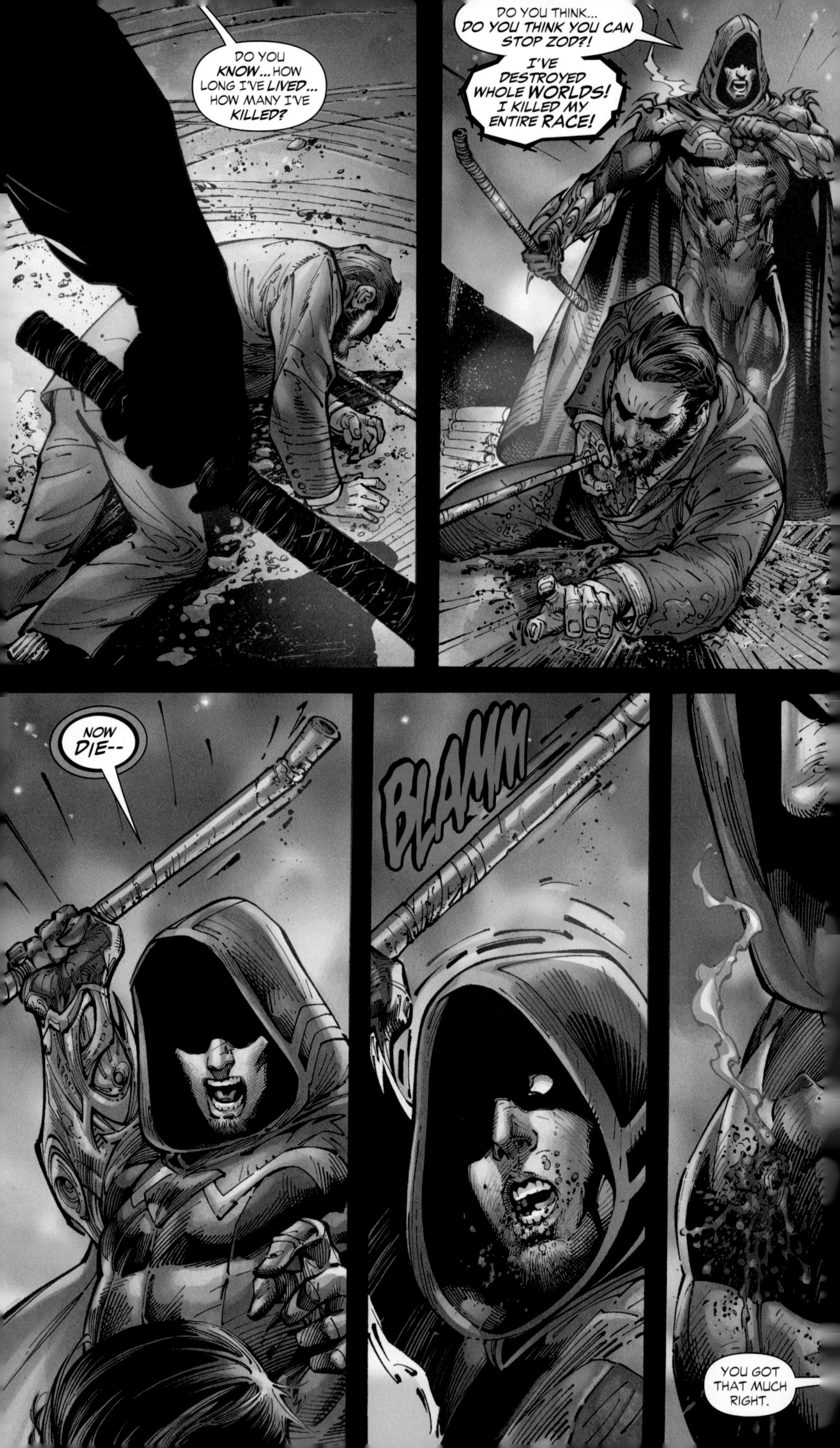
DO YOU KNOW... HOW LONG I'VE LIVED... HOW MANY I'VE KILLED?
DO YOU THINK... DO YOU THINK YOU CAN STOP ZOD?!
I'VE DESTROYED WHOLE WORLDS! I KILLED MY ENTIRE RACE!
NOW DIE--
BLAMM
YOU GOT THAT MUCH RIGHT.

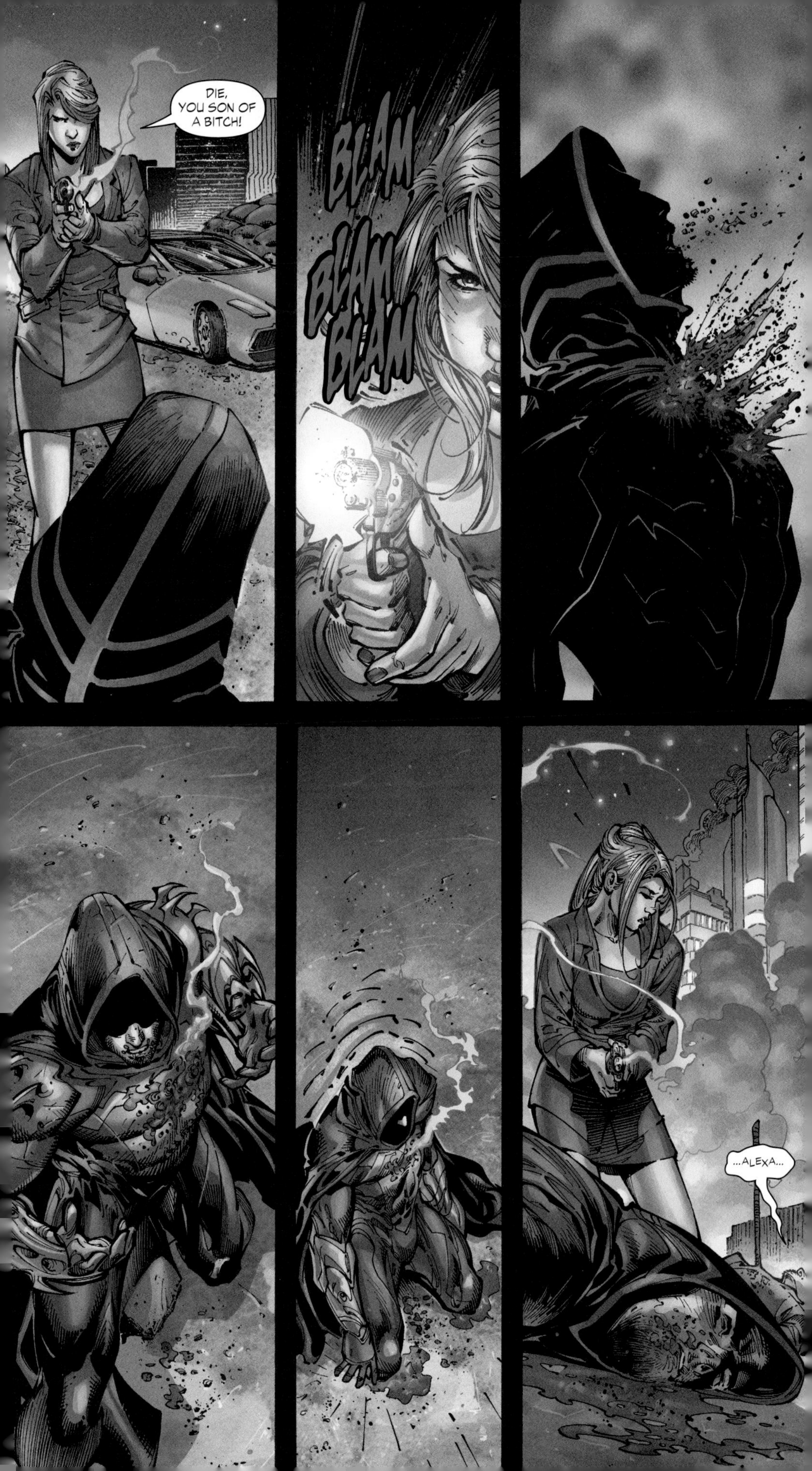
DIE, YOU SON OF A BITCH!
BLAM
BLAM
BLAM
...ALEXA...

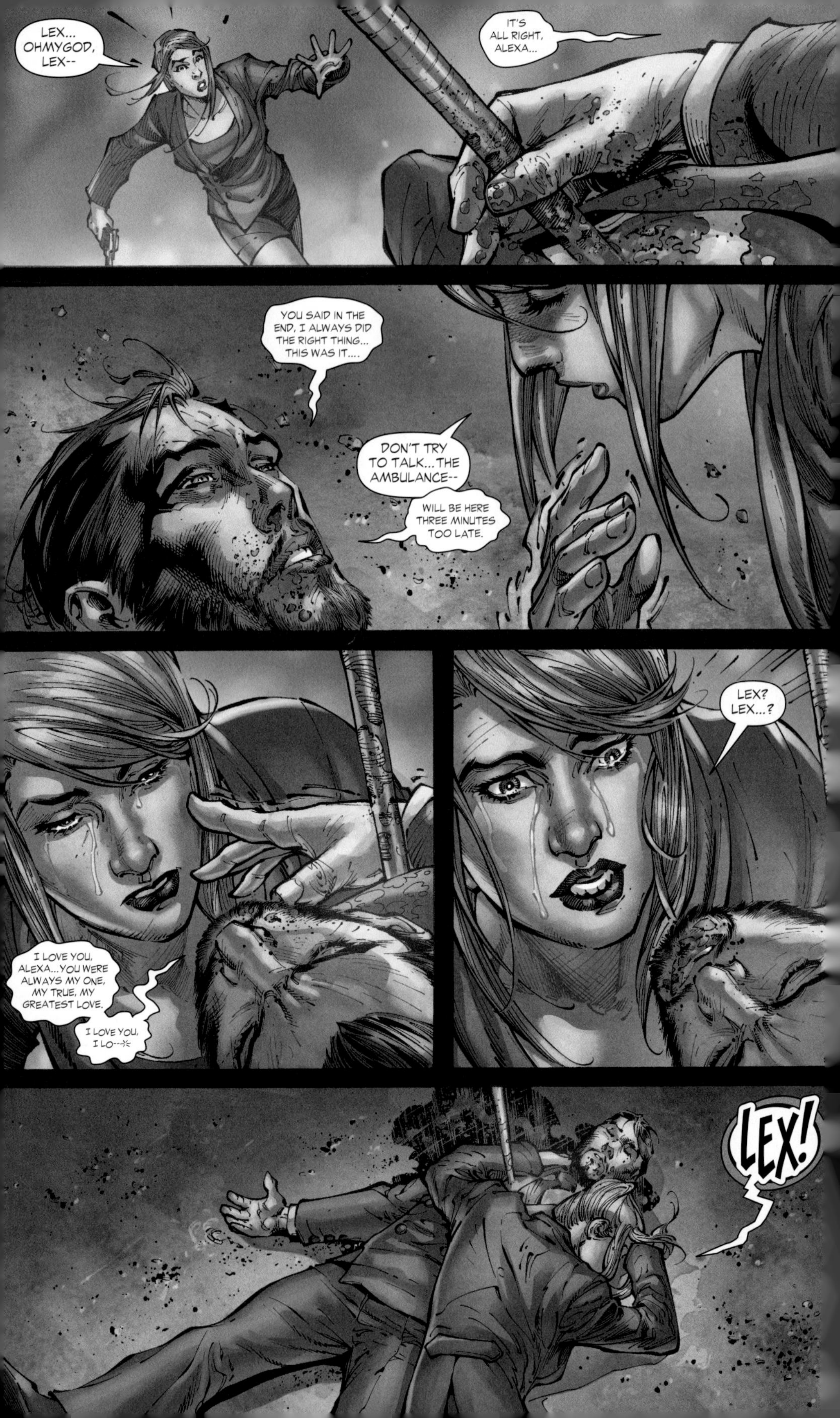
LEX... OHMYGOD, LEX--
IT'S ALL RIGHT, ALEXA...
YOU SAID IN THE END, I ALWAYS DID THE RIGHT THING... THIS WAS IT....
DON'T TRY TO TALK...THE AMBULANCE--
WILL BE HERE THREE MINUTES TOO LATE.
I LOVE YOU, ALEXA...YOU WERE ALWAYS MY ONE, MY TRUE, MY GREATEST LOVE.
I LOVE YOU, I LO--
LEX? LEX...?
LEX!

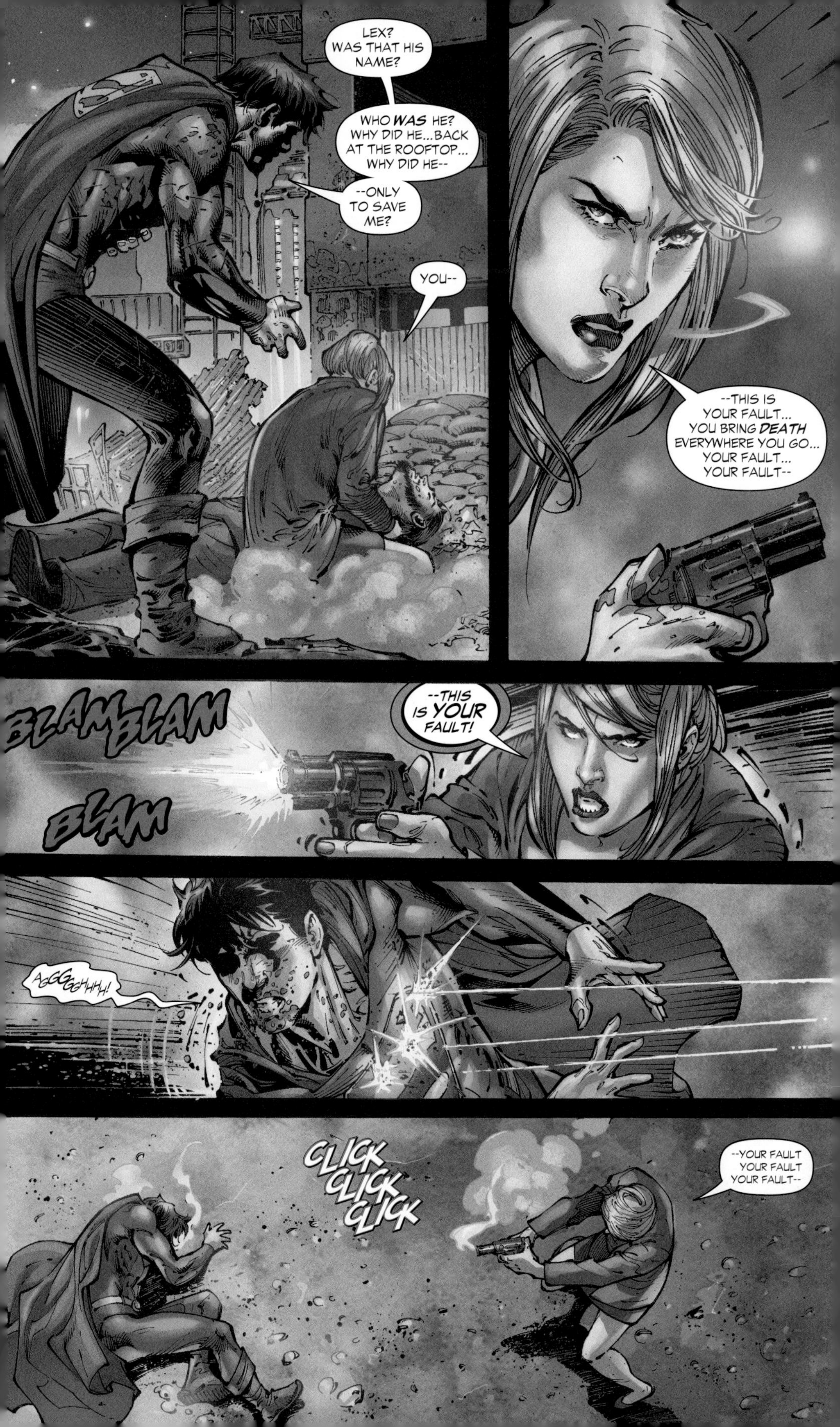
LEX? WAS THAT HIS NAME?
WHO WAS HE? WHY DID HE...BACK AT THE ROOFTOP... WHY DID HE--
--ONLY TO SAVE ME?
YOU--
--THIS IS YOUR FAULT... YOU BRING DEATH EVERYWHERE YOU GO... YOUR FAULT... YOUR FAULT--
BLAM BLAM
BLAM
--THIS IS YOUR FAULT!
AGGGGHHHH!
CLICK CLICK CLICK
--YOUR FAULT YOUR FAULT YOUR FAULT--

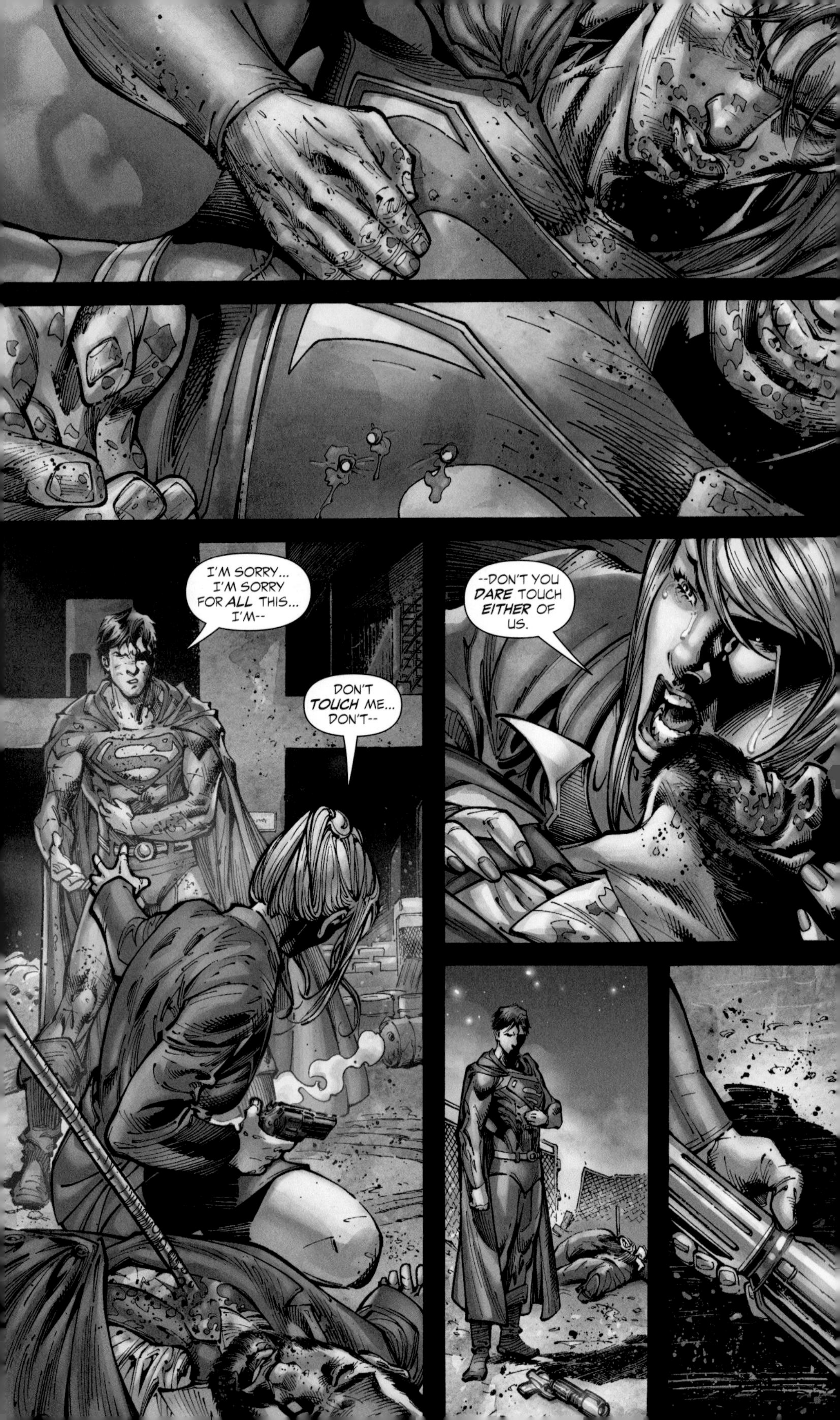
I'M SORRY... I'M SORRY FOR ALL THIS... I'M--
DON'T TOUCH ME... DON'T--
--DON'T YOU DARE TOUCH EITHER OF US.

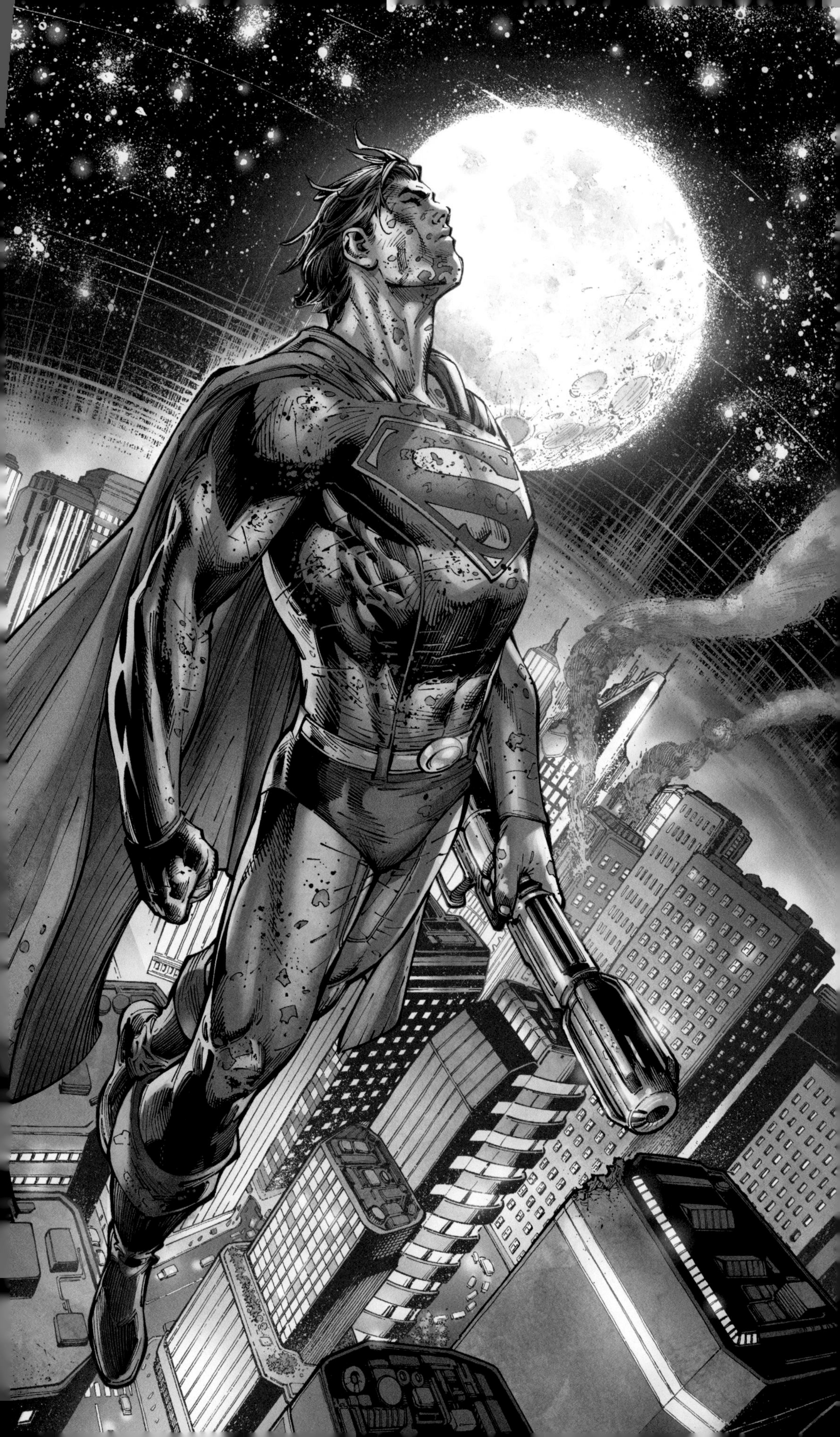

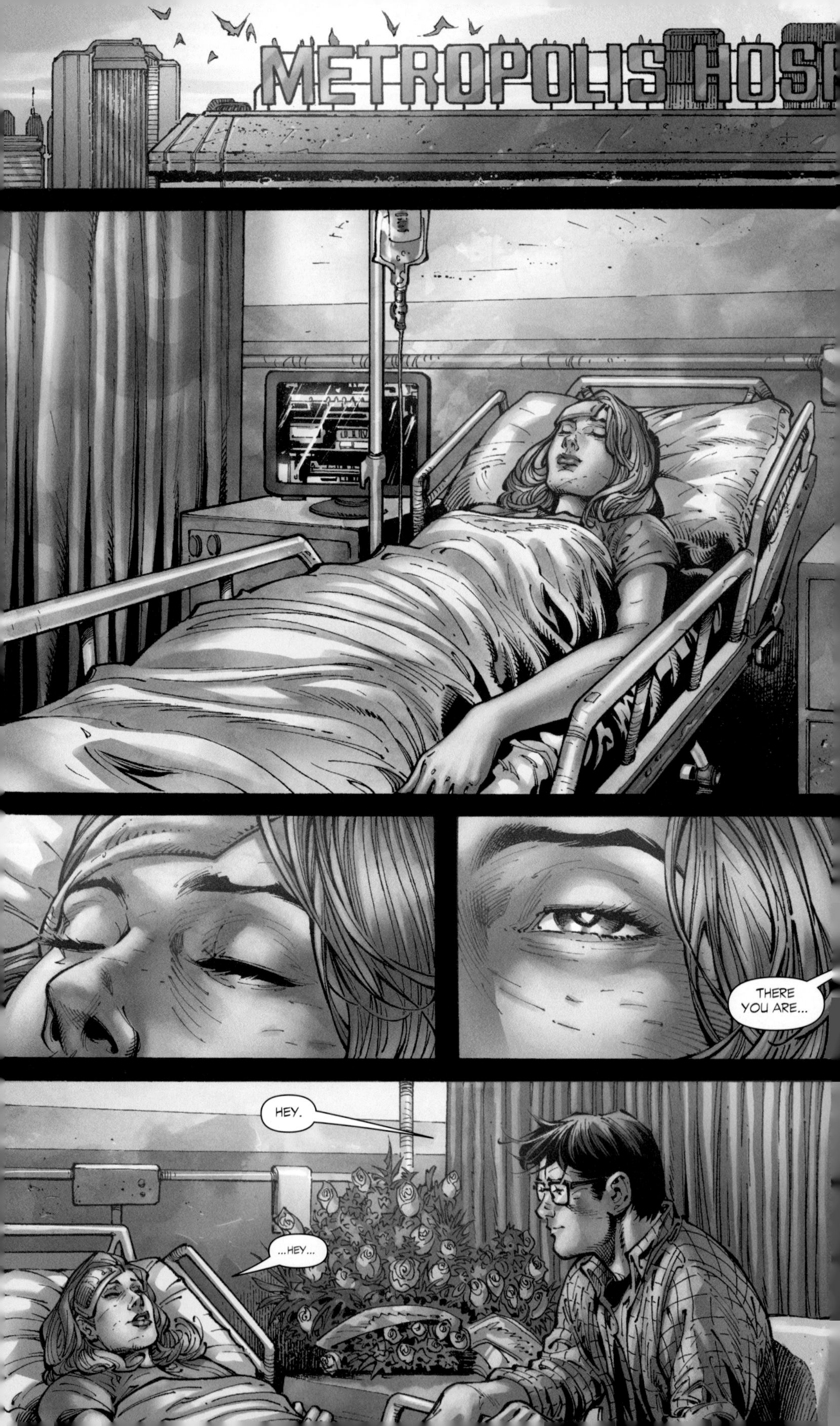
METROPOLIS HOSP
THERE YOU ARE...
HEY.
...HEY...

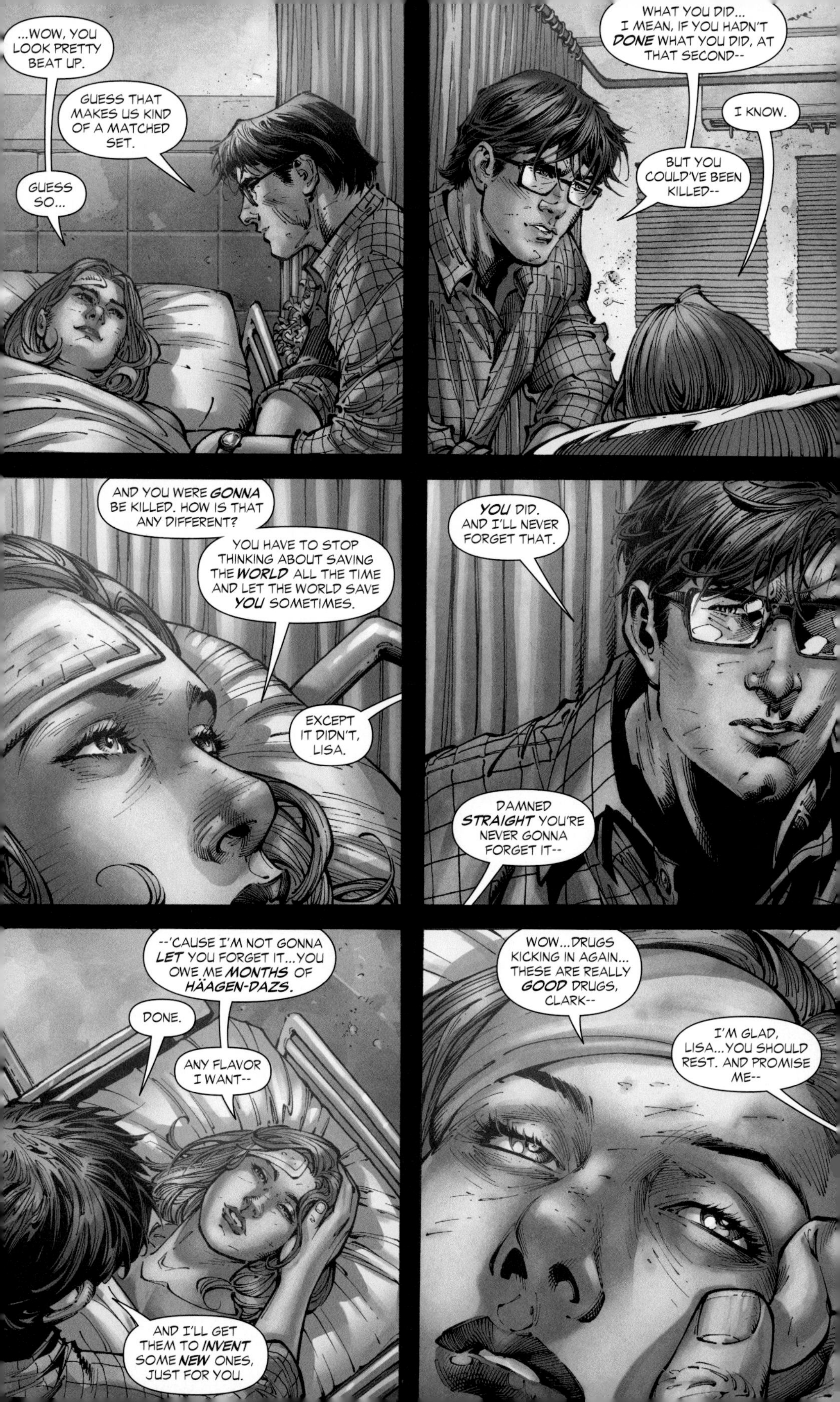

...WOW, YOU LOOK PRETTY BEAT UP.
GUESS THAT MAKES US KIND OF A MATCHED SET.
GUESS SO...
WHAT YOU DID... I MEAN, IF YOU HADN'T DONE WHAT YOU DID, AT THAT SECOND--
BUT YOU COULD'VE BEEN KILLED--
I KNOW.
AND YOU WERE GONNA BE KILLED. HOW IS THAT ANY DIFFERENT?
YOU HAVE TO STOP THINKING ABOUT SAVING THE WORLD ALL THE TIME AND LET THE WORLD SAVE YOU SOMETIMES.
EXCEPT IT DIDN'T, LISA.
YOU DID. AND I'LL NEVER FORGET THAT.
DAMNED STRAIGHT YOU'RE NEVER GONNA FORGET IT--
--'CAUSE I'M NOT GONNA LET YOU FORGET IT...YOU OWE ME MONTHS OF HÄAGEN-DAZS.
DONE.
ANY FLAVOR I WANT--
AND I'LL GET THEM TO INVENT SOME NEW ONES, JUST FOR YOU.
WOW...DRUGS KICKING IN AGAIN... THESE ARE REALLY GOOD DRUGS, CLARK--
I'M GLAD, LISA...YOU SHOULD REST. AND PROMISE ME--

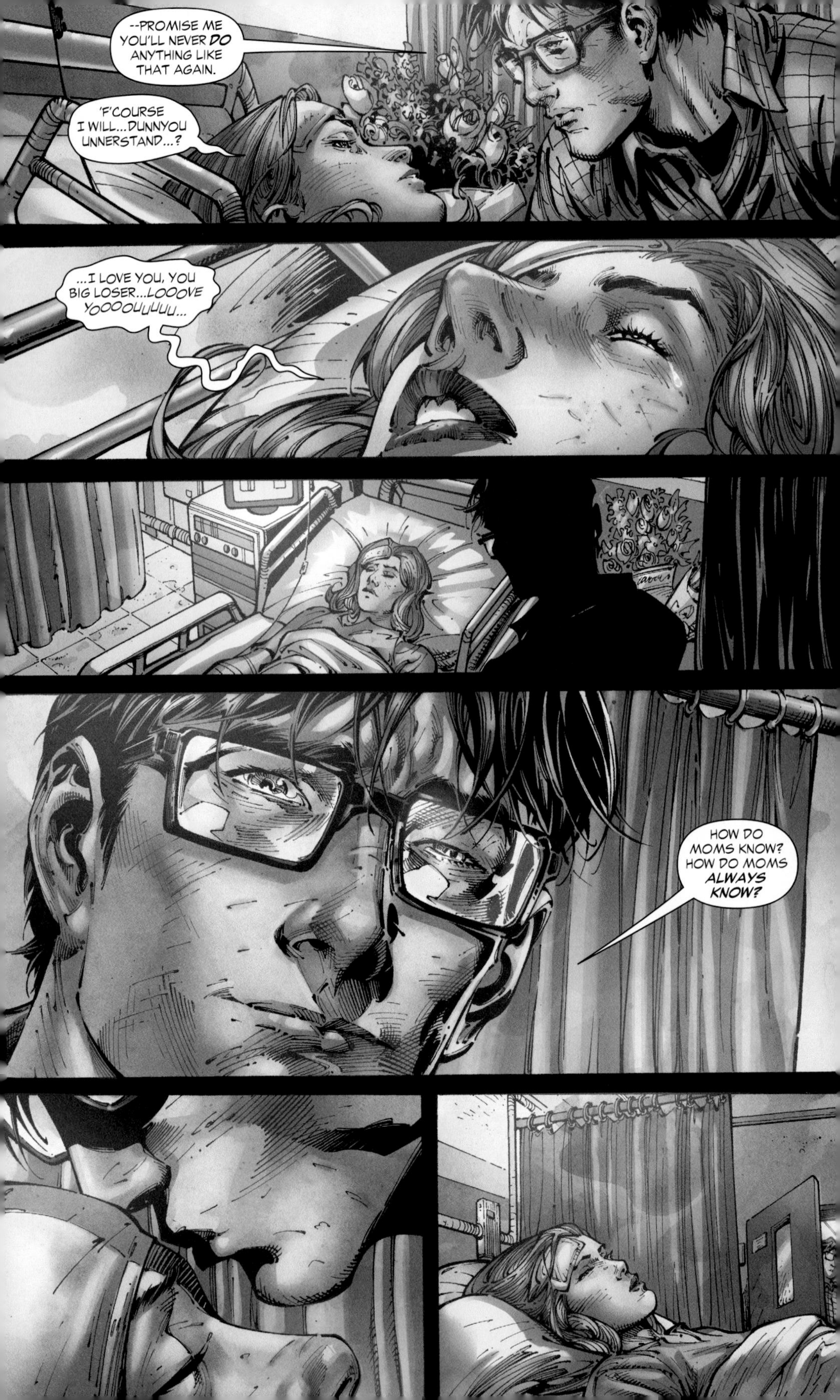
--PROMISE ME YOU'LL NEVER DO ANYTHING LIKE THAT AGAIN.
'F'COURSE I WILL...DUNNYOU UNNERSTAND...?
...I LOVE YOU, YOU BIG LOSER...LOOOVE YOOOOUUUUU...
HOW DO MOMS KNOW? HOW DO MOMS ALWAYS KNOW?

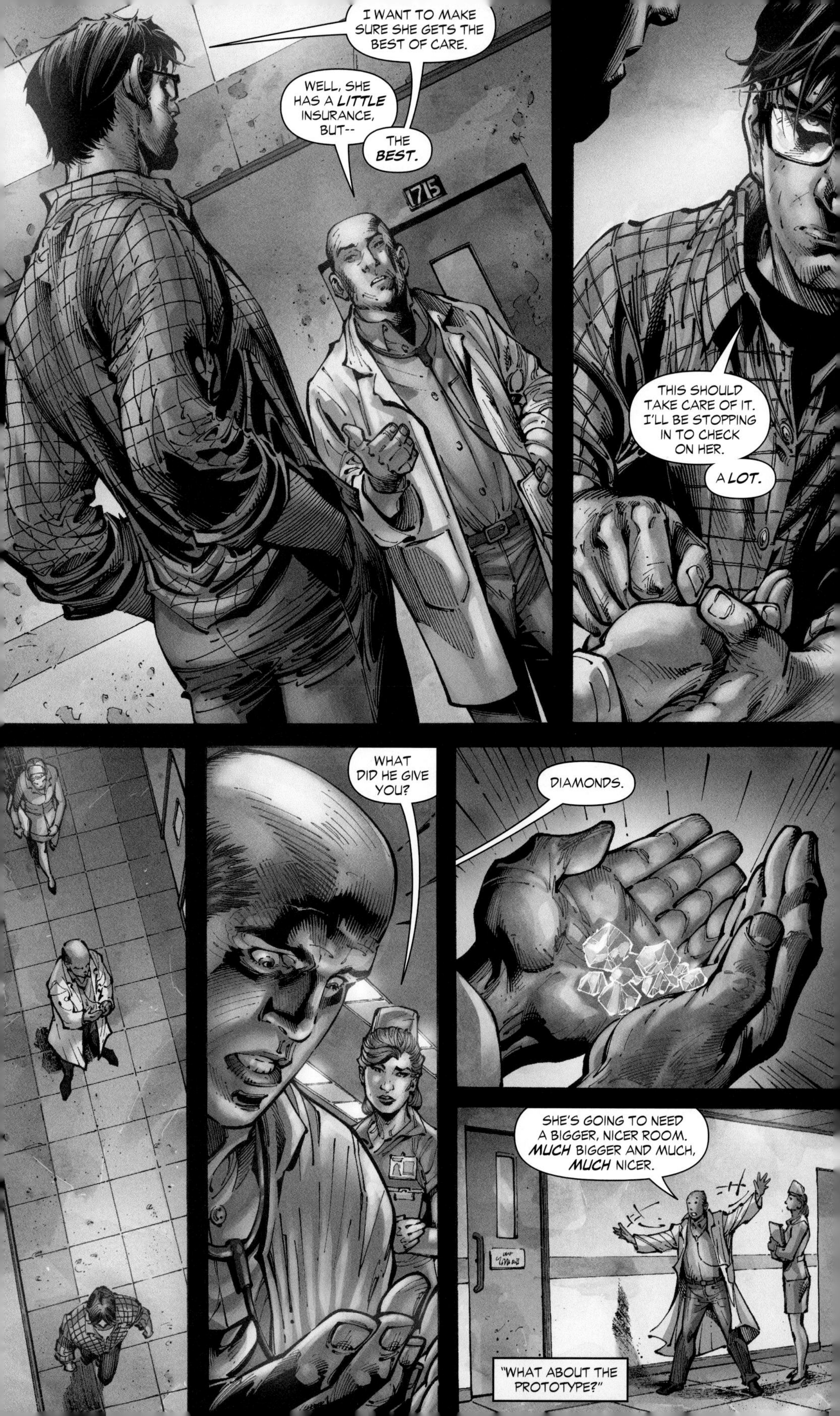

I WANT TO MAKE SURE SHE GETS THE BEST OF CARE.
WELL, SHE HAS A *LITTLE* INSURANCE, BUT--
THE *BEST.*
1715
THIS SHOULD TAKE CARE OF IT. I'LL BE STOPPING IN TO CHECK ON HER.
A *LOT.*
WHAT DID HE GIVE YOU?
DIAMONDS.
SHE'S GOING TO NEED A BIGGER, NICER ROOM. *MUCH* BIGGER AND MUCH, *MUCH* NICER.
"WHAT ABOUT THE PROTOTYPE?"

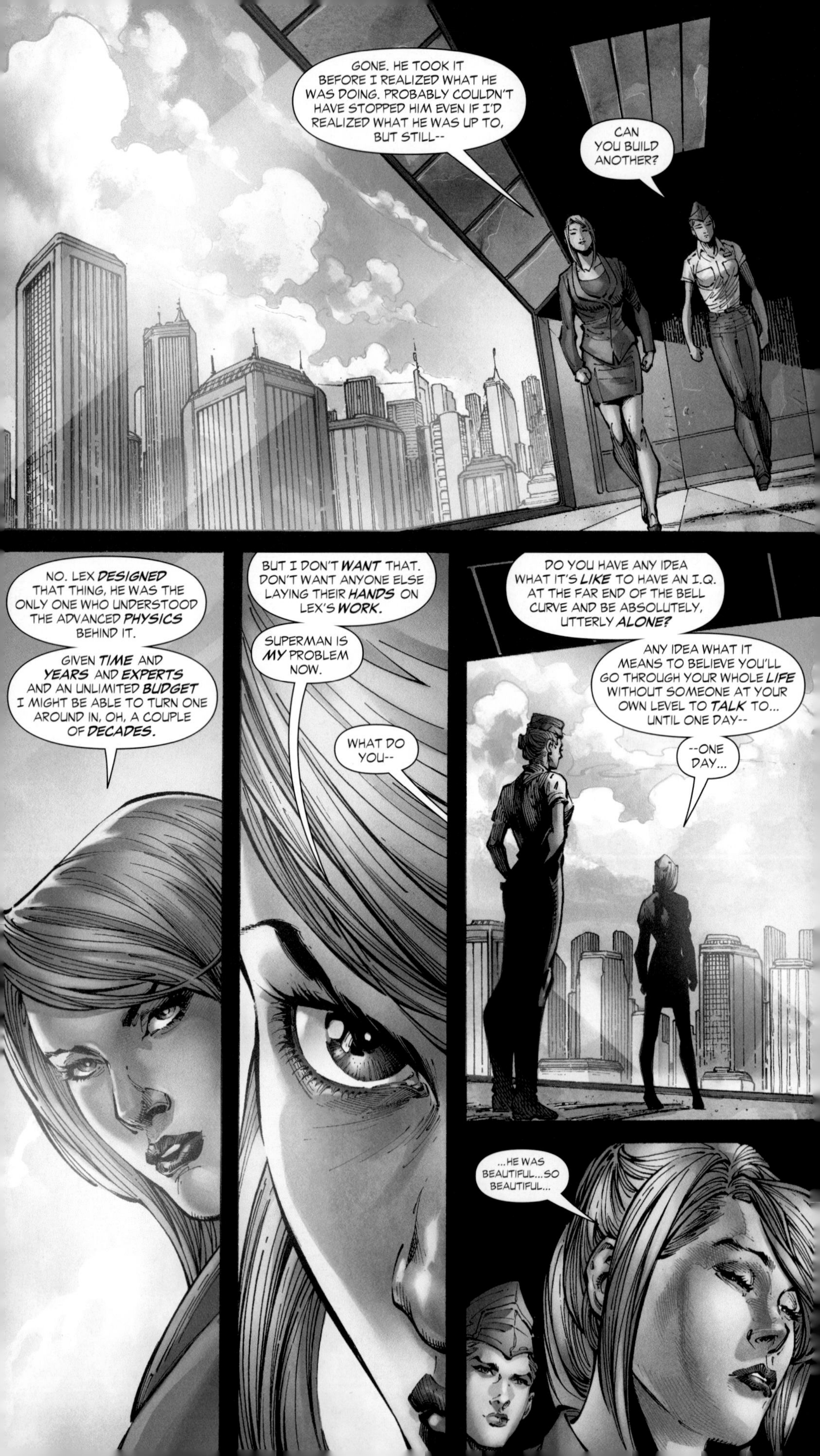

GONE. HE TOOK IT BEFORE I REALIZED WHAT HE WAS DOING. PROBABLY COULDN'T HAVE STOPPED HIM EVEN IF I'D REALIZED WHAT HE WAS UP TO, BUT STILL--
CAN YOU BUILD ANOTHER?
NO. LEX DESIGNED THAT THING, HE WAS THE ONLY ONE WHO UNDERSTOOD THE ADVANCED PHYSICS BEHIND IT.
GIVEN TIME AND YEARS AND EXPERTS AND AN UNLIMITED BUDGET I MIGHT BE ABLE TO TURN ONE AROUND IN, OH, A COUPLE OF DECADES.
BUT I DON'T WANT THAT. DON'T WANT ANYONE ELSE LAYING THEIR HANDS ON LEX'S WORK.
SUPERMAN IS MY PROBLEM NOW.
WHAT DO YOU--
DO YOU HAVE ANY IDEA WHAT IT'S LIKE TO HAVE AN I.Q. AT THE FAR END OF THE BELL CURVE AND BE ABSOLUTELY, UTTERLY ALONE?
ANY IDEA WHAT IT MEANS TO BELIEVE YOU'LL GO THROUGH YOUR WHOLE LIFE WITHOUT SOMEONE AT YOUR OWN LEVEL TO TALK TO... UNTIL ONE DAY--
--ONE DAY...
...HE WAS BEAUTIFUL...SO BEAUTIFUL...

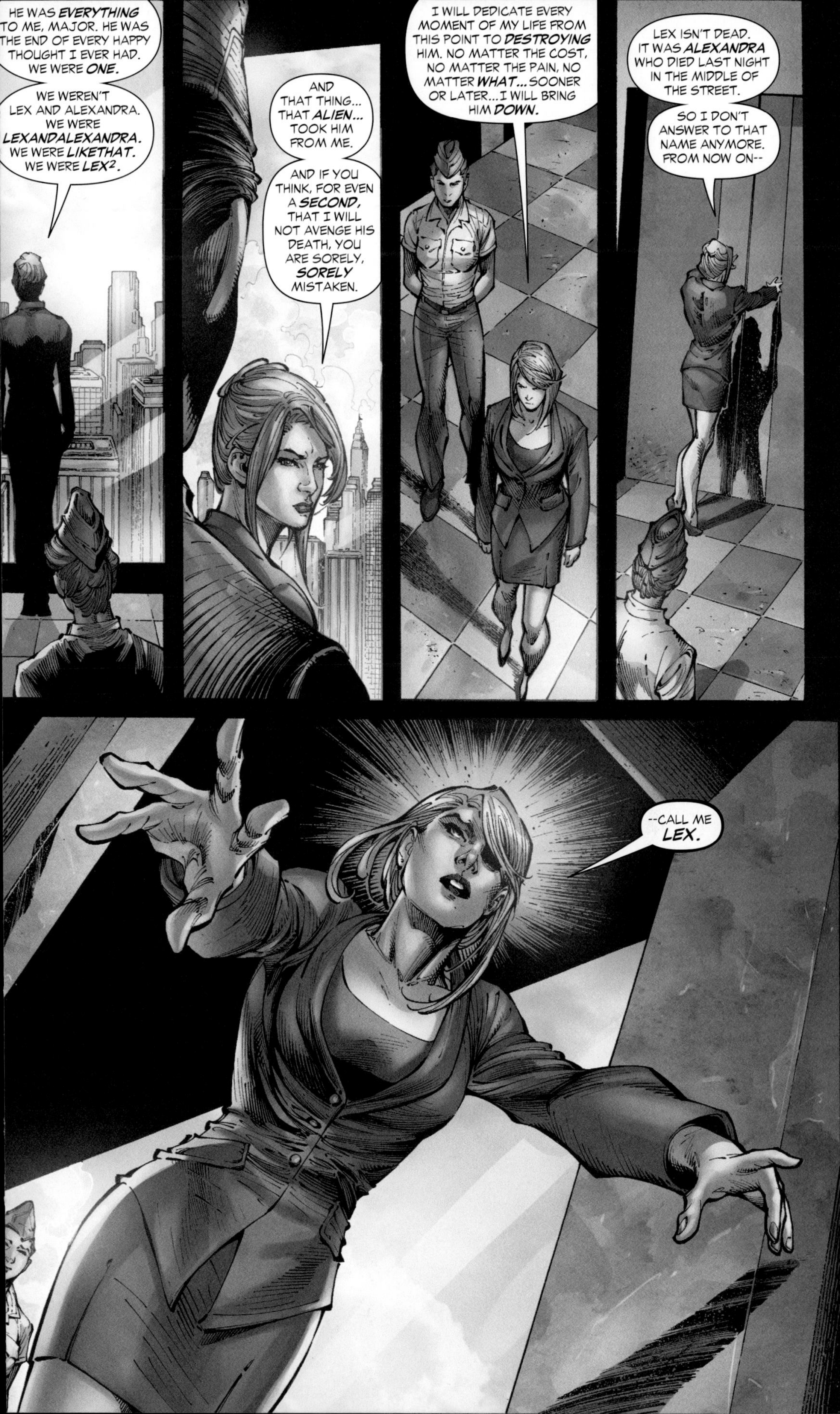
HE WAS EVERYTHING TO ME, MAJOR. HE WAS THE END OF EVERY HAPPY THOUGHT I EVER HAD. WE WERE ONE.
WE WEREN'T LEX AND ALEXANDRA. WE WERE LEXANDALEXANDRA. WE WERE LIKETHAT. WE WERE LEX².
AND THAT THING... THAT ALIEN... TOOK HIM FROM ME.
AND IF YOU THINK, FOR EVEN A SECOND, THAT I WILL NOT AVENGE HIS DEATH, YOU ARE SORELY, SORELY MISTAKEN.
I WILL DEDICATE EVERY MOMENT OF MY LIFE FROM THIS POINT TO DESTROYING HIM. NO MATTER THE COST, NO MATTER THE PAIN, NO MATTER WHAT... SOONER OR LATER... I WILL BRING HIM DOWN.
LEX ISN'T DEAD. IT WAS ALEXANDRA WHO DIED LAST NIGHT IN THE MIDDLE OF THE STREET.
SO I DON'T ANSWER TO THAT NAME ANYMORE. FROM NOW ON--
--CALL ME LEX.

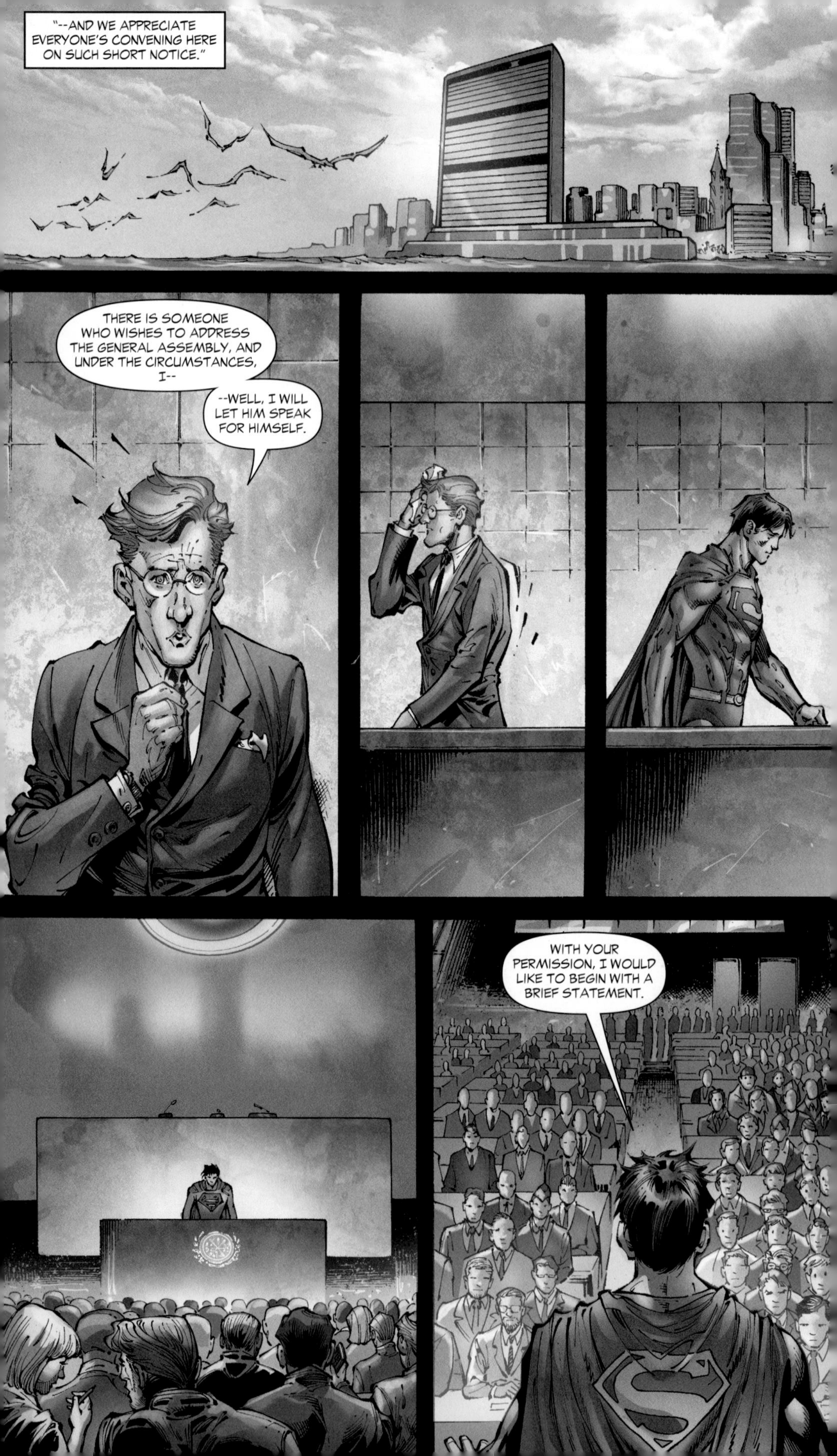
"--AND WE APPRECIATE EVERYONE'S CONVENING HERE ON SUCH SHORT NOTICE."
THERE IS SOMEONE WHO WISHES TO ADDRESS THE GENERAL ASSEMBLY, AND UNDER THE CIRCUMSTANCES, I--
--WELL, I WILL LET HIM SPEAK FOR HIMSELF.
WITH YOUR PERMISSION, I WOULD LIKE TO BEGIN WITH A BRIEF STATEMENT.

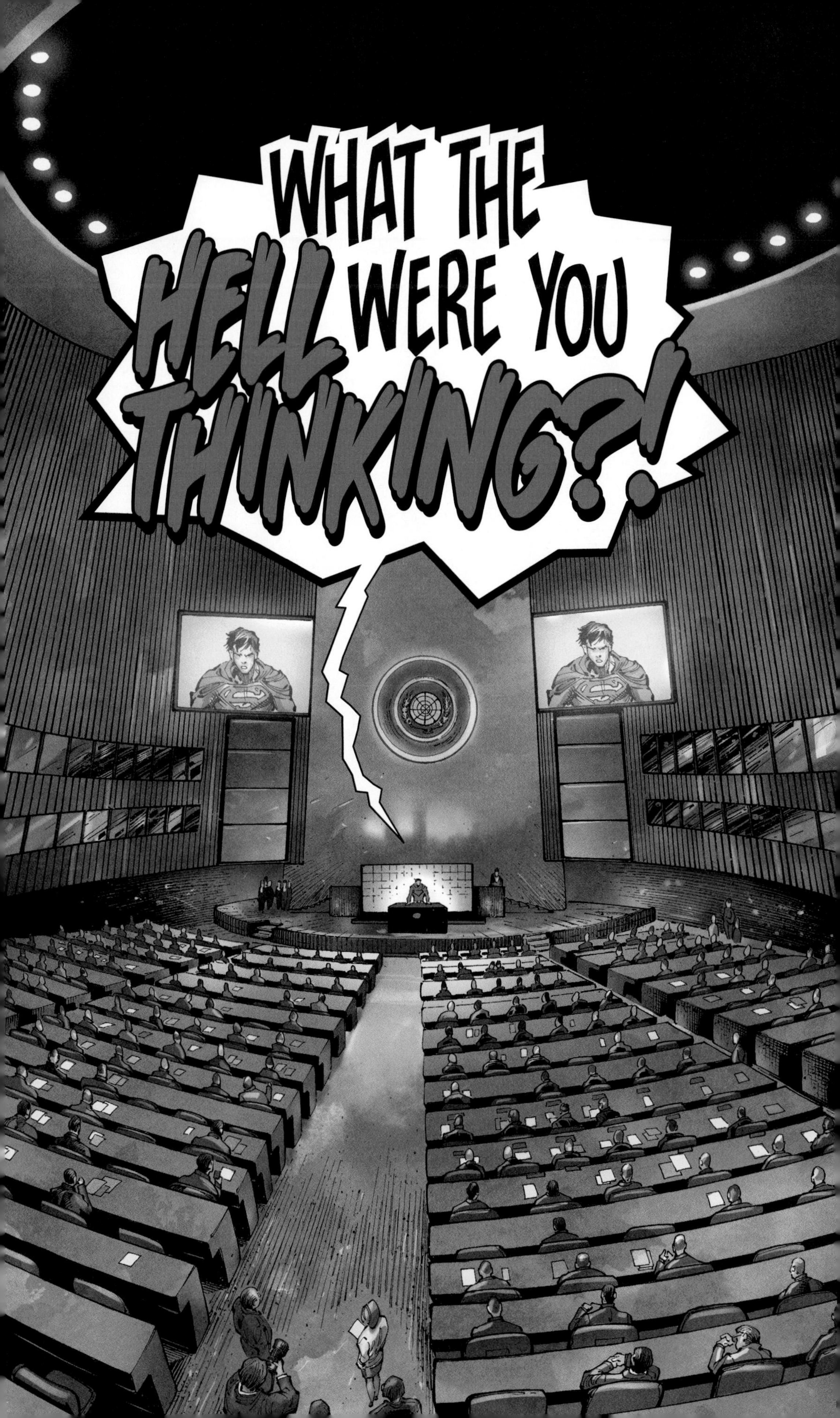
WHAT THE HELL WERE YOU THINKING?!

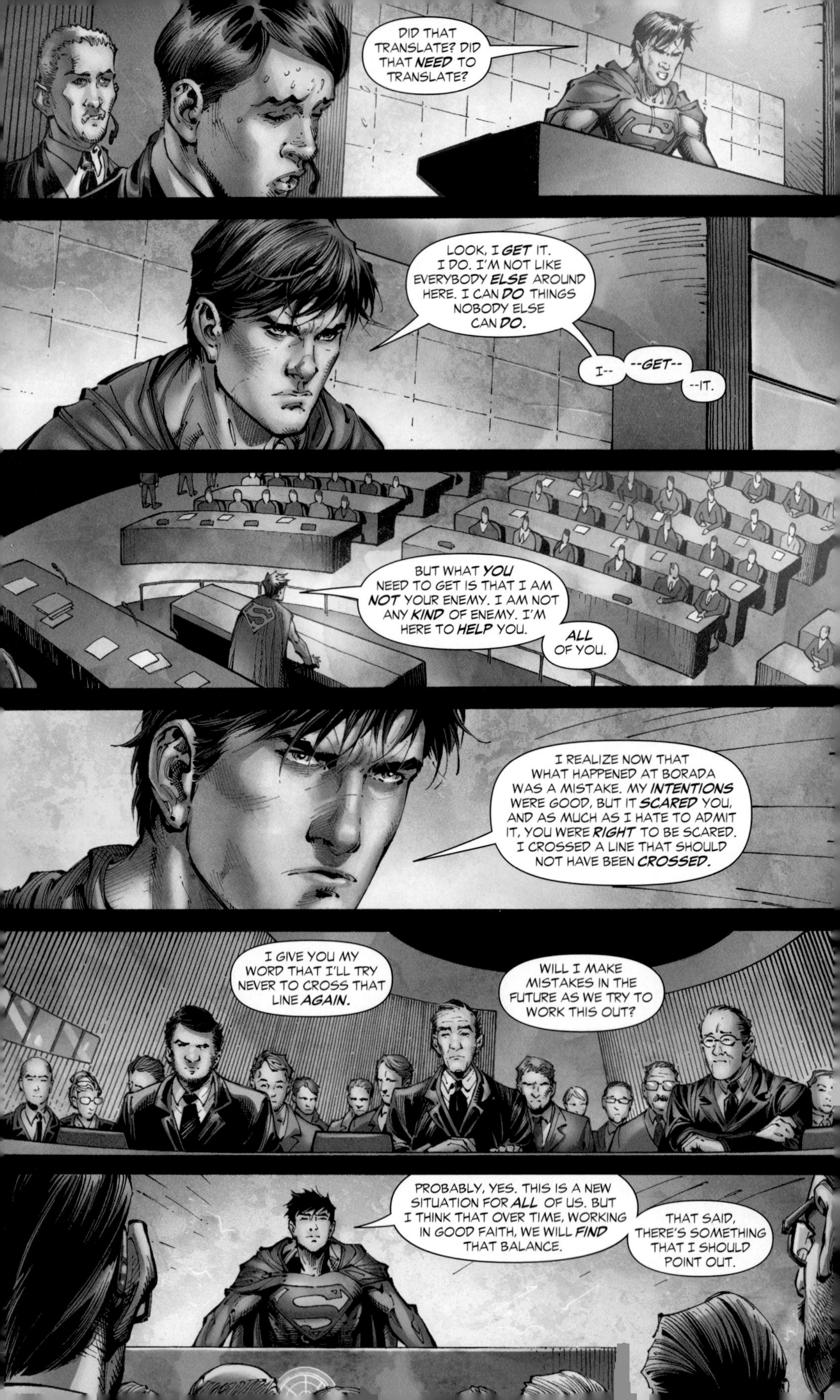
DID THAT TRANSLATE? DID THAT NEED TO TRANSLATE?
LOOK, I GET IT. I DO. I'M NOT LIKE EVERYBODY ELSE AROUND HERE. I CAN DO THINGS NOBODY ELSE CAN DO.
I--
--GET--
--IT.
BUT WHAT YOU NEED TO GET IS THAT I AM NOT YOUR ENEMY. I AM NOT ANY KIND OF ENEMY. I'M HERE TO HELP YOU.
ALL OF YOU.
I REALIZE NOW THAT WHAT HAPPENED AT BORADA WAS A MISTAKE. MY INTENTIONS WERE GOOD, BUT IT SCARED YOU, AND AS MUCH AS I HATE TO ADMIT IT, YOU WERE RIGHT TO BE SCARED. I CROSSED A LINE THAT SHOULD NOT HAVE BEEN CROSSED.
I GIVE YOU MY WORD THAT I'LL TRY NEVER TO CROSS THAT LINE AGAIN.
WILL I MAKE MISTAKES IN THE FUTURE AS WE TRY TO WORK THIS OUT?
PROBABLY, YES. THIS IS A NEW SITUATION FOR ALL OF US. BUT I THINK THAT OVER TIME, WORKING IN GOOD FAITH, WE WILL FIND THAT BALANCE.
THAT SAID, THERE'S SOMETHING THAT I SHOULD POINT OUT.

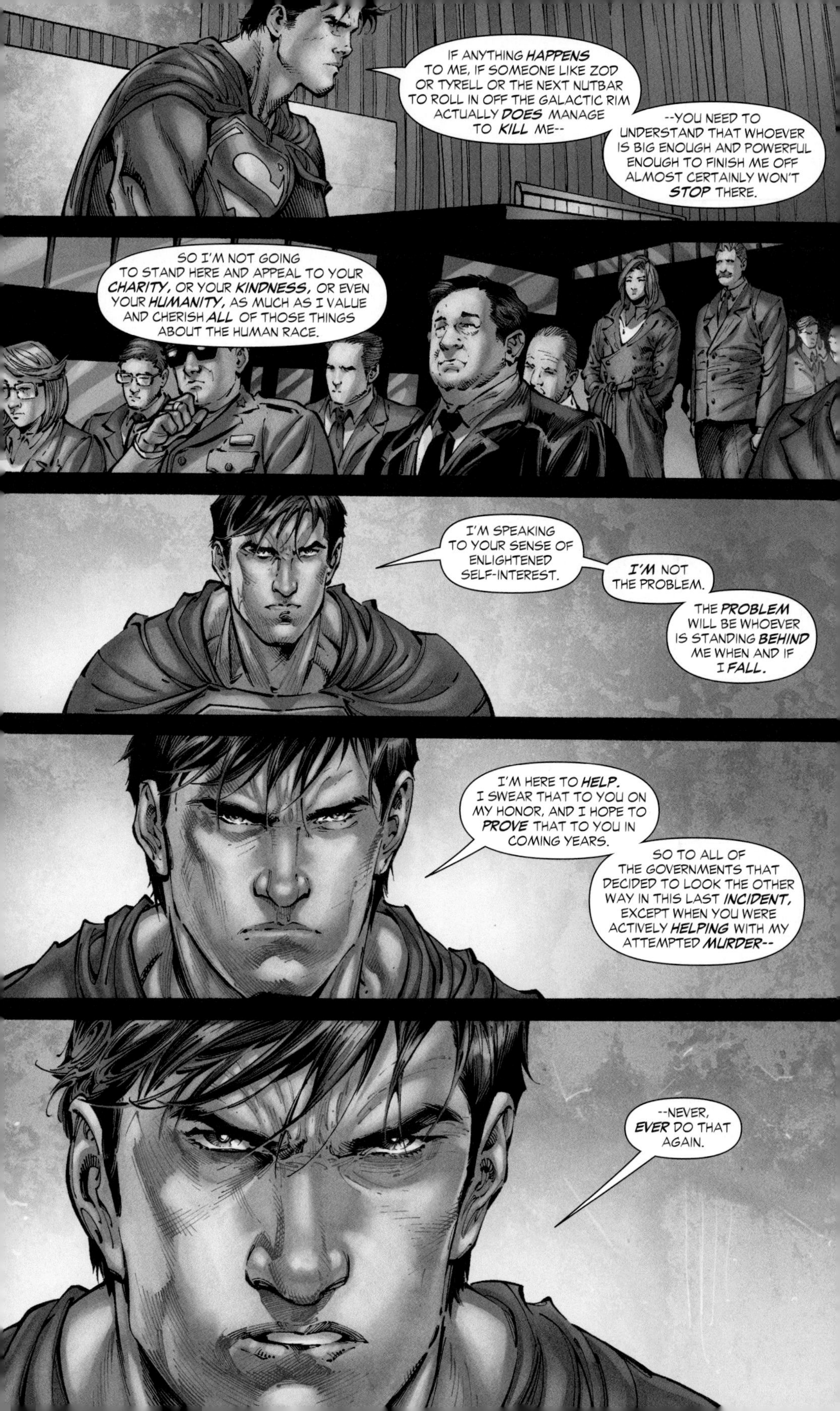
IF ANYTHING HAPPENS TO ME, IF SOMEONE LIKE ZOD OR TYRELL OR THE NEXT NUTBAR TO ROLL IN OFF THE GALACTIC RIM ACTUALLY DOES MANAGE TO KILL ME--
--YOU NEED TO UNDERSTAND THAT WHOEVER IS BIG ENOUGH AND POWERFUL ENOUGH TO FINISH ME OFF ALMOST CERTAINLY WON'T STOP THERE.
SO I'M NOT GOING TO STAND HERE AND APPEAL TO YOUR CHARITY, OR YOUR KINDNESS, OR EVEN YOUR HUMANITY, AS MUCH AS I VALUE AND CHERISH ALL OF THOSE THINGS ABOUT THE HUMAN RACE.
I'M SPEAKING TO YOUR SENSE OF ENLIGHTENED SELF-INTEREST.
I'M NOT THE PROBLEM.
THE PROBLEM WILL BE WHOEVER IS STANDING BEHIND ME WHEN AND IF I FALL.
I'M HERE TO HELP. I SWEAR THAT TO YOU ON MY HONOR, AND I HOPE TO PROVE THAT TO YOU IN COMING YEARS.
SO TO ALL OF THE GOVERNMENTS THAT DECIDED TO LOOK THE OTHER WAY IN THIS LAST INCIDENT, EXCEPT WHEN YOU WERE ACTIVELY HELPING WITH MY ATTEMPTED MURDER--
--NEVER, EVER DO THAT AGAIN.

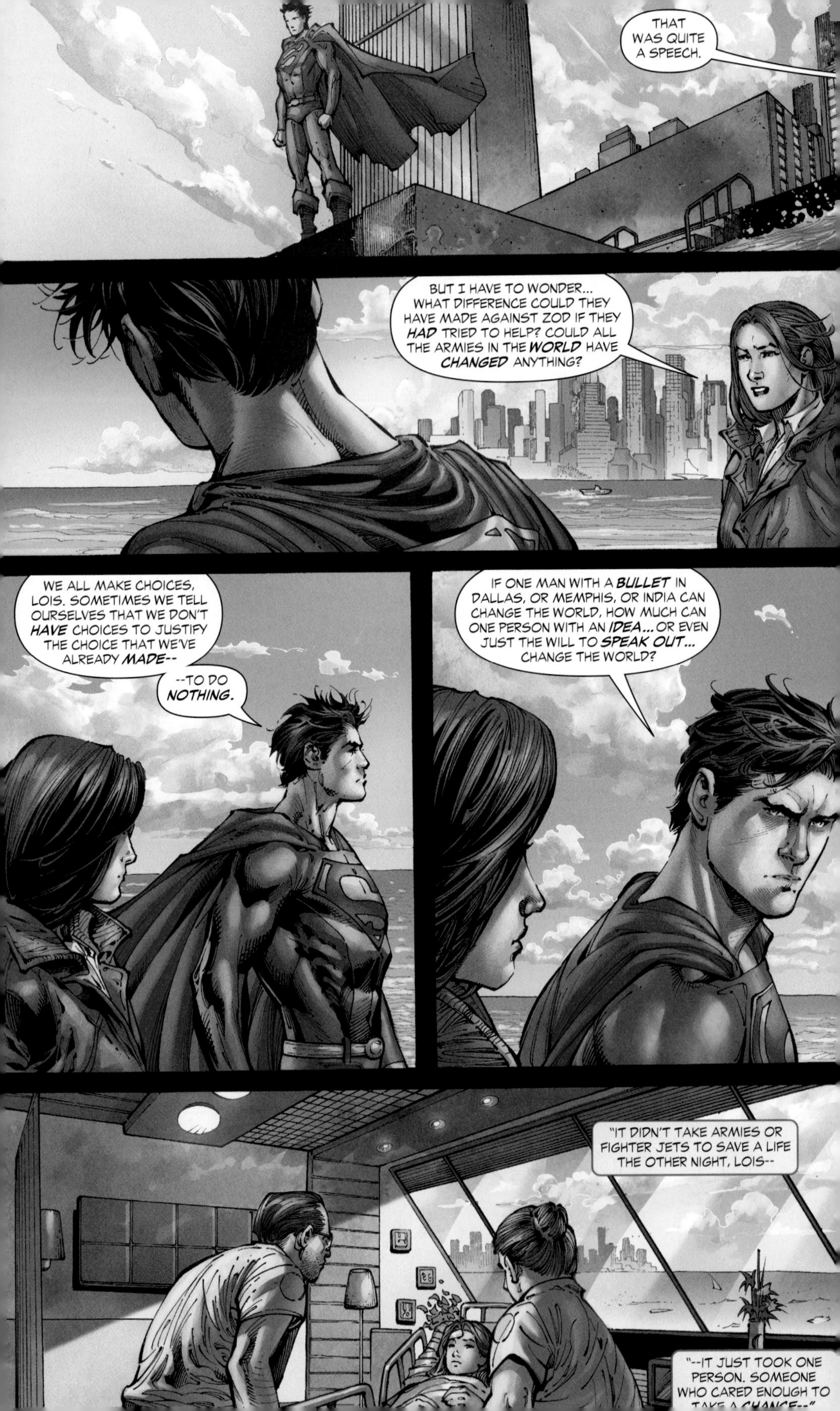
THAT WAS QUITE A SPEECH.
BUT I HAVE TO WONDER... WHAT DIFFERENCE COULD THEY HAVE MADE AGAINST ZOD IF THEY HAD TRIED TO HELP? COULD ALL THE ARMIES IN THE WORLD HAVE CHANGED ANYTHING?
WE ALL MAKE CHOICES, LOIS. SOMETIMES WE TELL OURSELVES THAT WE DON'T HAVE CHOICES TO JUSTIFY THE CHOICE THAT WE'VE ALREADY MADE--
--TO DO NOTHING.
IF ONE MAN WITH A BULLET IN DALLAS, OR MEMPHIS, OR INDIA CAN CHANGE THE WORLD, HOW MUCH CAN ONE PERSON WITH AN IDEA... OR EVEN JUST THE WILL TO SPEAK OUT... CHANGE THE WORLD?
"IT DIDN'T TAKE ARMIES OR FIGHTER JETS TO SAVE A LIFE THE OTHER NIGHT, LOIS--
"--IT JUST TOOK ONE PERSON. SOMEONE WHO CARED ENOUGH TO

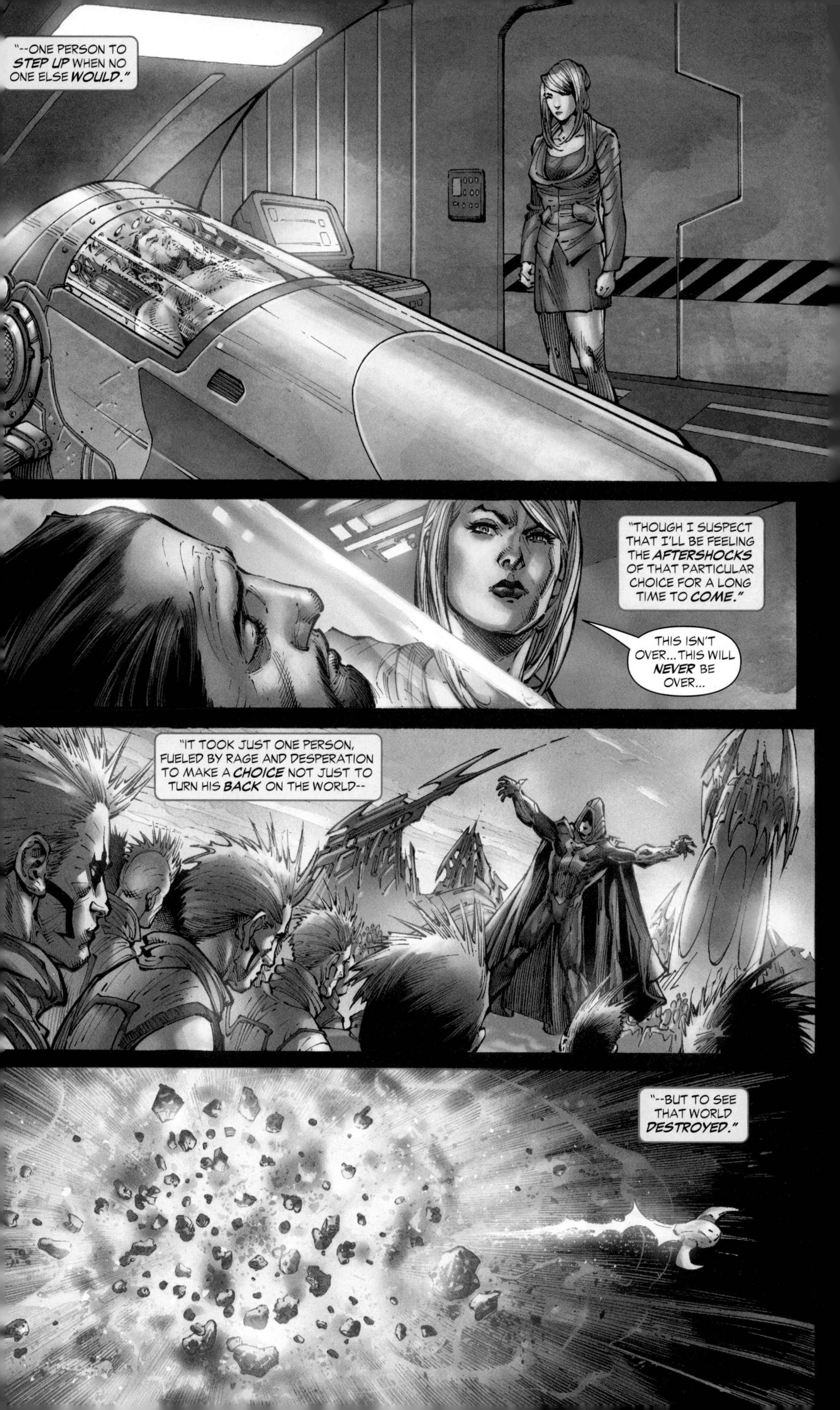
"--ONE PERSON TO STEP UP WHEN NO ONE ELSE WOULD."
"THOUGH I SUSPECT THAT I'LL BE FEELING THE AFTERSHOCKS OF THAT PARTICULAR CHOICE FOR A LONG TIME TO COME."
THIS ISN'T OVER... THIS WILL NEVER BE OVER...
"IT TOOK JUST ONE PERSON, FUELED BY RAGE AND DESPERATION TO MAKE A CHOICE NOT JUST TO TURN HIS BACK ON THE WORLD--
"--BUT TO SEE THAT WORLD DESTROYED."

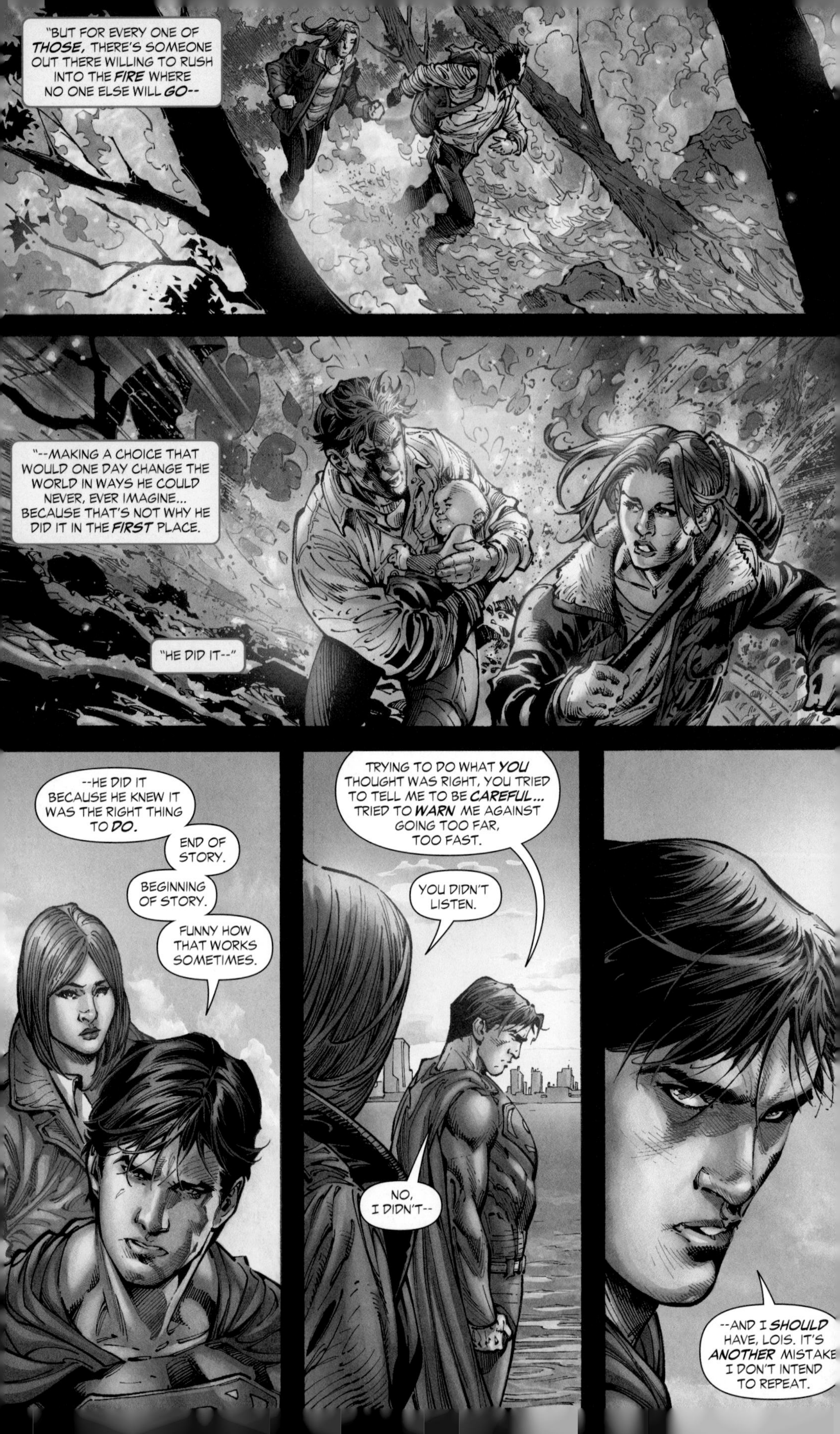
"BUT FOR EVERY ONE OF THOSE, THERE'S SOMEONE OUT THERE WILLING TO RUSH INTO THE FIRE WHERE NO ONE ELSE WILL GO--
"--MAKING A CHOICE THAT WOULD ONE DAY CHANGE THE WORLD IN WAYS HE COULD NEVER, EVER IMAGINE... BECAUSE THAT'S NOT WHY HE DID IT IN THE FIRST PLACE.
"HE DID IT--"
--HE DID IT BECAUSE HE KNEW IT WAS THE RIGHT THING TO DO.
END OF STORY.
BEGINNING OF STORY.
FUNNY HOW THAT WORKS SOMETIMES.
TRYING TO DO WHAT YOU THOUGHT WAS RIGHT, YOU TRIED TO TELL ME TO BE CAREFUL... TRIED TO WARN ME AGAINST GOING TOO FAR, TOO FAST.
YOU DIDN'T LISTEN.
NO, I DIDN'T--
--AND I SHOULD HAVE, LOIS. IT'S ANOTHER MISTAKE I DON'T INTEND TO REPEAT.

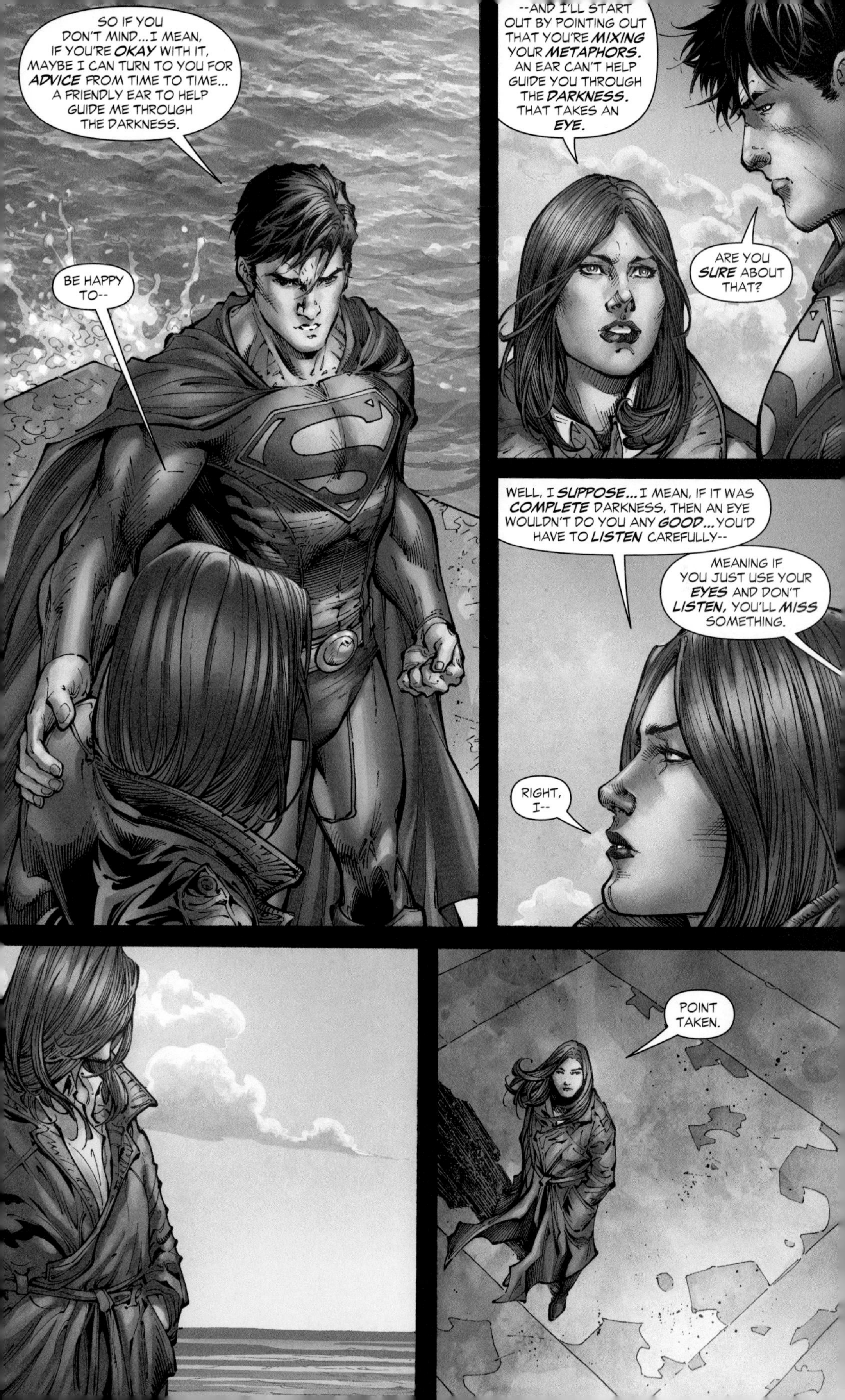
SO IF YOU DON'T MIND...I MEAN, IF YOU'RE OKAY WITH IT, MAYBE I CAN TURN TO YOU FOR ADVICE FROM TIME TO TIME... A FRIENDLY EAR TO HELP GUIDE ME THROUGH THE DARKNESS.
BE HAPPY TO--
--AND I'LL START OUT BY POINTING OUT THAT YOU'RE MIXING YOUR METAPHORS. AN EAR CAN'T HELP GUIDE YOU THROUGH THE DARKNESS. THAT TAKES AN EYE.
ARE YOU SURE ABOUT THAT?
WELL, I SUPPOSE...I MEAN, IF IT WAS COMPLETE DARKNESS, THEN AN EYE WOULDN'T DO YOU ANY GOOD...YOU'D HAVE TO LISTEN CAREFULLY--
MEANING IF YOU JUST USE YOUR EYES AND DON'T LISTEN, YOU'LL MISS SOMETHING.
RIGHT, I--
POINT TAKEN.

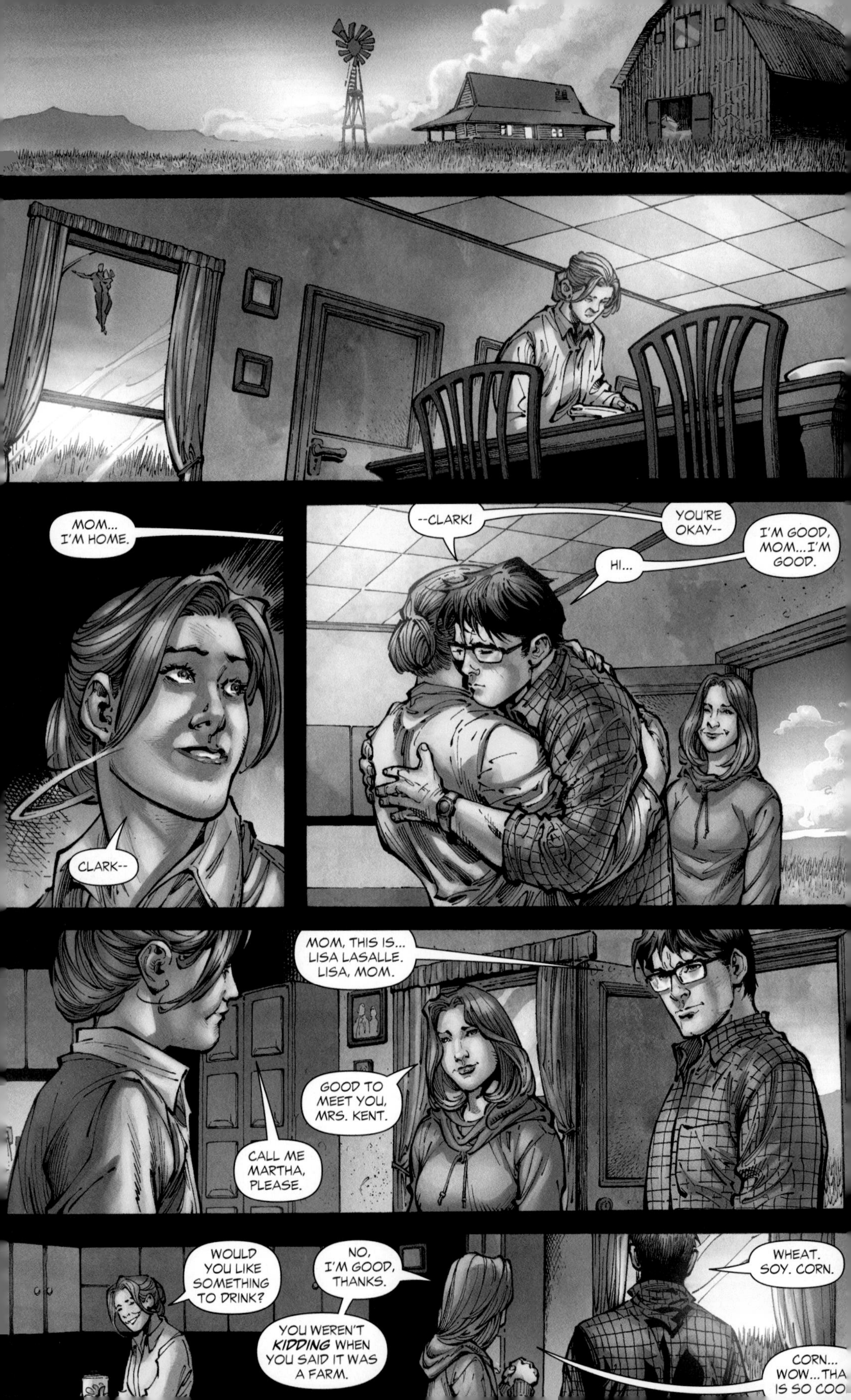
MOM... I'M HOME.
CLARK--
--CLARK!
YOU'RE OKAY--
HI...
I'M GOOD, MOM...I'M GOOD.
MOM, THIS IS... LISA LASALLE. LISA, MOM.
GOOD TO MEET YOU, MRS. KENT.
CALL ME MARTHA, PLEASE.
WOULD YOU LIKE SOMETHING TO DRINK?
NO, I'M GOOD, THANKS.
YOU WEREN'T *KIDDING* WHEN YOU SAID IT WAS A FARM.
WHEAT. SOY. CORN.
CORN... WOW...THA IS SO COO

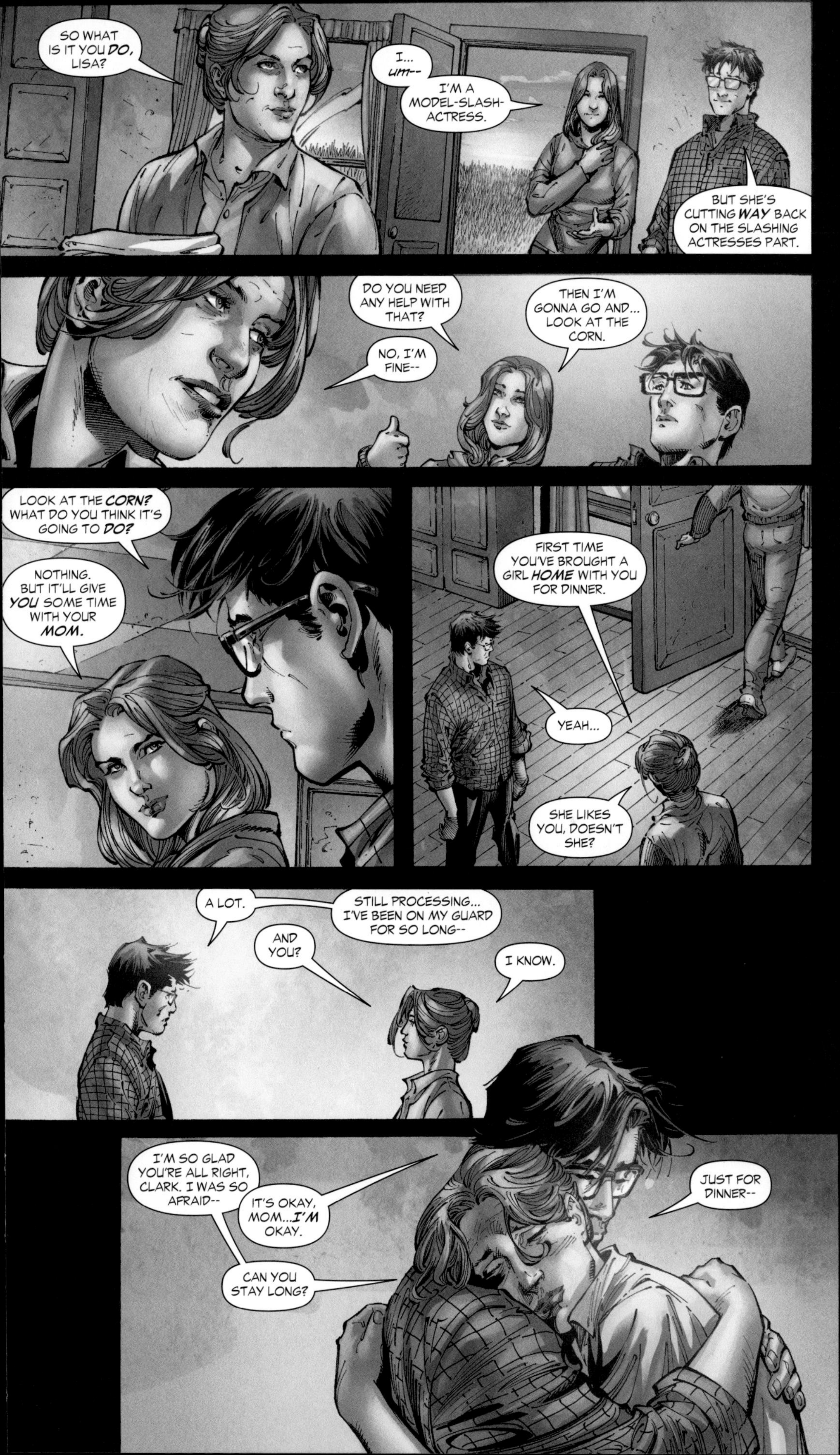
SO WHAT IS IT YOU *DO,* LISA?
I... *UM--*
I'M A MODEL-SLASH-ACTRESS.
BUT SHE'S CUTTING *WAY* BACK ON THE SLASHING ACTRESSES PART.
DO YOU NEED ANY HELP WITH THAT?
NO, I'M FINE--
THEN I'M GONNA GO AND... LOOK AT THE CORN.
LOOK AT THE *CORN?* WHAT DO YOU THINK IT'S GOING TO *DO?*
NOTHING. BUT IT'LL GIVE *YOU* SOME TIME WITH YOUR *MOM.*
FIRST TIME YOU'VE BROUGHT A GIRL *HOME* WITH YOU FOR DINNER.
YEAH...
SHE LIKES YOU, DOESN'T SHE?
A LOT.
AND YOU?
STILL PROCESSING... I'VE BEEN ON MY GUARD FOR SO LONG--
I KNOW.
I'M SO GLAD YOU'RE ALL RIGHT, CLARK. I WAS SO AFRAID--
IT'S OKAY, MOM...*I'M* OKAY.
CAN YOU STAY LONG?
JUST FOR DINNER--

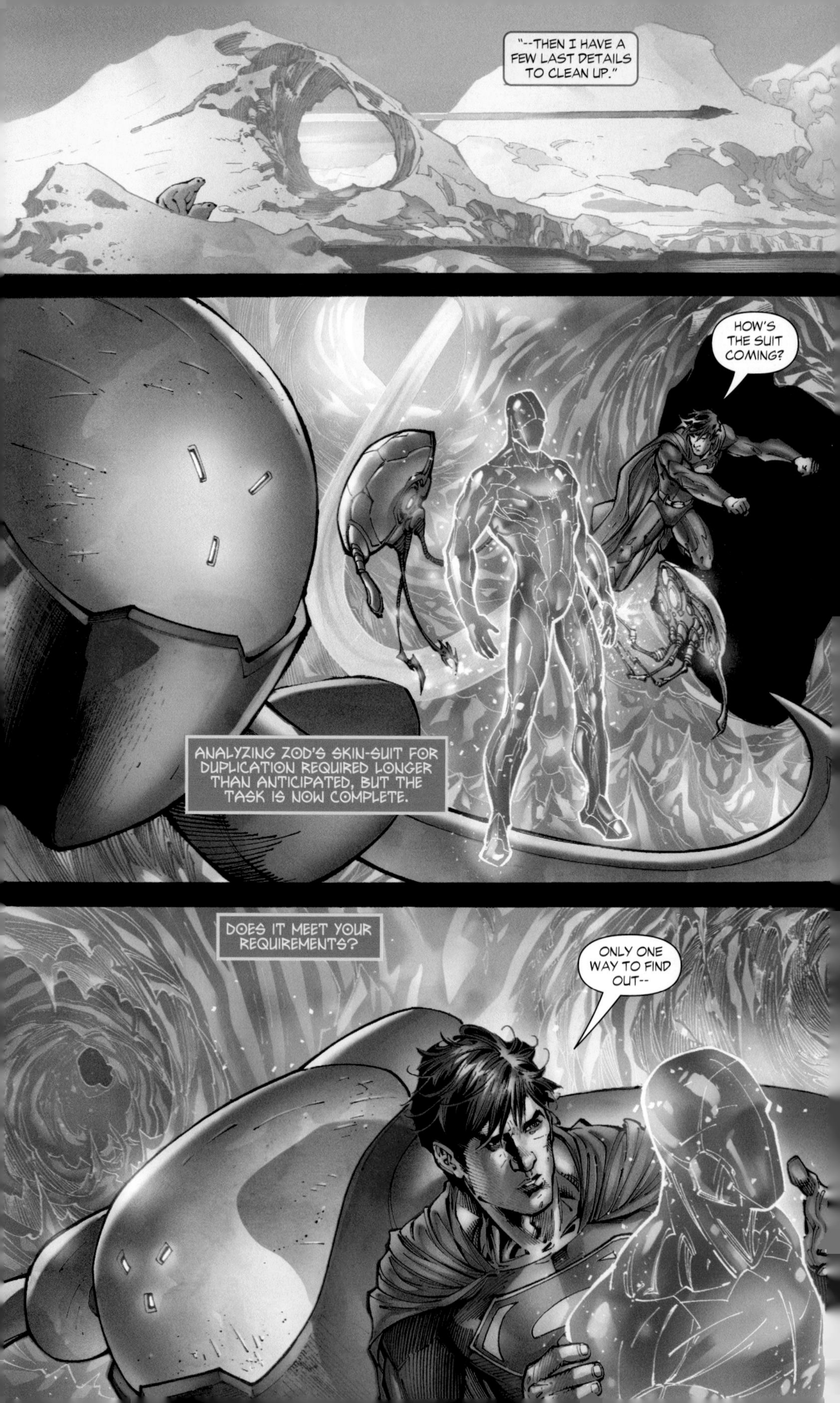
"--THEN I HAVE A FEW LAST DETAILS TO CLEAN UP."
HOW'S THE SUIT COMING?
ANALYZING ZOD'S SKIN-SUIT FOR DUPLICATION REQUIRED LONGER THAN ANTICIPATED, BUT THE TASK IS NOW COMPLETE.
DOES IT MEET YOUR REQUIREMENTS?
ONLY ONE WAY TO FIND OUT--

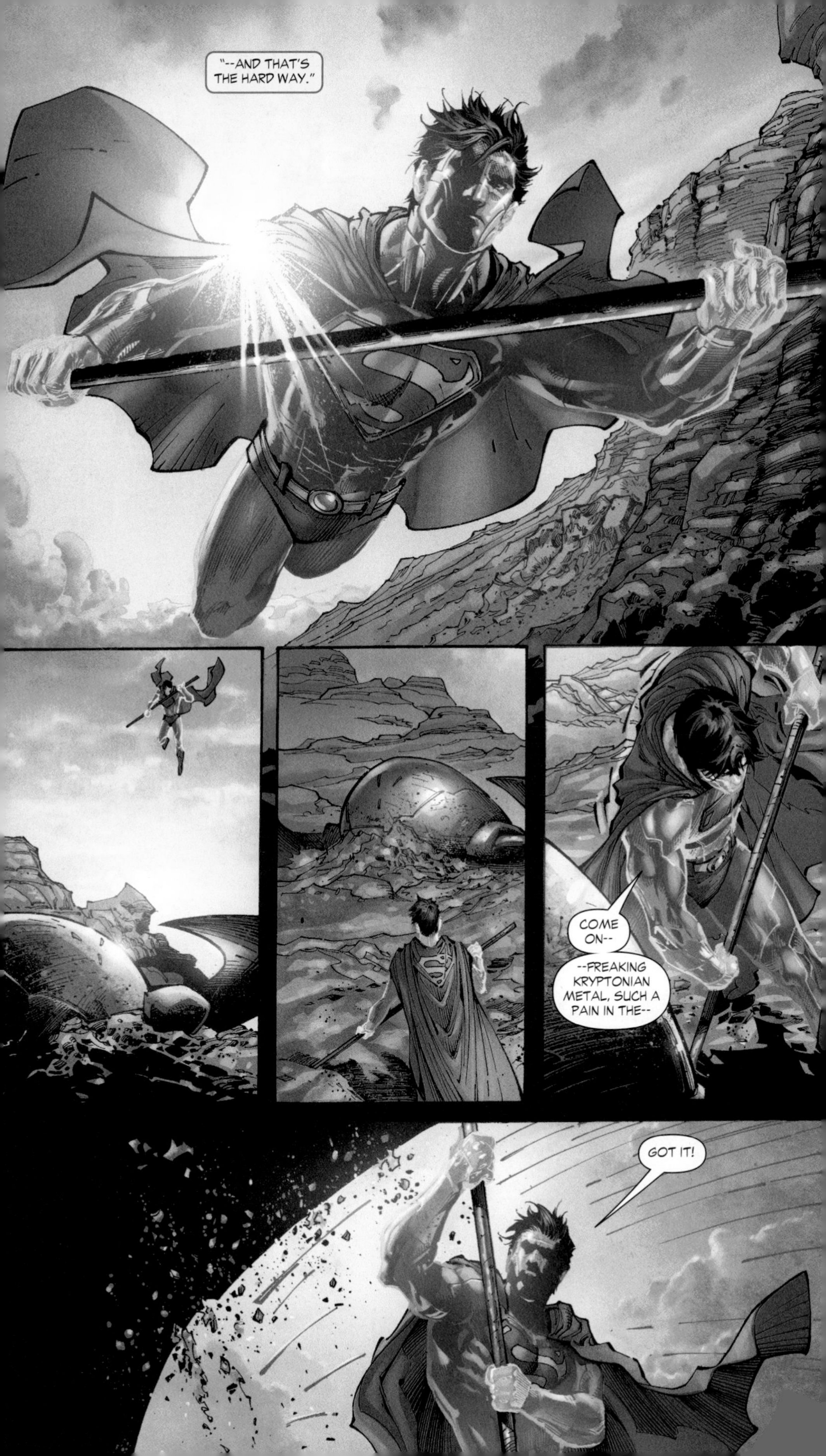
"--AND THAT'S THE HARD WAY."
COME ON--
--FREAKING KRYPTONIAN METAL, SUCH A PAIN IN THE--
GOT IT!

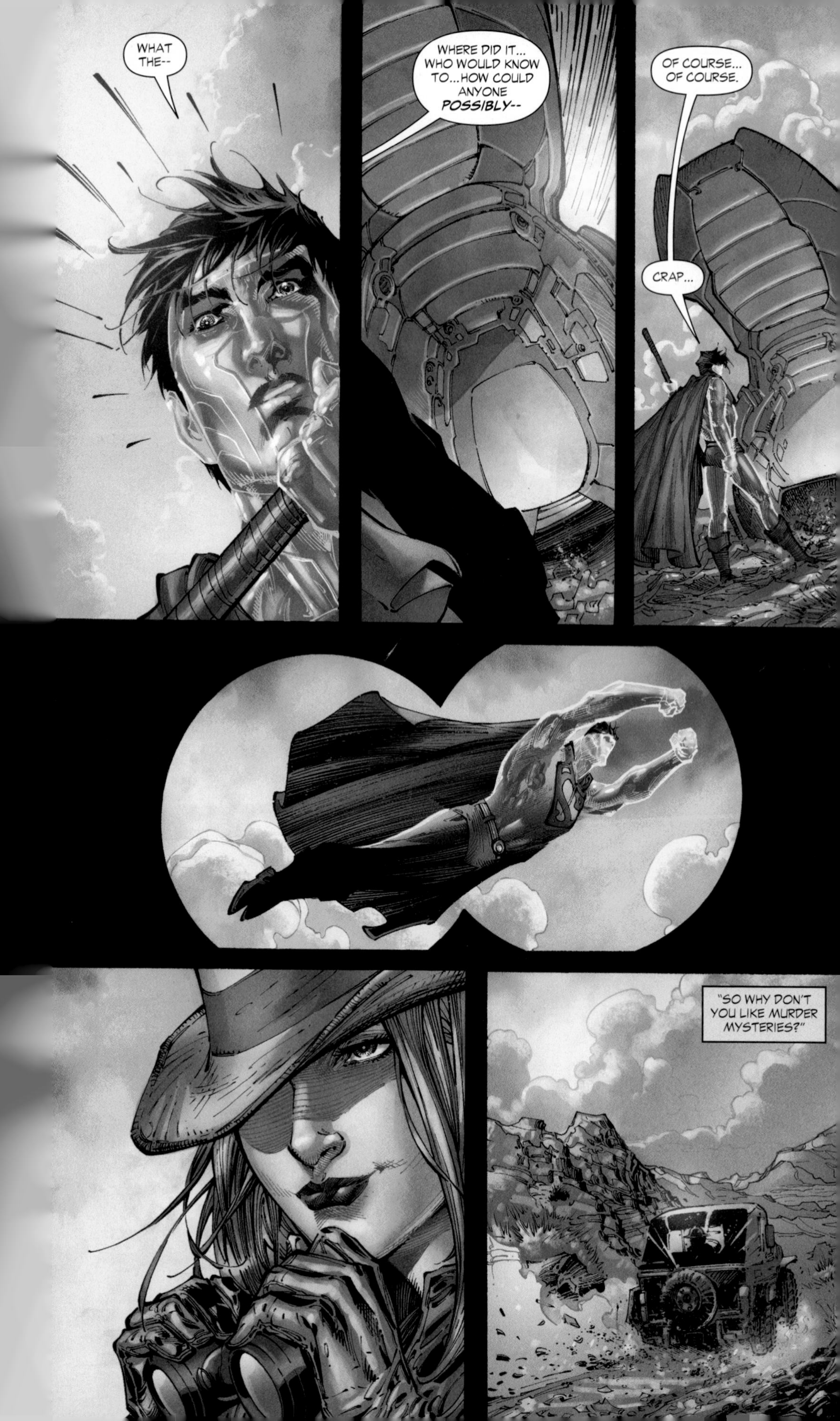
WHAT THE--
WHERE DID IT... WHO WOULD KNOW TO...HOW COULD ANYONE POSSIBLY--
OF COURSE... OF COURSE.
CRAP...
"SO WHY DON'T YOU LIKE MURDER MYSTERIES?"